Clients with Complex Needs:
Interprofessional Practice

Clients with Complex Needs: Interprofessional Practice

J. Keene

Professor of Primary Care
University of Reading

Blackwell Science

© 2001 by
Blackwell Science Ltd
Editorial Offices:
Osney Mead, Oxford OX2 0EL
25 John Street, London WC1N 2BS
23 Ainslie Place, Edinburgh EH3 6AJ
350 Main Street, Malden
  MA 02148 5018, USA
54 University Street, Carlton
  Victoria 3053, Australia
10, rue Casimir Delavigne
  75006 Paris, France

Other Editorial Offices:

Blackwell Wissenschafts-Verlag GmbH
Kurfürstendamm 57
10707 Berlin, Germany

Blackwell Science KK
MG Kodenmacho Building
7–10 Kodenmacho Nihombashi
Chuo-ku, Tokyo 104, Japan

Iowa State University Press
A Blackwell Science Company
2121 S. State Avenue
Ames, Iowa 50014-8300, USA

First published 2001

Set in 10/12.5 Sabon
by DP Photosetting, Aylesbury, Bucks
Printed and bound in Great Britain by
MPG Books Ltd, Bodmin, Cornwall

The Blackwell Science logo is a trade mark of
Blackwell Science Ltd, registered at the
United Kingdom Trade Marks Registry

DISTRIBUTORS

Marston Book Services Ltd
PO Box 269
Abingdon
Oxon OX14 4YN
(*Orders:* Tel: 01235 465500
            Fax: 01235 465555)

USA
Blackwell Science, Inc.
Commerce Place
350 Main Street
Malden, MA 02148 5018
(*Orders:* Tel: 800 759 6102
            781 388 8250
            Fax: 781 388 8255)

Canada
Login Brothers Book Company
324 Salteaux Crescent
Winnipeg, Manitoba R3J 3T2
(*Orders:* Tel: 204 837 2987
            Fax: 204 837 3116)

Australia
Blackwell Science Pty Ltd
54 University Street
Carlton, Victoria 3053
(*Orders:* Tel: 03 9347 0300
            Fax: 03 9347 5001)

A catalogue record for this title is available
from the British Library

ISBN 0-632-05223-6

Library of Congress
Cataloging-in-Publication Data
Keene, Jan.
    Clients with complex needs:
Interprofessional practice/J. Keene.
        p. cm.
    Includes bibliographical references and
index.
    ISBN 0-632-05223-6
    1. Social medicine.   2. Medicine and
psychology.   3. Medical cooperation.
4. Human services.   5. Human services
personnel.   6. Social service.   I. Title.
RA418.K43 2001
362.1–dc21   2001035379

For further information on
Blackwell Science, visit our website:
www.blackwell-science.com

For Bill

Contents

Acknowledgements

With thanks to: Sue Bailey, Darren Howell, Jan Janacek, Deborah Martin, Mark Owers, Louise Swift, and Margaret Woolgrove for data collection and statistical advice.

But most thanks go to the public service managers, practitioners, database workers and clients without whom the research would not have been possible.

Introduction

This book is concerned with bringing about a major beneficial change in the way that professionals in health and social care and the criminal justice system deal with adult clients/patients with complex needs. (For brevity, both patients and clients will be referred to throughout as 'clients'.) The book is aimed at professional practitioners, but also at those responsible for managing and planning, as well as providing, services.

The book examines the limitations of service provision for clients with complex needs and demonstrates that it is not only worthwhile for professionals but also cost-effective for agencies to assess psychosocial problems, prioritise service provision for shared clients and provide psychosocial maintenance support as well as psychological change programmes. (For a general review of the psychosocial perspective see Woods and Hollis 2000 and for a useful discussion of maintenance see Davies 1985.)

The first part of the book outlines the problems of complex needs clients in a psychosocial context. It builds on a comprehensive literature search and a collaborative multiagency database and places these in the context of contemporary policy and planning. The second part is concerned with gaining a greater understanding of the obstacles to comprehensive multidisciplinary care through qualitative in-depth interviews with different professionals and clients. It examines contemporary practice, highlighting how needs are often assessed in isolation and how interventions can be limited, not only by narrow assessments but also by time-limited specialist models of intervention. It then considers potential ways of multidisciplinary working. The third part examines the usefulness and limitations of a psychological approach to individual change and proposes an additional model of psychosocial maintenance. It then deals with the management of clients with complex needs in this psychosocial context; it gives clear guidelines for working with these clients in terms of assessment, psychological change models and psychosocial maintenance methods.

By combining these three parts, this book presents research findings on complex needs and psychosocial problems and public service responses. It considers why traditional professional philosophies and practice models

1

might be less effective with these clients and considers additional or alternative approaches.

BACKGROUND

The provision of care for clients with complex needs is undertaken by a large and varied number of statutory and voluntary agencies; public order and safety are the responsibility of the criminal justice system. The wide experience of these agencies and their considerable resources are employed to deal with millions of men and women each year. It is, however, common knowledge that many individuals fail to receive the comprehensive help and support that they need and that many do not benefit from what is provided, despite making repeated demands of a wide range of agencies. These people are often the most vulnerable and socially excluded members of our society (Woogh 1990; Brach *et al.* 1995).

Service provision for clients with multiple problems can be fragmented and uncoordinated, handicapped by philosophical differences, incompatible treatment methods, categorical funding and inadequate staff training (Sommerville 1985; Woogh 1990). The combination of frequent service use and non-compliance by clients (Brach *et al.* 1995) is perhaps the greatest challenge to both treating the problem and monitoring it, rendering epidemiological information sparse and services ineffective (Woogh 1990). Treatment is confined often to services for discrete disorders, and conventional methods of monitoring have been largely limited to treatment samples in specialist agencies (Barbee *et al.* 1989). As a consequence, purchasers and providers lack information about the true extent and characteristics of this group among wider social and health care populations, making it extremely difficult to construct a comprehensive profile of needs.

Problems in multidisciplinary and multiagency working have been attributed to a variety of causes, for example from social workers ignoring health problems (Corney 1985) to health workers ignoring social and other non-health problems (Sommerville 1985). However, one of the main obstacles to multidisciplinary agency working is the lack of information about overlapping populations and shared patients. Whilst each agency had some evidence of particularly problematic patient groups which repeatedly attended their own agency and did not appear to benefit (Brach *et al.* 1995), they remained unaware of the extent to which these problematic patients were shared with other agencies.

Recent changes in policy and practice have placed greater emphasis on multiagency development of policy, planning and collaborative working (see, for example, in the UK, DoH 1998a, b). Issues of anti-discriminatory and anti-oppressive practice need to be confronted (see, for example,

Collins and Keene 2000). The development of joint primary health and social care systems depends increasingly on information concerning the needs of social and health care populations and services provided by each agency. In addition, the increasingly close collaboration with the criminal justice system in Britain in the context of the Crime and Disorder Act 1998 relies on understanding of the social and health care needs of criminal populations. However, distinct individual agendas determine both practice and research policies within each agency.

The author strongly believes that professionals can overcome obstacles to multidisciplinary and interprofessional working if these constraints are clearly identified and there is accurate information about the clients they are sharing (or could be sharing). One of the major problems has been the lack of comprehensive and accurate quantitative data about the shared clientele of agencies and understanding of the theories, beliefs and roles of professional groups. While there is growing awareness, based on anecdotal evidence, that professionals have clients or patients in common, the organisational and professional boundaries between agencies have inhibited the development of common systems of information. It was to remedy this major gap in the delivery of services that the Tracking Project database was established and this book written.

The book emphasises the needs of clients with multiple problems. It establishes the principles of shared data and shared practice methods when working with shared clients. It provides a base of information designed to bring different professionals and agencies together in order to identify and define common problems and to plan their solutions.

Each agency is accustomed to a particular model of working and defines its role in specific terms and from a professionally established perspective. For example, a man or woman experiencing a serious drug dependency will be treated by a GP as a medical problem, by a drug agency as needing treatment or a harm minimisation programme and by the police as a possible threat to public order. Each agency will assess every patient/client in terms of its perceived remit and allocate them an appropriate priority (a 'tariff'), depending on the agency's conception of the severity of the problems in their specific area. *Little, if any, account is taken of problems presented by the same people to other agencies.* As a consequence, men and women with multiple problems, who make the greatest demands on resources, may often receive a package of support that is inadequate and not cost-effective.

This book is concerned with identifying these problems, both in face-to-face contact with individual clients and within agency populations as a whole. Once we have information about this group of shared clients and a clearer understanding of the psychosocial context of complex problems, it becomes possible to consider realistic practical solutions.

The book is divided into three parts, as outlined here.

PART I   UNDERSTANDING COMPLEX NEEDS: A PSYCHOSOCIAL APPROACH

Part I examines what we know about adult clients with complex needs and then analyses their service use and contact with a range of professionals responsible for psychological and social interventions. It explores the type of characteristics and problems of this group and the kind of professional help they receive.

Researchers have identified a significant group of vulnerable men and women with complex health, psychological and social problems who move more or less continually through social, mental health and health care agencies, homeless hostels, drug and alcohol agencies and the criminal justice system. They constitute a disproportionate part of the caseloads of health, social care and criminal justice professionals. Many of them are vulnerable, deprived and often labelled as 'revolving door' clients. It is clear that this group is shared by a range of different professions each of which may have multiple contacts with each client.

Part I examines assessed needs and service use within total populations (across a range of agencies) in order to identify obstacles to effective service provision, and opportunities for developing better services for this group and improving cost-effectiveness. Whilst there are, of course, clients with psychosocial needs who only contact one service or none, this work focuses more closely on shared populations of clients.

Finally, the implications for planning and policy are considered.

Chapter 1   Clients with complex psychosocial problems

Chapter 1 reviews the literature on psychosocial problems and complex needs. It demonstrates how clients attending more than one agency often have both psychological and social problems in conjunction with those problems for which they present.

For example, research indicates that significant proportions of mentally disordered individuals have a substance misuse problem (up to 75%) and that this is associated with poor prognosis, higher relapse, more non-compliance; service costs are greater and clinical and social outcomes are less favourable. In addition to mental health and substance abuse problems, complex needs clients have been shown to have a range of social problems. Studies suggest that these people may also have unstable accommodation, a history of criminal offences, hostile behaviour and recent aggression, particularly among young single males.

Chapter 2 Shared clients: complex needs and multiple service use

Adult clients with complex needs cross professional boundaries including health, social care and low threshold self-referral agencies, together with the criminal justice system. This chapter examines the patterns of service use of clients with complex needs. It reports the findings of the 'Tracking' research multiagency database, providing evidence of the extent to which different professionals share clients with complex needs and the characteristics of this group of clients.

The Tracking Project was established in 1996. It was designed to provide an innovative method of collating and analysing data within overlapping agency populations. The amalgamated database contains the total county populations (over 800 000 anonymised subjects) of the following 23 partner agencies: social services, health authority, county hospital health trust, community health trust, community mental health trust, ambulance trust, GPs, housing, hostels, night shelter, county police, probation and prison services, together with a range of non-statutory agencies including all drug and alcohol services in one county.

In this way it has been possible to identify and characterise complex needs or 'revolving door' clients who consistently reused different services and were in contact with the criminal justice system. Data for three years reveal significant overlaps in services, together with identifying and characterising a group of men and women with psychosocial problems who repeatedly use a wide range of agencies. This is the first time in the UK that such a database has been created, providing a foundation for interagency working with clients who have multiple problems. It demonstrates not only that there is a need to examine shared clients more closely, but also that it is feasible for planners and professionals to do so.

Chapter 3 Planning comprehensive care: assessed needs across populations

This chapter considers the policy and planning perspective, largely devoted to assessing needs and managing services for *single specialist agency* populations. It analyses the underlying assumptions and constraints in specialist agency policy and planning which limit comprehensive service delivery for populations of complex needs clients.

It examines how needs assessments for specific agency populations are constructed for needs-led planning. It demonstrates how a multiagency approach to policy and planning can be based on assessed health and psychosocial needs across populations. It considers the limitations of assessing needs in one agency population only, rather than examining assessed needs of total or shared populations. The values and priorities of planners in different agencies are analysed to show how their approaches (and therefore also their data collection) may reflect their attitudes to prioritising services.

Using the 'Tracking' method to examine assessed need and service provision across overlapping agency populations

Having identified the existence of a group of shared clients with complex psychosocial needs across total social and health care populations and considered the implications for monitoring assessed needs and planning services for them, this chapter will demonstrate how the 'Tracking' method can be used to monitor assessed need and service provision in any area. The method can be used for combining any number of agency populations for any area, whether this includes all health, social and criminal justice populations or simply overlapping social and health care populations.

The chapter then examines how agencies and professionals can work together more effectively to prioritise services for clients with complex needs, through the development of multiple agency needs assessments for interagency service planning and interagency tariffs.

PART II   THE LIMITATIONS OF SPECIALIST PERSPECTIVES: A PSYCHOSOCIAL APPROACH TO MULTIDISCIPLINARY WORKING

The research findings outlined in Part I raise a series of questions and highlight a need for greater understanding of different professional responses to this group. Part II goes some way towards answering these questions. It will provide a qualitative picture of the different perspectives of clients and professionals and between different professional groups, in order to give insight and understanding into the problems and needs of this group and the obstacles and opportunities for professional practice.

It examines professional and client perspectives in order to provide greater understanding of the usefulness and limitations of different professional models for this group. It becomes clear that professionals within each type of agency define the problems within the context of the academic base and priorities of their profession and that they use methods derived from this base. Each agency has its own professional perspective, ideology, methods of working, plans and priorities. Individual agency agendas and priorities are often in conflict with other agencies. So, for example, the probation service might see problems in terms of criminal behaviour and successful outcome in terms of reconviction rates, whereas health agencies may focus only on clinical diagnosis and see health gain as an appropriate criterion. Similarly, criminal justice workers might see severity or frequency of crime as the main criteria for allocating services, medical practitioners might see severity of diagnosis as the determining criterion for prioritising treatment services, whereas social care workers might see deprivation indicators as more relevant.

So professionals (like planners) assess predefined needs in their specialised populations, using criteria and priorities which are pertinent to their specialisms. They do this in isolation from each other. As planners assess and manage needs in particular populations, professionals also assess and manage appropriate clinical or other needs in terms of their predetermined caseload. Specialist professionals may recognise that some clients have more than one problem, but often regard them as 'inappropriate' and not part of their remit or not qualifying for their services in terms of lack of severity of the particular specialist problem.

Alternatively, professionals may not recognise a range of problems; this may involve differential diagnosis or a focus on specific problems about which the specialist has the expertise to deal. Consequently, many clients with complex psychological and social needs fail to receive the comprehensive help they require.

The findings highlight the psychosocial context of complex needs and suggest additional or alternative philosophies and practice theories which contribute to better understanding and more effective methods for assessing needs and working with this group.

Chapter 4   Understanding client perspectives: the need for maintenance support

Chapter 4 examines the underlying assumptions in specialist professional assessments which limit comprehensive and ongoing help for complex needs clients. It explores the need for maintenance.

It reports findings from a series of in-depth interviews with a range of different clients and professionals. It highlights the major themes arising from these data, particularly the understandings and aims of clients and compares them with the models and aims of different professionals.

It considers the limitations of professional practice for complex needs clients. It asks if problems should be seen in terms of 'inappropriate clients' or 'inappropriate services'. Different professional perspectives and attitudes to presenting clients are considered to reveal how they reflect what is seen as an appropriate client and appropriate use of services. It focuses on specialist practitioner approaches to assessment and the underlying assumptions in professional interventions which limit *ongoing* help for complex needs clients.

Chapter 5   Understanding professional perspectives: the need for new models of multidisciplinary care

Chapter 5 examines similarities and differences between different professional models and how each delimits interprofessional working and comprehensive care.

The chapter will build on the discussion of obstacles to multi-professional working and highlight the reasons why a psychosocial perspective is necessary to a comprehensive understanding of complex needs. It will consider the opportunities for developing an interdisciplinary approach to psychosocial problems.

PART III   COMPREHENSIVE PRACTICE: A PSYCHOSOCIAL APPROACH TO CHANGE AND MAINTENANCE

This part of the book moves on from a critique of the limitations of services for complex needs clients to solutions. While it is suggested that professionals should work from the population planning framework outlined in Part I to develop comprehensive assessment and ongoing care, it provides guidelines for individual practitioners independently of policy issues.

Part III discusses in detail how individual professionals can provide a comprehensive service for clients with complex needs. The need for concurrent and/or consecutive psychological and social interventions and ongoing support through time is explored. This part is designed to inform readers how to use their own professional skills in conjunction with ongoing psychological and social support. Detailed guidelines are provided in three main areas: psychosocial assessment, psychological change models and psychosocial maintenance methods. In this way it is hoped to prioritise services for this group and to provide appropriate psychosocial care and support over sufficient time periods.

Chapter 6   Comprehensive psychosocial assessment

Chapter 6 gives clear guidelines for carrying out psychosocial assessments and care plans. It proposes the notion of developing additional generic psychosocial assessment criteria across professional groups. It describes the essential components of a comprehensive psychosocial assessment and demonstrates how it provides the framework for change and/or maintenance. The chapter highlights the importance of placing all problems within a psychosocial framework in order to draw up comprehensive assessment criteria. It considers the specific additional psychosocial criteria that are essential to comprehensive assessments across different professions.

Chapter 7   Psychological change-orientated methods

Chapter 7 gives a description of a range of different psychological change or treatment models and methods. It explains each approach and the types of problems each is used for. It then considers the limitations of both the psychological perspective without social context, and change models without maintenance methods.

Chapter 8   Psychosocial maintenance methods

As in the previous chapter, a description of a range of different 'maintenance' methods is provided. Maintenance methods are concerned with individual clients coping or maintaining themselves at a certain level, rather than changing or improving themselves. The chapter considers the importance of coping skills and supportive environments, low threshold and outreach services, prevention and relapse prevention services and crisis support.

Chapter 9   New models of ongoing psychosocial care

Chapter 9 draws together the final recommendation for policy and practice with complex needs clients.

Part I
Understanding Complex Needs: a Multidisciplinary Approach

This first part of the book will set the context for the analysis of professional and client perspectives and of practice models that follows in Parts II and III. As the title of the book makes clear, the approach is multidisciplinary and psychosocial. As such, it stands in contrast to specialist approaches that characterise the individual professions responsible for providing health and social care and maintaining the criminal justice system.

The subject area is largely identified and established through the substantive body of literature, mostly research-based, which has been produced in the last two decades of the twentieth century, dealing with the care and support of men and women whose needs have brought them into direct contact with the many agencies providing the services. These individuals can be seen as constituting a continuum. At one end are those who appear once at one agency with one problem; at the other are the vulnerable persons who have multiple and usually intractable problems and who seek their solution by attending a number of agencies on many occasions. As we shall see, the former make up the majority and the latter a minority, but a minority that is very demanding of resources. The strategy adopted in this book is to concentrate on the men and women with complex needs, since they exemplify the issues of multiple problems and shared care that preoccupy the relevant policy makers, planners and services providers at national and local levels.

Almost all the literature reviewed in the first chapter points to a situation where, in both the UK and the USA, service provision is disjointed and less effective than is necessary. The reasons for this are examined. One important factor is the failure by the relevant agencies to share information, which is an essential precondition for comprehensive collaboration.

A means of establishing a common information database is described in Chapter 2, together with practical proposals for using it as the basis for multiagency joint assessments and methods of establishing priorities.

A common database is also one of the major prerequisites of a collaborative system of policy making and planning. How policy is made and how planning is undertaken are the subject matter of Chapter 3, leading to a consideration of 'joined up working' that is a major strategic aim of many governments at present.

Chapter 1
Clients with Complex Psychosocial Problems

INTRODUCTION

This chapter sets out to examine the present state of our knowledge of clients with complex needs through a literature search. As noted in the introduction to this part of the book, these vulnerable men and women lie at one end of a continuum and at the other end there are those who have a single 'simple' need. In between there are many whose needs vary from the relatively straightforward to much less so. By directing our attention to the most difficult and intractable group who make heavy use of services, we intend to provide an apt illustration of problems. The issue, nevertheless, for policy makers and planners is how to design and deliver a service that deals with this great variety.

This is followed by an account of treatment and other services, which concludes that there are problem areas concerning matters of appropriateness, which may be viewed as to do with inappropriate clients, inappropriate service delivery or the services themselves. The chapter ends with a general discussion.

The recent literature on complex needs is fragmented and, as we shall see, tends to approach this difficult area from the standpoint of a specific professional interest. This is not surprising since, as we demonstrate in a later chapter, professional areas of concern and their boundaries are a significant element of policy and practice. The research indicates that clients with complex needs and psychosocial problems are those frequently attending a range of different agencies but less likely to be helped by any one agency. The research findings identify a group of repeat attenders with health and psychosocial problems across a range of professional services, who use a disproportionate amount of agency resources, apparently without gaining much benefit. Therefore there is need to improve service provision both to provide more appropriate help to this client group and to make services more cost-effective.

TYPES OF COOCCURRING PROBLEMS

To provide an order to the review, complex needs and multiple problems are examined as follows:

(1) Psychological, mental health and other problems.
(2) Learning and developmental difficulties and other problems.
(3) Social problems, homelessness and other problems.
(4) Crime and other problems.
(5) Drug and alcohol misuse and other problems.

The list of topics is not exhaustive, by its nature is not logically exclusive, and is not in any order of importance.

This is then followed by an analysis of research on diagnosis, particularly dual diagnosis, which has attracted major interest in its own right.

Psychological and mental health problems

Psychological and mental health problems are reported as constituting between a fifth and a third of the workload of GPs in Britain. Matson & Bamberg (1998) in the USA argue that emotional and behavioural problems are a major source of additional handicap for adolescents and adults with learning difficulties. As we shall show in the next chapter, mental illness is a frequent component of a range of problems found in those men and women who make heavy and repeated use of services – the 'revolving door' phenomenon. Research regarding suicide attempts demonstrates that 90% of suicides have mental health problems (DoH 1996).

A study of a group of women with post-traumatic stress disorder (PTSD) is reported by Najavits *et al.* (1999). When compared with women suffering from PTSD who were not substance abusers, the authors found that the dual diagnosis respondents consistently had a more severe clinical profile, including worse life conditions (e.g. physical appearance, opportunities in life) both as children and adults, more criminal behaviour, a higher number of lifetime suicide attempts, a greater number with a sibling with a drug problem and fewer outpatient psychiatric treatments. The two groups did not differ in number or type of lifetime traumas, PTSD onset or severity, family history of substance misuse, coping style, psychiatric symptoms or sociodemographic characteristics. Ouimette *et al.* (1998) state that PTSD is commonly associated with substance misuse and that, although this is well documented, relatively little is known about effective treatment. Psychological counselling and referrals for family treatment and self-help group participation are among the treatment practices that are recommended.

In the 1990s there were a number of studies of particular psychological disorders found in association with other problems. Schubiner *et al.* (1995) state that it is now recognised that attention-deficit/hyperactivity disorders (ADHD) may persist into adult life. A number of studies have discovered an association between ADHD and substance misuse. Tucker (1999) found that ADHD is associated with later development of substance misuse and reviews the evidence for the mediating role of antisocial behaviour in this association. He concludes that such behaviour may have a predominating role and casts doubt on the possibility that individuals may be self-medicating. Marshall (1997) points out that the relationship between panic disorder and substance misuse is well known but not understood. He suggests that individuals may be self-medicating for anxiety symptoms or may be generically predisposed to this dual diagnosis. Both conditions must be taken into account when making a treatment plan.

Grella (1997) states that women who abuse alcohol or drugs are more likely than men to be diagnosed with a psychiatric disorder, particularly depression or a personality disorder. The interaction of substance misuse, pregnancy and mental illness creates complex needs that often go unrecognised by treatment providers. Jerrell & Wilson (1997) examine the differences between white and ethnic client psychosocial functioning, psychiatric and substance abuse symptomatology and service use costs. In a longitudinal study they showed that clients from ethnic backgrounds received less supportive treatment although their overall outcomes were the same as those for white clients after six months.

Polcin (1997) asserts that recent epidemiological studies indicate that alcohol-related problems are widespread and include multiple medical, psychological, family and social consequences. The author analyses the many debates and controversies about aetiology, diagnosis and disease versus syndrome concepts. It is argued that if the field of psychology is to make an effective contribution to alcohol treatment, clinicians must deploy specific diagnostic and intervention strategies.

The significance of mental illness in men and women with complex needs is demonstrated in the review below of dual diagnosis. It is also considered further in Chapter 5.

Learning and developmental difficulties and other problems

The difficulties of providing adequate services for individuals with learning difficulties have only been recognised relatively recently. As a group they have been characterised as a 'Cinderella' service, lacking any political power and attracting much public stigma. They do, however, demonstrate the intractable problems that often face vulnerable men and women with complex needs. Part of the difficulty arises from the institutional vagueness of the boundary between intellectual disability and mental illness and the possibility that mental health problems occur more often among those with learning difficulties than in the general population (Anon 1999).

It is also suggested that this group may pose problems of challenging behaviour taking into account the difficulties of psychiatric diagnosis in persons with developmental disabilities (Sturmey 1998; Clark & Bukstein 1999). The literature suggests that it has been 'standard practice' to ignore comorbidity in men and women where learning difficulties and mental illness coexist and that differential diagnosis gives priority to a single causation within the many presenting symptoms. Given that persons with learning disabilities are now normally located within the community rather than in institutions, new client management issues are apparent, centring on obtaining funds and access to services, establishing effective treatment plans and ensuring interdisciplinary communication (Fuller & Sabatino 1998). Treatment to control self-injury, physical aggression, property damage and hyperactivity is not clearly established and there is no guidance on how behavioural and psychopharmacological treatment should be combined (Pyles *et al.* 1997).

Social problems, homelessness and other problems

Recent government initiatives in the UK have been directed towards reducing the amount of homelessness; in particular the establishment of the Rough Sleepers Unit. Homeless people are, of course, a highly visible group in western society and one whose numbers increased throughout the 1980s and 1990s. Ducq *et al.* (1997) in their comprehensive review of the literature have examined the substantial number of epidemiological surveys in the UK, Australia, Canada and particularly the USA, which have established a relationship between homelessness and mental illness. The authors show that the disparity of epidemiological methods in making any assessment is compounded by a lack of agreement on the definition of homelessness and by the very varied use of means of psychiatric evalua-tion. One third of homeless adults had a history of hospitalisation for mental illness and rates of psychosis range up to 70%; 4–7% of homeless people suffer from affective disorders and a substantial number of them have problems of substance misuse. The authors also comment that their data highlight the 'Anglo-Saxon' debate between those who identify deinstitutionalisation as a cause of homelessness and those who see it as a more general consequence of social and economic malaise.

Other studies estimate that up to a third of homeless people have a history of criminal offences, antisocial behaviour and recent aggression, particularly young single males (Leff 1993; Menezes *et al.* 1996).

Lambert & Caces (1995) argue that sociodemographic indices of drug misuse among the general household population may be less accurate when applied to homeless people and transients. A study of 908 homeless and transient people in Washington DC showed that three key socio-economic correlates of drug misuse in the general population – educational attainment, employment status and marital status – were not significant predictors of drug misuse among the homeless. Those that were significant included institutionalisation during the previous year, location within the metropolitan area and stage of homelessness.

This relatively recent interest in homeless people is also reflected in a number of studies which examine their use of services. Marshall *et al.* (1994) established that early loss of contact with services for homeless people in Oxford was strongly predicted by substance (mainly alcohol) dependence in the month before the first attendance at the clinic and that homeless people with mental disorders who were also alcohol dependent were five times more likely to lose contact with caring agencies than those who were not similarly dependent. The authors conclude that homeless people with mental illness who are substance dependent tend to be more mobile than those who are not substance dependent.

Studies in the USA examine ambitious projects for providing services to the homeless with multiple problems, which report encouraging results (Krueger *et al.* 1997; Bebout *et al.* 1997).

Crime and other problems

The link between criminal behaviour and the other problems that feature prominently in the lives of men and women with complex needs – mental illness, substance abuse, homelessness, unemployment, etc. – is well established and thoroughly documented. For example, a survey by Sestoft (1996) of 25 years' research on forensic psychiatry in Denmark, covering 30 studies, demonstrates that criminal recidivism is common among forensic patients, of whom more than half have a dual diagnosis. A review undertaken recently by Thomson (1999) examines the evidence for an association between crime and substance abuse and the probable synergistic role of mental illness in aggression.

The strength of the link is evident in the study by Hoptman *et al.* (1999) in their study of patient characteristics with a clinical prediction of assaultive behaviour in a New York forensic psychiatric hospital. In this investigation, psychiatrists were asked to predict which of a sample of 183 newly admitted male patients were likely to show assaultive behaviour over a period of three months. These predictions were compared with reported assaults. The psychiatrists correctly predicted in 71% of the sample, with a diagnostic sensitivity of 54% and a diagnostic specificity of 79%. The characteristics associated with the accurate prediction were race, transfer from a civil facility following violence, education, arrests for violent offences, childhood physical abuse, hostility and inability to follow ward routines. The characteristics associated with actual assaults were transfer from a civil hospital, dual diagnosis of schizophrenia and substance abuse or dependence, childhood physical abuse, age, thought disorder and temper. All these characteristics were rated independently. Some of the characteristics associated with clinical prediction, such as race, ability to follow ward routine and arrest history were not associated with actual assaults and the clinicians did not use dual diagnosis as a predictor. Nevertheless, these results are striking.

Other American studies support the view that crime is closely associated with multiple problems. Peters *et al.* (1997) examine the few studies of female offenders with substance misuse that show women with varied psychosocial problems and treatment needs and who have been subjected to frequent sexual abuse and violence. The authors undertook a study of a sample of 1655 prisoners with a history of substance misuse, 26% of whom were female and 74% male. They found that female inmates experienced employment problems more often, had lower incomes, more frequently reported cocaine as the primary drug of choice and were more likely to report depression, anxiety, suicidal behaviour and a history of physical and sexual abuse. Edens *et al.* (1997) report that 3–11% of prison inmates in the USA have mental illness and substance abuse.

These findings accord generally with an Australian study of 194 schizophrenic patients with substance misuse. The sample was predominantly male, had instability in accommodation and almost half had a history of criminal offences, most often drug or alcohol-related (Fowler *et al.* 1998).

This research is, as we shall see, consistent with the evidence presented in the next chapter from a major study in an English county.

Drug and alcohol misuse and other problems

Research indicates that high proportions of substance misusers have multiple problems ranging from psychological or serious mental health problems to social and housing problems (Kozarickovacic *et al.* 1995). Clear links have been established between mental health problems, drug misuse and crime (Bean & Wilkinson 1988; Hammersley *et al.* 1990; Keene 1997). Associations between alcohol misuse and mental illness have also been highlighted by Barbee *et al.* (1989) who identified 50% of schizophrenics as having drug or alcohol problems and Woogh (1990) who identified a link between major functional disorders and drug and alcohol misuse.

Studies suggest that clients/patients with drug and/or alcohol misuse together with mental health problems also have unstable accommodation (a third of homeless people are estimated to have prior histories of drug or alcohol misuse) (Leff 1993; Menezes *et al.* 1996), a history of criminal offences, recent hostile behaviour and aggression, particularly among young single males (Swanson *et al.* 1990). Bartels *et al.* (1991) identified a link between substance misuse, mental illness and violence, suggesting that violence was more common among the mentally disordered who misused drugs. Self-neglect and consequent deterioration in health are linked to alcohol abuse and mental health (Quinton *et al.* 1995). Whilst this research tells us little about service use as a whole, it suggests that drug and alcohol agency clients will have contact with a range of different non-specialist, generic agencies.

Kadden & Kranzler (1992) examine the way in which diagnosis of comorbid psychiatric disorders in substance abuse patients is complicated by the fact that many abused substances induce transient symptoms that mimic independent disorders. The authors developed criteria designed to distinguish 'independent' comorbid disorders from those that may have been 'substance-induced', to determine the impact on rates of diagnosis and on concurrent and predictive validity. They show that of those with symptoms sufficient to meet criteria for comorbid depression (12%) or anxiety diagnoses (26%), fewer than 25% were considered to have independent disorders, and these patients did not constitute a category of greater severity. It is apparent that further research is needed to establish criteria that will provide a clinically meaningful distinction.

Substance misuse is also recognised as frequently related to previous and contemporary experience of abuse. A recent study typifies this well-established finding. Individuals in drug treatment, particularly women, often record high levels of past sexual and physical abuse. Although histories of sexual and physical abuse are associated with greater prevalence and severity of depression, anxiety, phobias and interpersonal difficulties for individuals seeking substance-related treatment, a number of investigations failed to demonstrate that prior sexual or physical abuse compromised short-term drug treatment outcomes (Fiorentine *et al.* 1999).

Similarly, a study by Jarvis & Copeland (1997) revealed that women with a history of childhood sexual abuse had higher levels of psychological distress and were more likely to have attempted suicide if they were being treated for substance misuse than those in treatment who had no such experience. The authors comment that their findings point to the need for better collaboration between drug and alcohol agencies and other health services.

SINGLE, DUAL AND MULTIPLE DIAGNOSIS

It is necessary, first, to explore briefly the significance of the use of the term 'diagnosis', in anticipation of further extended analysis in later chapters.

When medicine and related professions formally assign a label to problematic behaviour, assessed need or right to services, the label is referred to as a 'diagnosis'. To justify this labelling process, clinicians and other members of the helping professions have constructed elaborate and sophisticated sets of criteria which are normally claimed to be based on theory or experience. From a sociological perspective, these professional practices can be seen as the medicalisation of deviant behaviour, by which clinicians attempt to redefine 'badness' as 'illness' (Conrad 1992; Conrad & Schneider 1992). Similarly, McKeown *et al.* (1998) argue that until recently the term has been loosely defined with consequences for the targeting of services. Using a postmodernist perspective they see the usage as a form of social control and as evidence of the increasing medicalisation of social life. In the same way, psychological diagnosis or assessment can be seen to define problems narrowly in terms of individual psychological processes.

An important corollary to this argument is that clinical diagnosis of substance misuse is derived mainly from cultural norms. So that, for example, drinking behaviour that is considered 'alcoholic' is that which deviates from the acceptable; acceptability in turn is determined by a number of social factors. What is 'normal' for young men is often seen as deviant for, say, middle-aged women.

Single diagnosis

With this very important caveat in mind, we now return to a review of the literature. A useful example for illustrating the limitations of single diagnosis is substance abuse. In much of the western world, this is perceived by professionals as a disease and is treated accordingly by doctors. (In much of the literature the 'disease' model is not synonymous with the 'medical' model.) This is particularly the situation in the USA, where '... the predominant model for understanding alcoholism and other addictions is the view that these disorders are diseases' (Yalisove 1998; Toombs 2000). In addition, in countries where the disease model is less prevalent, many treatment programmes are based on a medical model and are therefore supervised by physicians. The notion is also strongly established in the UK and much of western Europe. This is therefore often an example of single diagnosis – it is seen as 'primary disease' or addiction that is not the result of another condition (Talbott 1989).

In much the same way, aberrant behaviour has been categorised as mental illness and become the territory of psychiatry (Szasz 1976). As an illness it is identified and categorised by (single) diagnosis. Where substance misuse and mental illness are the subject of single diagnosis, their respective treatments are based on different aetiologies and may have little in common with each other and in fact may even conflict.

Dual diagnosis

Dual diagnosis has been increasingly used in practice, in research and in the literature to describe users of services who have mental health problems and who are substance misusers. A notable example from the USA is the *Diagnostic and Statistical Manual of Mental Disorders* (American Psychiatric Association 1994). In this manual, substance dependence is defined in terms of seven major symptoms, any three of which justify the diagnosis of dependence.

Dual diagnosis is not used to describe those men and women who are diagnosed as having mental illness and problems other than substance misuse, or persons with physical illness who are substance misusers and have other problems.

Comorbidity between alcohol and other drug misuse and mental illness has been a major subject of study, particularly in the USA, since the early 1990s. Research indicates that significant proportions of mentally disordered individuals have a substance misuse problem and that this is associated with poor prognosis, higher relapse and more non-compliance; service costs are greater and clinical and social outcomes are less favourable. Conversely, high proportions of substance misusers have a mental health problem, frequently associated with non-compliance, higher service costs and poor social outcomes.

For example, results from the Epidemiological Catchment Area Study in the USA show that substance misuse problems cooccur with psychiatric illness at a rate far in excess of that predicted by chance (Regier *et al.* 1990). In a population of 20 000, 20% had at least one pychiatric disorder, whereas among those with an alcohol disorder the rate rose to 37% and among those with a drug misuse disorder it rose to 50%. For patients being treated for a substance abuse problem, who had a psychiatric illness, the rate varied from 67% to 95%, depending on whether the diagnosis involved alcohol, drugs or both (Ross *et al.* 1990). Other studies have resulted in different rates, both in the UK and the USA. (Menezes *et al.* 1996; Soyka 1996; Pozzi *et al.* 1997; Launay *et al.* 1998). The variance in rates reported is substantial – from 20% to 75% – (which is clearly problematic), but all the studies show much higher rates of comorbidity than would occur by chance.

It does not, of course, follow that there is a causal relationship at work here, and if there is, it is not possible to determine causal direction. Substance misuse may result from mental illness or it may cause a mental illness. A common factor may be responsible for both, or a reciprocal relationship may exist in which the two sets of problems influence one another in a synergistic manner (Toombs 2000). Attempts have been made to illuminate the nature of the relationship by examining the order in which they occur. Ross (1988) established in a treatment sample that the onset of antisocial personality disorder nearly always came before alcohol abuse. For other psychiatric illnesses, the percentages were lower: schizophrenia 60%, phobia 60% and panic disorder 58%. In turn, alcohol abuse appeared more likely to come before the onset of major depression (57%) and obsessive-compulsive disorder (54%). These sorts of findings have led some researchers to suggest a self-medication theory where, for example, drugs or alcohol are used in an attempt to cure depression.

In addition to mental health and substance abuse problems, these patients have been shown to have a range of social problems. Studies in Europe replicate those in the USA, suggesting that patients with dual diagnosis have unstable accommodation (a third of homeless people are estimated to have prior histories of dual diagnosis), a history of criminal offences, hostile behaviour and recent aggression, particularly among young single males. Populations which cross professional boundaries are frequently characterised by dual diagnosis, including low threshold self-referral agencies (such as accident and emergency departments) and the criminal justice system.

The substantial amount of research in this area has still left a number of uncertainties and disagreements. Mueser *et al.* (1998), for example, argue that the aetiology of the high prevalence of substance abuse disorders in patients with schizophrenia and bipolar disorder is unclear. There are several theories of increased comorbidity: one asserts that the evidence points to antisocial personality disorder; a second posits that biological vulnerability of psychiatric disorders results in sensitivity to alcohol and drugs that produces problems of substance misuse. Tsuang *et al.* (1995) examined how the comorbidity of substance misuse or dependence and psychiatric illness can complicate assessment and treatment. They examined substance misuse and psychopathology in an outpatient setting among 391 men and women evaluated at an anxiety and affective disorders clinic. In sharp contrast to findings in other settings, there were no significant differences in the severity of psychopathology between patients with and without substance abuse disorders and dependence.

Hien *et al.* (1997) examined those patients with clearly established major depression and alcohol abuse. They argued that, although assumptions are often made about the relationship between these two conditions, there is very little empirical evidence on the effects of changes in depression on the course of alcohol dependence in patients presenting at psychiatric facilities. A study of the five-year history of alcohol problems in 127 patients showed that changes in the status of depression had strong significant effects on the course of alcoholism, with an increased chance of remission and reduced chance of relapse. A study by Luke *et al.* (1996), using a range of instruments, concluded that dual diagnosis is extremely heterogeneous and requires individualised treatment programmes.

Multiple diagnosis

While dual diagnosis is firmly located in the world of medicine, experience has shown that medical problems are also associated with a variety of psychological and social problems. A number of studies of dual diagnosis have incorporated these problems into the research design and others, more broadly-based, have attempted to explore the range of problems encountered by substance abusers. Some studies are summarised here as examples of 'multiple diagnosis' since they share in common a generally positivist/scientific approach aimed at producing treatment solutions.

Luke *et al.* (1996) rated 467 patients admitted to a state psychiatric hospital with a dual diagnosis in terms of psychological, social and community functioning, scoring medical, employment, alcohol, drug, legal, family and psychiatric functioning. They were able to divide patients into seven groups for possible treatment programmes. Mowbray *et al.* (1999) undertook a study of 486 dually diagnosed patients from an urban psychiatric hospital, based on a comprehensive array of clinical, social and community functioning measures. The majority of the respondents had serious economic and employment problems, poor living arrangements, family and social relationships that were limited or subject to conflict and many had criminal records. The Addiction Severity Index (ASI) revealed that the problems requiring support were: psychiatric, alcohol and drug abuse, employment, family/social, legal and medical. Some sub-group differences based on gender, age and race were found to have implications for community treatment planning.

Sloan and Rowe (1995) looked at the psychosocial correlates of those persons who had a history of any type of psychiatric treatment and who were identified by staff as suitable candidates for an outpatient dual diagnosis programme. They reviewed 1303 consecutive patients who applied for substance abuse or dual diagnosis treatment at a Veterans Administration hospital in the USA. Data were collected on admission and on even the broadest definition (having a history of any kind of treatment for psychiatric illness), dual diagnosis was shown to be associated with high rates of homelessness, disconnection from social support systems, unemployment and vocational disability and treatment chronicity. Finally, it should be pointed out that even the concept of multiple diagnosis has limitations, since the very notion of diagnosis limits assessment of associated problems.

TREATMENT AND OTHER SERVICES

While we know that patients/clients have multiple problems, we know very little about multiple service use. Almost all the detailed research on dual and multiple diagnosis is based on data from drug or alcohol agencies or mental health clinic populations. There is also some limited research concerning two overlapping agencies, but this cannot be used, for example, to identify and characterise the full service use patterns of drug agency clients who are clients of social service departments, or are on probation or who use the varied services of the NHS. It is, however, apparent that populations which cross professional boundaries are frequently characterised by mental health and/or drug and alcohol problems, including low threshold self-referral agencies (such as accident and emergency departments) and the criminal justice system.

It will be evident from this brief review of recent research that care and support for men and women with complex needs and psychosocial problems are dominated by concepts of diagnosis and the importance given to treatment. Where those problems concern or are part of health, mental illness or substance abuse, then their definition as falling within the realm of medicine ensures that diagnosis and assessment lead almost always to some form of treatment. The first part of this section examines recent research and identifies some of the major issues that arise from this approach. This has important implications for both assessment and intervention. Diagnosis and assessment for treatment focus on a primary problem that can be treated and interventions are accordingly narrow and time-limited. These issues are discussed in more detail in Parts II and III.

Screening, identification and assessment

Treatment first requires screening, identification and assessment. The major concentration on dual diagnosis has brought about a substantial number of research studies in this area. Zeidonis and Brady (1997), for example, analyse the process of identification and assessment. They assert that the initial phase includes engaging the patient in the clinician's concerns and providing the patients with information about the problems as well as the possibility of change. This is seen as particularly important in the development of a realistic treatment plan, which must attempt to evaluate and treat the substance misuse and the psychiatric and medical illnesses. (Here is a very clear example of the dominance of the professional perspective and the accompanying assumptions about the patient's view. We shall return to this issue in Part II.)

Sturmey (1998) undertakes a short historical review of psychiatric diagnosis in persons with development disabilities who have mental illness and substance misuse. Definitions are examined and some of the problems identified. Common issues in the process of collecting and combining information to make a diagnosis are described. Gafoor and Rassool (1998) argue that mental health nurses have a key role to play in the early identification and management of dually diagnosed patients. They also address treatment strategies for such patients. ElandGoossensen *et al.* (1997) compare two instruments used in the assessment of dually diagnosed patients, using the ASI and the Composite International Diagnostic Interview (CIDI). This study of 327 patients demonstrated that there were large areas of disagreement. Breakey *et al.* (1998) state that professionals often miss the presence of substance misuse in patients with disabling mental illness, and argue that this could be substantially improved by the use of a simple screening instrument. A research study appeared to confirm this finding.

A study which involved patient participation was undertaken in 1999. A cohort of 264 consecutively admitted patients entered into a dual diagnosis treatment programme were questioned about their perceptions of their problems and need for treatment before and after the programme. Most patients acknowledged a substance misuse or mental health problem and the need for treatment. Patients with substance induced mental health disorders were more likely to acknowledge a substance misuse problem and need for treatment. After treatment, changes in perception of mental illness were greater for substance induced mental disorder patients compared to patients with a primary mental illness. Persons with a more severe substance misuse problem were more likely to acknowledge it and the need for treatment. The author concludes that in-patient stay presents a prime opportunity to treat substance misuse.

Bartels *et al.* (1995) in a major study assessed the long-term course of substance misuse and dependence among severely mentally ill patients. A prospective seven-year follow-up of severely mentally ill outpatients successfully located and reassessed 79.1% ($n = 148$) of the patients from the original study group. They were assessed for alcohol and drug use at baseline and seven-year follow-up. Analysis showed that there was little change in the prevalence of active substance use disorder from baseline to follow-up. Alcohol use or dependence was present in 24% of patients at baseline and 21% at follow-up; drug abuse or dependence was present in 20% at baseline and 17% at follow-up. However, those with initial alcohol abuse had a higher rate of remission (67%) than those with initial alcohol dependence (33%). Similarly, those with initial drug abuse had a higher rate of remission (54%) than those with initial drug dependence (31%). These differing rates suggest that distinguishing between abuse and dependence may have important implications for assessment and prognosis.

Dual diagnosis treatment programmes

Interventions for dual diagnosis, as might be expected, are within a medical treatment framework, attempting to provide parallel therapeutic solutions to the two problems.

Bellack and Gearon (1998) and Drake *et al.* (1998) are examples of a substantial number of studies expressing dissatisfaction at the state of treatment for dual diagnosis. Bellack and Gearon argue that, while there is widespread agreement on the need to integrate psychiatric and substance abuse treatments, there are no programmes with solid empirical support. Drake *et al.* state that dual diagnosis patients traditionally received care from two different sets of physicians in parallel treatment systems.

For the UK, there are varying proposals for future development. Holland (1996) looked to new patterns of joint working between mental health and drug and alcohol services. He also suggests (1999) that specialised dual diagnosis teams should be established, based on examples from the USA. Hall and Farrell (1997) and Smith and Hucker (1993) propose that dual diagnosis should remain within the umbrella of general psychiatric services. Such views are examined in more detail in Chapter 5, where dual diagnosis is used as a detailed example of professional differences and practice solutions.

Multidisciplinary treatment

The realisation that patients with mental illness and substance misuse often experience a range of other problems – in other words they have complex psychosocial needs that do not necessarily indicate dual diagnosis as the prime starting point for a treatment programme – has given rise to models that are broad-based and eclectic. Such initiatives are as yet rare.

One example is the study by Moggi *et al.* (1999) who examine a model of treatment for substance abuse and dependence for patients with substance use disorders and concomitant psychiatric disorders. The model focuses on five interrelated sets of variables (social background, intake functioning, dual diagnosis treatment orientation, patients' change on proximal outcomes and aftercare participation) that are hypothesised to affect dual diagnosis patients' one-year post-treatment outcomes.

A total of 981 male dual diagnosis patients completed assessment at intake, discharge and one-year follow-up. The relative importance of each set of variables as predictors of outcome was estimated by constructing block variables and conducting path analyses. Dual diagnosis patients had a higher abstinence rate at follow-up (39%) than at intake (2%); they also improved on freedom from psychiatric symptoms (from 60% to 68%) and employment (from 20% to 29%). At follow-up, patients in programmes with a stronger dual diagnosis treatment orientation showed a higher rate of freedom from psychiatric symptoms (71%) than did patients in weaker dual diagnosis treatment oriented programmes (65%); they were also more likely to be employed (34% compared with 25%). More change on proximal outcomes and more aftercare participation were also associated with better one-year outcomes. Patients with less severe psychiatric disorders improved more and responded better to dual diagnosis oriented treatments than did patients with more severe psychiatric disorders.

A study by Keene *et al.* (1999) set out to compare the progress of clients attending two substance misuse agencies. A wide range of problems were recorded at one, three to six and twelve-month intervals; these included measures of substance misuse and dependence together with social problems and physical and mental health problems. Differences in outcome between the two agencies were entirely attributable to the number and severity of a range of problems rather than simply to severity of dependence or differences between the agencies. This raised questions of how treatment outcome is understood and explained and the usefulness of therapeutic models.

Maisto *et al.* (1999) examine ways of changing patterns of substance misuse among individuals with cooccurring schizophrenia and substance use disorder, who tend to have medical and social problems and to make slower progress in treatment than those who have either disorder alone. The purpose of this study was to collect qualitative data as a way to help identify techniques that might help to change patterns of substance use in the seriously mentally ill. The participants were 21 men and women who were psychiatric clinic out-patients and who had a current schizophrenia spectrum diagnosis. A total of 18 participants had a lifetime diagnosis of alcohol abuse or dependence, and 21 other lifetime drug diagnoses were recorded for the sample. These individuals participated in focus group discussions about topics related to substance misuse and people's experiences of trying to quit. The results showed that participants identified several therapeutic and extratherapeutic factors that helped them to initiate and maintain changes in their substance misuse, as well as factors that hindered change. The findings are related to knowledge about the effectiveness of substance misuse disorder treatment techniques in general, and implications of the data are discussed for the conduct of integrated treatment of individuals with severe mental illness and a substance use disorder.

Friedman *et al.* (1999) argue that providing health services to drug abuse treatment clients improves their outcomes. Using data from a 1995 national survey of 597 outpatient drug abuse treatment units in the USA, they examine the relationship between these units' organisational features and the degree to which they provided on-site primary care and mental health services. Units with more dual diagnosis clients provided more on-site mental health but fewer on-site HIV/AIDS treatment services. Organisational features appear to influence the degree to which health services are incorporated into drug abuse treatment. Fully integrated care might be an unattainable ideal for many such organisations but quality improvement across the treatment system might increase the reliability of clients' access to health services.

Finally, it may be observed at this point that the important areas of aftercare, relapse and relapse prevention are neglected in the literature.

INAPPROPRIATE CLIENTS, INAPPROPRIATE SERVICE USE OR INAPPROPRIATE SERVICES?

The extensive literature on diagnosis and treatment, examples of which have been reviewed above, is normally based on the fundamental premise that clients/patients are expected to comply with the account of the problems defined and specified by professionals and with the solutions that are produced to solve those problems. The 'good patient/client' is one who accepts the professional view. Those who do not are often categorised as non-compliant or 'inappropriate' and it is only very recently that the examination of inappropriate service use and delivery has been raised. Obstacles to provision include incompatible treatment methods, bureaucratically devised funding procedures, inadequate staff training and few central guidelines (Brach *et al.* 1995). It is also clear that whilst these 'revolving door' clients take up a disproportionate amount of resources, they are not making efficient use of services; researchers report frequent re-entry into services, non-compliance and failure (Woogh 1990). Significant proportions of mentally disordered individuals have a substance misuse problem which is associated with poor prognosis, higher relapse and non-compliance; service costs are greater and outcomes are less favourable. The combination of fragmented service provision in a range of social, health care and criminal justice agencies together with frequent service use and non-compliance by clients provide major obstacles to treating the problem and monitoring it, rendering services wasteful and ineffective (and epidemiological information sparse).

Treatment compliance

A substantial amount of research has been undertaken on compliance. A characteristic example is provide by Bebbington (1995) who states that compliance is adherence to a prescribed and *appropriate* (my emphasis) treatment, not necessarily pharmacological. Non-compliance may occur in up to 50% of patients with schizophrenia who are prescribed neuroleptics. It may be more common in young people, particularly if male or from certain ethnic minority groups, but demographic factors are relatively unimportant. Clinical features such as positive symptoms are associated with non-compliance but the strongest clinical relationship is with a 'dual diagnosis', usually with an associated alcohol abuse. Patients' and relatives' beliefs about schizophrenia and about medication are of considerable importance in determining compliance, and can be understood in terms of the 'health belief model'. However, a full understanding of non-compliance must take into account the relationship between patients and doctors in the context of the sick role. Several techniques for increasing compliance have been described, but they contain common elements – the provision of information within the context of a warm and equitable therapeutic relationship, preferably maintained over some time, and the use of the relationship to encourage and prompt compliance and to establish more productive views of the illness and medication. The costs of poor compliance to sufferers and to society alike are considerable, and effective ways of improving it are a crucial part of good management.

Other research studies with a similar perspective are Horvath (1994), Levy *et al.* (1996), Bogenshutz and Siegfried (1998), Hoff and Rosenheck (1998) and Salloum *et al.* (1998). In much the same vein, Breen and Thornhill (1998) state that non-compliance remains one of the greatest challenges when prescribing psychotropic medication and can render any treatment regimen wasteful and ineffective. While rates of non-compliance vary widely, treatment costs are clearly increased and the duration of hospitalisation prolonged. Furthermore, non-compliance has a human cost in terms of morbidity and mortality. The reasons for non-compliance can be divided into three categories: medication-, patient- and provider-specific factors.

Adverse effects are likely to be the most common reason for patients not to comply with prescribed medication regimens. Ineffectiveness, complexity of the regimen and cost are also important medication-related factors contributing to non-compliance. The use of newer effective medications that have fewer adverse effects, with drug holidays and low-dose treatment strategies, may ameliorate adverse effects. In some cases, the complexity of regimens and the cost of medications can be reduced. The symptoms of a psychiatric disorder, the presence of substance abuse, and culture and attitude are patient-specific factors that may interfere with compliance. Non-compliance related to patient attitudes can be remedied through improving the patient-provider relationship, using depot antipsychotics and possibly medicating patients by force of judicial orders. Treatment of dual diagnosis, greater understanding of a patient's culture and the involvement of families in treatment can all be used to foster increased compliance. Psychosocial rehabilitation can also help increase compliance.

Non-compliance increases when practitioners' views of their patients' prognosis or the effectiveness of treatment differ from those of their patients. How physicians communicate and what information they present to the patients and their families plays a significant role in determining compliance. Physicians who believe in the medications they are prescribing and actively involve their patients in treatment decisions are likely to increase compliance. Expressing an understanding, empathic and caring manner will further promote compliance. Compliance should increase when good and clear lines of communication exist and patients feel free to ask questions. Specialised treatment options that practitioners can use to increase compliance include education, cognitive behavioural interventions, behaviour modification techniques, and using direct rewards for compliance. Psychotherapy can also be used as a tool to improve the practitioner-patient relationship.

Inappropriate service use

The combination of frequent service use and non-compliance is perhaps the greatest challenge to both monitoring the problem and treating it, resulting in wasteful and ineffective services. Conventional methods of monitoring have been largely limited to treatment samples in specialist agencies and treatment itself confined to services for discrete disorders; as a consequence there is a lack of information about the true extent and characteristics of this group among wider social and health care populations. A major remaining obstacle is the lack of information across social, health care and criminal justice agencies; with these data it will be possible to assess need and examine the cost-effectiveness of dual (or multiple) disorder services that integrate diverse systems.

DISCUSSION

This review has identified the existence of clients with complex needs; it has shown the range of complex needs and the factors common to these clients. It has then examined the constraints of service provision for this group and examined why they are difficult to help.

The starting point has been those problems which are most commonly found together among people who have complex needs, particularly substance misuse and mental health difficulties. However, this book moves far beyond this particular form of comorbidity and broadens its remit to include other issues that are not encompassed within the medical model.

It has also been suggested that we should reconceptualise the notion of complex needs and consider their solution in terms not only of medical and psychological change taken in isolation, but also by adopting a social perspective that includes other responses, particularly maintenance. The review of the literature brings out the dominance of the treatment paradigm and the importance of dual diagnosis. These will be discussed in detail in Part II.

The following chapter will demonstrate a new method for providing interagency data to inform interagency planning and report on its findings. It is then necessary to consider the implications for planning for the clients identified in this way. Chapter 3 therefore will summarise the nature of policy and planning and will consider the implications for clients with complex needs and psychosocial problems.

Chapter 2

Shared Clients: Complex Needs and Multiple Service Use

INTRODUCTION

The previous chapter reviewed the research literature to provide an up-to-date conspectus of the prevailing views of complex problems and their treatment and support services. The dominance of the medical model and of professional definitions was demonstrated.

It will be clear from that analysis that, in spite of calls for a comprehensive approach to complex problems and a response from the relevant agencies that reflected it, little has been done. This is largely the consequence of a lack of accurate, interagency data that enable informed planning in order to provide a structure or context for developing interprofessional and multiagency working; that is, it is difficult to plan without up-to-date information concerning assessed needs *across* agency populations and interprofessional working is severely handicapped by a lack of such planning.

This chapter will describe a methodology for monitoring interagency assessed need and service provision and will report on the initial findings of a three-year project in order to demonstrate the feasibility and practical utility of doing this. The project was the first pilot of this method and demonstrated the practical feasibility of establishing anonymised multiagency databases. The findings identified populations of shared complex needs clients and indicated the extent of the overlapping agency populations.

BACKGROUND

The project developed from a growing awareness among professionals and agencies in an English county that they had clients in common. Whilst professionals believed that they were most likely to share those with multiple problems and complex needs, they were often unsure about developing interprofessional and multiagency working as they lacked concrete information to substantiate intuition and anecdotal evidence concerning shared populations of clients. This situation is widespread in the UK.

This local interest should be placed in the context of recent changes in policy and practice which have placed greater emphasis on multiagency development of policy, planning and collaborative working between agencies. The establishment in the UK of primary health care groups (and more recently primary care trusts) and the development of joint health and social care systems depend increasingly on information concerning the needs of social and health care populations and services provided by each agency. In addition, the increasingly close collaboration with the criminal justice system in the context of the Crime and Disorder Act relies on understanding the social and health care needs of criminal populations.

Increases in the number of services and options of help, new agencies and organisations and the growing involvement of the private and voluntary sector have compounded the problem, and mean that it becomes imperative for different professional groups and agencies to work together when they have clients in common. This is reflected in the aims of the Community Care Act 1990, where there is an emphasis on assessment of needs and matching appropriate services to clients. This issue is particularly significant for easy access, multiproblem agencies, such as accident and emergency departments, or the new primary care trusts, where recent controversies regarding inappropriate patients are being reformulated in terms of inappropriate service provision.

TRACKING PROJECT METHODS

There are many problems in studying use of services (McKinlay 1972). Problems of combining survey data with professional databases are difficult to resolve (Kitsuse & Cicourel 1963). The major work carried out on overlapping agency populations in the UK has been the work of Acheson on record linkage (Acheson 1967; Acheson & Baldwin 1978). However these data linking medical records did not attempt to examine overlapping social and criminal justice records. The method used in this study allows for the first time analysis of data regarding multiple agency attendance and shared clients.

The Tracking Project provided a feasibility study for this innovative method of collating and analysing data within overlapping agency populations. The amalgamated database contained more than 800 000 anonymised subjects, 245 377 of whom had attended an agency other than their GP. All the agencies insisted on the use of anonymous identifiers on both legal and ethical grounds. The format of data collected was uniform and computer compatible. A software programme was used by agency staff to anonymise data prior to access. This software was distributed to all participating agencies and IT support offered to instruct agency staff in its use and to devise means for each agency to extract and anonymise data for transfer in a useable form. All the problems of combining a variety of individual agency data within a common database were resolved through time (using a range of different databases and software programs) and the project therefore served as a successful feasibility study for this innovative method of collating data within overlapping agency populations. The database included the following common variables: anonymous identifier; date of reception; date of birth and gender.

Quality checks and data validation procedures were created. The majority of agencies streamlined the anonymisation and transfer process, so reducing the time needed to carry out this procedure to less than an hour or two once every three months. The project has provided annual reports to all participating agencies.

It should be stressed that the database and its analysis were carefully structured to ensure that each agency's individual data were secure and protected. The confidentiality of agencies was ensured because information about one agency's population was confidential to that agency. The confidentiality of individuals was achieved by attaching very limited data to anonymous identifiers and by deleting information on groups of less than ten. If it was desirable to extend the amount of detail in the databases it would be necessary to keep each database secure and separate, in order to protect individual and agency confidentiality.

It should be noted that agencies did not collect data in the same form and that substantial differences in definition and range became apparent. The great majority of agency datasets could not therefore be combined fully and effectively and so each individual agency could only receive detailed information about its own population. Each agency-specific report was therefore designed to provide confidential information for each agency about its own population. It utilised only the variables transferred by each particular individual agency to give proportions of particular client groups overlapping with each other agency and proportions of 'heavy repeaters' in each client group. The reports therefore identified the types of patients or clients most likely to overlap with each other 'cluster' and the types most likely to be classified as 'heavy repeaters' in terms of the agencies' own data.

The information reported below concerns the amount of overlap between different types of agency population clusters and the proportions of heavy repeaters or clients shared between more than one cluster. Information concerning assessed needs was confidential to each agency concerned and therefore could not be reported. However, each individual agency could combine information concerning assessed needs within its own population with any other agency.

RESULTS

Table 2.1 provides a summary of the amount of overlap between the 20 agencies (with 28 databases) in the county that participated in the Tracking Project over a period of up to three years. To give a clear overall picture, the agencies were grouped into 'clusters', that is agencies of a similar type, so that, for example, the five drug agencies form one cluster.

Table 2.1 Proportion of each cluster population that overlaps with each other cluster.

	Total no.	MH	CH	A&E	SS	Drg	Alc	Hsg	CJS A	CJS J	NS
MH	27480		6836	6755	5213	413	795	1506	2319	551	96
			25%	25%	19%	2%	3%	6%	8%	2%	1%
CH	106824	6836		23549	13273	147	247	2562	1615	291	29
		6%		22%	12%	1%	1%	2%	2%	1%	1%
A&E	91911	6755	23549		6597	607	750	4834	6434	1381	183
		7%	26%		7%	1%	1%	5%	7%	2%	1%
SS	33031	5213	13273	6597		265	331	807	1211	350	95
		16%	40%	20%		1%	1%	2%	4%	1%	1%
Drg	3081	413	147	607	265		139	340	1014	475	123
		13%	5%	20%	9%		5%	11%	33%	15%	4%
Alc	2107	795	247	759	331	139		231	805	317	46
		34%	12%	36%	16%	7%		11%	38%	15%	2%
Hsg	14012	1506	2562	4834	807	340	231		2298	687	106
		11%	18%	35%	6%	2%	2%		16%	5%	1%
CJS A	29360	2319	1615	6434	1211	1014	805	2298		3719	241
		8%	6%	22%	4%	4%	3%	8%		13%	1%
CJS J	4567	551	291	1381	350	475	317	687	3719		89
		12%	6%	30%	8%	10%	7%	15%	81%		2%
NS	548	96	29	183	95	123	46	106	241	89	
		18%	5%	34%	34%	23%	8%	19%	44%	17%	

Key
MH   = Mental health services
CH   = Community health services
A&E   = Accident and emergency services
SS   = Social services
Drg   = Drug services
Alc   = Alcohol services
Hsg   = Housing
CJS A = Adult criminal justice services
CJS J = Juvenile criminal justice services
NS   = Night shelter/hostel services

(Details are given at the foot of Table 2.1.) This avoids the danger of double counting, for example between different drug agencies or between police and the probation service, but it should also be noted that the figures in the table show the *minimum* amount of overlap as some boundaries are not identical for all agencies. The table shows that all the clusters overlap with each other and a similar tabulation for each individual agency would reveal that they all overlap. This is the first time that this pattern, known to professionals from their experience but necessarily anecdotal, had been quantified, giving objective evidence that each agency shared its clients with each other to some degree.

As Table 2.1 shows, the amount of overlap varied considerably and this is, of course, in large part a reflection of the great variations in numbers – from well over 100 000 in the community health services to 546 in the night shelter/hostel. However, by expressing these numbers in percentages, the table shows clearly that the *degree* of overlap for each cluster (and also in fact for each agency) was substantial. So, for example, while alcohol agencies had an overlap of 2.57% with the mental health services, if this proportion is inverted and seen from the perspective of these small agencies, the overlap with the mental health services was over a third of their clients (33.46%). In other words, each row gives the amount of overlap for each cluster.

The table also displays the amount of overlap between the major areas of the statutory and voluntary services, mental health, health, social care and the criminal justice system. These are, necessarily, the realms of major policy concerns by government at national, regional and local levels. The Crime and Disorder Act 1998, directed at bringing all these areas into close collaboration and a unified direction, is an important example.

Health and social care

The interface between health and social care has been an area of policy development for over half a century and has been characterised by difficult problems of collaboration and interprofessional working. The relevant statutory agencies in this area provide services for large populations. Overlap here is therefore of substantive importance. It can be seen that there was much sharing of clients between social services, community health and accident and emergency. Two-fifths of social services clients contacted community health and slightly more than one in eight community health clients contacted social services.

Mental health, health and social care

This is also an area where there have been major changes in policy and practice, with radical developments in the field of mental health. Once again, the statutory agencies serve large populations. It can be seen from Table 2.1 that there was much overlap between mental health, community health and social services. A quarter of mental health patients contacted the community health services and almost a fifth contacted social services.

Accident and emergency services

Accident and Emergency departments (A&E) are of particular interest as they provide a major low-threshold, rapid access service to the general public. It is therefore notable that between a fifth and a quarter of each of mental health, social services and community health patients had contacted A&E. It can also be seen from the table that the A&E department had much overlap with both drug and alcohol clusters. Whereas all these figures form fairly low proportions of the A&E population, as a consequence of its large numbers of patients it can be seen when these figures are inverted that very high proportions of drug and alcohol agencies had contact with A&E. Additional information concerning frequency of attendance at A&E may be useful to clarify this picture.

Drug and alcohol agencies, mental health and criminal justice

Drug and alcohol agencies have some interesting similarities and differences. Both cluster types had high overlap of more than a third with criminal justice agencies; however this was greater for alcohol agencies than drug agencies. Similarly, both types of agencies had high levels of contact with mental health. However, whereas only 13% of drug agency clients had contact with mental health services, more than a third of alcohol agency clients did so.

Criminal justice, mental health and housing

Whilst the proportion of clients in contact with the criminal justice system and attending mental health varies with different agencies within the cluster, the overall figure of 8% points to a closer examination of the overlap for each individual criminal justice agency. Almost half (44%) of night shelter/hostel clients and nearly a fifth (17%) of city council housing list clients had contact with some part of the criminal justice system.

Bar charts

The bar charts in Figs 2.1 to 2.9 illustrate the pattern of overlap for each cluster.

It can be seen from Fig. 2.1 that the mental health services had their greatest proportion of overlap with community health, social services and

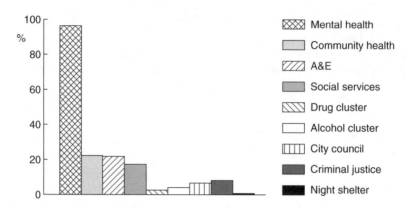

Fig. 2.1 Proportions of mental health population contacting other agencies.

accident and emergency. However there was also important overlap with criminal justice. Although the relative proportion of overlap with other agencies was low, it is important to stress that when these figures are seen from the perspective of drug and alcohol clients, those attending the mental health services were very high (see Figs 2.5 and 2.6 below).

Figure 2.2 records that for community health services, overlap with the accident and emergency department was highest. Again, as this population was very large, to identify high levels of overlap with mental health, social services and city council housing see Figs 2.1, 2.4 and 2.7.

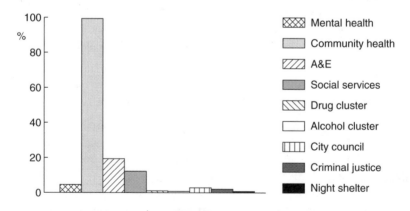

Fig. 2.2 Proportions of community health population contacting other agencies.

Figure 2.3 shows proportionally small overlaps for accident and emergency department clients due to the size of the population. When the other agency bar charts are examined it can be seen that almost all clusters showed very high overlap of between a quarter and a third with this department.

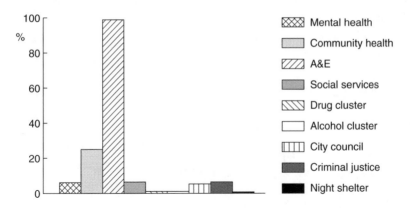

Fig. 2.3 Proportions of accident and emergency population contacting other agencies.

Social services (Fig. 2.4) show the largest overlap (40%) with the community health services. In addition overlap with mental health and other health services was high, whereas overlap with the criminal justice system was low.

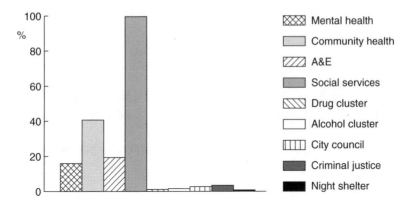

Fig. 2.4 Proportions of social services population contacting other agencies.

Drug agencies (Fig. 2.5) had high levels (approximately a third) of overlap with criminal justice agencies and a quarter with accident and emergency. Contact with mental health services was also fairly high (13%).

More than a third (39%) of alcohol agency clients (Fig. 2.6) had contact with criminal justice services, about a third (33%) with mental health agencies and more than a third (36%) with accident and emergency. In addition, nearly a sixth of this client population had contact with social services and a tenth with city council housing.

Just under a fifth (18%) of the city council housing population (Fig. 2.7)

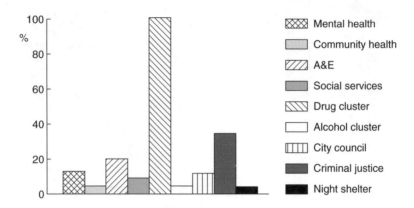

Fig. 2.5   Proportions of drug agency population contacting other agencies.

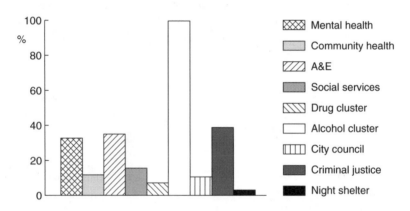

Fig. 2.6   Proportions of alcohol agency population contacting other agencies.

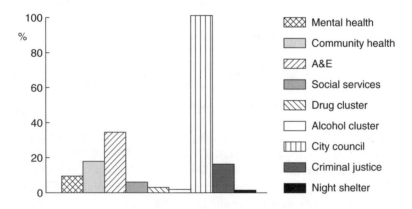

Fig. 2.7   Proportions of city council housing population contacting other agencies.

had contact with the community health services and a tenth (11%) had contact with mental health services. However, this population encompasses a wide range of clients and should be examined more closely in terms of the individual agency populations for greater clarity.

The night shelter/hostel population (Fig. 2.8) was small but of much relevance as this population has much overlap with others. Nearly half (44%) had contact with the criminal justice system, a third (33%) had contact with accident and emergency, and approximately a fifth had contact with each of the following; mental health services (18%), social services (17%), city council housing (19%).

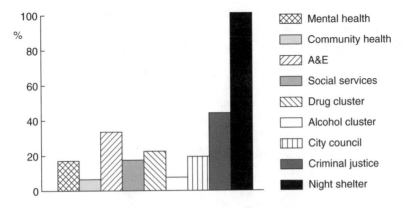

Fig. 2.8 Proportions of night shelter/hostel population contacting other agencies.

When all the criminal justice agencies were grouped together (Fig. 2.9), it can be seen that overlap with accident and emergency was high, though this may be explained by the dual role of health and police in attending incidents. Perhaps more relevant is the overlap of 8% with mental health

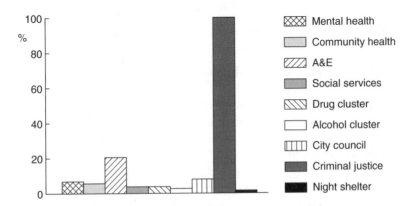

Fig. 2.9 Proportions of criminal justice population contacting other agencies.

services. As with the health care agencies, the large size of the criminal justice system meant that, although the relative proportion of overlap with other agencies was low, when the bar charts for other agencies are examined, the proportions of other agency populations can be seen to be high: 44% of the night shelter population, more than a third of drug and alcohol agency populations and nearly a fifth of the city council housing population had criminal justice contact.

It should be emphasised that the criminal justice cluster encompasses a wide range of different client populations and should be examined more closely in terms of each criminal justice agency for greater clarity.

Figure 2.10 shows the overall picture, indicating the proportion of each cluster population that overlapped with at least one other cluster. It can be seen that nearly a quarter of the total population of people in the county using agency services, other than their GP, used more than one type of service (cluster).

Overall ($n = 238\,535$)

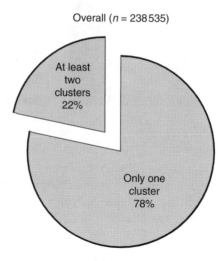

Fig. 2.10 Proportion of each cluster population that overlaps at least one other cluster.

CHARACTERISTICS OF SHARED 'REPEATER' CLIENTS

This section identifies the proportions of clients that repeatedly attended different agencies, by classifying four distinct types of heavy repeater (see below) and calculating the proportions of each type in agency populations.

The total number of clients of at least one agency (other than a GP) over the three years was just short of a quarter of a million. Of these, females constituted a little more than half, outnumbering males by a quarter of one per cent. As for age, the over 65s amounted to just over 35% of all agency users.

The group of 'heavy repeaters' is defined in four ways:

(1) *Number of attendances.* Clients who had attended eight or more times at any agency (this may be eight attendances at the same agency or at many different agencies).
(2) *Number of agencies.* Clients who had attended four or more agencies (this may be four attendances at the same type of agency (e.g. criminal justice) or at many different types of agency).
(3) *Number of clusters.* Clients who had attended three or more clusters, or different *types* of agency.
(4) *'Super repeaters'.* Clients who had attended at least eight times and had contact with at least four agencies and at least three clusters.

Table 2.2 shows the proportions of shared clients who repeatedly used a range of different agencies. It shows the groups of heavy repeaters in each of the four categories listed above, and indicates that there are clear differences in the age of heavy repeaters. Older client groups had higher proportions of heavy repeaters. It can be seen, for example, that whereas younger clients (aged 16–24 years) were more likely to attend at least four agencies, those aged 65 and over had higher proportions of heavy repeaters for three categories. A tenth of this group (10.2%) had attended at least eight times at any agency, 6.5% had attended at least three clusters, and 2% fulfilled all three criteria and were categorised as 'super repeaters'. It is clear that older people were more likely to make heavier demands on the agencies and, as their numbers are expected to increase substantially, this has important policy and practice implications for service delivery. It is worth noting that in the general population of the county, this age group is projected to have the largest increase in the first two decades of the present century.

Whilst gender differences were less consistent, it can be seen that men

Table 2.2 Proportions of heavy repeaters across all cluster populations.

	All	Repeaters attendance >8 No.	Repeaters attendance >8 %	Repeaters agencies >4 No.	Repeaters agencies >4 %	Repeaters clusters >3 No.	Repeaters clusters >3 %	Super repeaters All previous No.	Super repeaters All previous %
	245377	15734	6.4	6237	2.5	13320	5.4	4106	1.7
Male	117338	6706	5.7	3389	2.9	6211	5.3	2129	1.8
Female	123629	9085	7.3	2847	2.3	7107	5.7	1976	1.6
Age									
<25	32998	1395	4.2	1109	3.4	1588	4.8	504	1.5
25–64	125655	5528	4.4	2683	2.1	6136	4.9	1832	1.5
>64	86724	8871	10.2	2445	2.8	5596	6.5	1770	2.0

were more likely to be heavy repeaters in two of the four categories; 2.9% had attended at least four agencies, and 1.8% fulfilled all three criteria and were categorised as 'super repeaters'. In contrast, women were more likely to have attended at least eight times at any one agency (7.3%), and to have attended at least three different clusters (5.7%).

Table 2.2 focuses attention on the high proportions of heavy repeaters among different age groups, who made the greatest demands on resources and who made extensive use of a wide range of agencies. These data raise questions concerning differences in age and sex and types of service use; for example, one might expect that the young would be more closely implicated in the criminal justice system and the older men and women in the major statutory providers of health care.

It is also the case that the proportion of heavy repeaters and the category of heavy repeaters varied depending on the type of agency or cluster. These differences are illustrated in Table 2.3 where it can be seen, for example, that there were high proportions of frequent attenders and super repeaters in the city council housing and mental health populations. For housing 4.1% (578) and for mental health 3% (836) were categorised as

Table 2.3   Proportions of heavy repeaters in each cluster.

	Total population	Attendances >=8		Agencies >=4		Clusters >=3		Super repeaters	
		%	No.	%	No.	%	No.	%	No.
Mental health	**27480**	**7.42**	**2040**	**4.89**	**134**	**8.66**	**2381**	**3.04**	**836**
16–24	2373	8.30	197	7.88	18	11.00	261	4.85	115
25–64	18350	4.82	884	4.25	77	7.50	1376	2.63	483
65 and over	6757	14.19	959	5.59	37	11.01	744	3.52	238
Male	11430	8.28	946	6.96	79	10.59	1211	4.24	485
Community health	**106824**	**1.64**	**1755**	**1.00**	**106**	**1.77**	**1887**	**0.50**	**531**
16–24	4731	3.04	144	2.03	9	3.38	160	1.25	59
25–64	44462	1.91	850	0.96	42	2.08	925	0.69	305
65 and over	57631	1.32	761	0.94	54	1.39	802	0.29	167
Male	38723	1.81	700	1.23	47	1.97	764	0.62	242
Female	68101	1.55	1055	0.87	59	1.65	1123	0.42	289
A&E	**91911**	**5.95**	**5467**	**1.91**	**175**	**2.95**	**2708**	**1.16**	**1063**
16–24	15469	2.88	445	2.29	35	2.22	344	1.00	155
25–64	54635	3.31	1807	1.64	89	2.89	1577	1.12	613
65 and over	21807	14.73	3213	2.32	50	3.61	787	1.35	295
Male	50852	4.50	2288	2.10	106	2.78	1414	1.23	624
Female	41005	7.75	3176	1.69	69	3.16	1294	1.07	439

Contd

Table 2.3 *Contd.*

	Total population	Attendances >=8		Agencies >=4		Clusters >=3		Super repeaters	
		%	No.	%	No.	%	No.	%	No.
Social services	33031	14.74	4870	2.72	89	5.88	1942	1.98	653
16–24	1222	19.55	239	9.41	11	12.03	147	6.98	85
25–64	9079	17.60	1598	5.99	54	11.09	1007	4.71	428
65 and over	22730	13.12	2982	1.06	24	3.47	788	0.61	139
Male	12856	14.54	1870	4.29	55	7.39	950	3.11	400
Female	20162	14.87	2998	1.72	34	4.92	991	1.25	253
Drug agencies	3080	17.47	538	13.83	42	15.84	488	10.68	329
16–24	619	26.01	161	21.32	13	20.03	124	15.99	99
25–64	2438	15.42	376	12.06	29	14.85	362	9.43	230
65 and over	23	4.35	1	0.00		8.70	2	0.00	0
Male	1341	28.64	384	22.60	30	25.50	342	17.38	233
Female	527	29.03	153	23.34	12	27.51	145	18.22	96
Alcohol agencies	2107	23.92	504	17.42	36	24.25	511	13.10	276
16–24	219	27.40	60	20.55	4	16.44	36	10.96	24
25–64	1831	23.65	433	17.37	31	25.23	462	13.54	248
65 and over	57	19.30	11	7.02		22.81	13	7.02	4
Male	1390	26.62	370	20.22	28	26.40	367	15.11	210
Female	644	20.81	134	13.35	8	22.36	144	10.25	66
City council	14012	8.86	1242	5.87	82	8.69	1218	4.13	578
16–24	3201	9.65	309	7.31	23	8.37	268	4.06	130
25–64	8337	9.54	795	6.48	54	10.02	835	4.89	408
65 and over	2474	5.58	138	1.98	4	4.65	115	1.62	40
Male	7044	10.73	756	7.65	53	9.88	696	5.25	370
Female	6967	6.98	486	4.08	28	7.49	522	2.99	208
Criminal justice	30329	3.27	991	2.37	71	4.80	1456	1.55	471
16–24	12451	1.60	199	1.04	13	2.45	305	0.67	84
25–64	17407	4.45	774	3.33	57	6.50	1132	2.19	381
65 and over	471	3.82	18	2.12	1	4.03	19	1.27	6
Male	24447	2.88	704	2.07	50	4.20	1026	1.30	319
Female	5858	4.90	287	3.64	21	7.32	429	2.59	152
Night shelter	546	28.94	158	27.29	14	30.95	169	23.26	127
16–24	105	31.43	33	30.48	3	35.24	37	24.76	26
25–64	436	28.21	123	26.61	11	29.82	130	22.94	100
65 and over	5	40.00	2	20.00		40.00	2	20.00	1
Male	387	33.85	131	32.04	12	36.18	140	26.87	104
Female	69	39.13	27	36.23	2	42.03	29	33.33	23

super repeaters compared to 0.5% (531) of community health, 1% (1063) of accident and emergency, 2% (653) of social services and 1.6% (471) of criminal justice populations.

When specialist drug and alcohol clusters are examined it can be seen that there were much higher proportions of super repeaters among these populations. The proportion of super repeaters among drug agencies was 10.7% and for alcohol agencies it was 13.1%. If the night shelter/hostel population is examined, it can be seen that nearly a quarter (23.3%) were classified as heavy repeaters.

It can also be seen that the age and sex profile for heavy repeaters is different for each cluster. Detailed information concerning the characteristics of heavy repeaters within each agency population was given to each agency. This included not only age and gender profiles for each type of repeater, but also client characteristics such as assessed need and service type profiles where these were available.

DISCUSSION

Purchasers and providers/practitioners need information about their agency populations, the former to plan and develop services and the latter to identify and target clients. This project established for the first time in quantitative terms the exact degree and nature of overlap between agencies in one county. It is the only record of interagency overlap and shared clients in the UK and provides a baseline for all future work with individual agencies.

At this stage the Tracking Project has been successful in establishing the proportion of populations which overlap between different agencies and in demonstrating the existence of a group who repeatedly use a range of services. At present, the project has identified the amount of shared care for a range of client groups, but not what care would be appropriate. While those groups of clients that appeared to be resource intensive were most likely to be those with the most serious, complex problems, this may not always be the case and there may reasons to develop or change existing provision. The question of whether clients and/or services are 'appropriate' is a matter for professionals: however it is now possible for the project to inform this debate within each agency through further development of this method.

SUMMARY

The Tracking Project was the first project in the UK to combine total population databases from a range of social, health care and criminal justice agencies. The multi-agency database covered one county for a three-year period.

The initial Tracking Project was established to provide agencies with information about their overlapping populations, while retaining confidentiality for individual clients and individual agencies. It did this by collecting only limited data and combining these data on one database to identify extent of overlap and characteristics of heavy repeaters. The general report for all agencies provided information about the extent of overlapping agency populations and the characteristics of groups of heavy repeaters or shared clients. The report demonstrated a substantial overlap between agencies and quantified it, detailing the amount of overlap between different agency types or clusters. In addition, a group of heavy repeaters across all agencies were characterised to enable analysis of the nature of repeating behaviour and the different types of heavy repeater.

Overlapping populations

The extent of overlap has not only been quantified for the first time, but also tried and tested for three separate years. It remained consistent for each year. This will provide a baseline for more detailed work within each individual agency in terms of agency specific population data such as assessed need and service provision over time.

Heavy repeaters

The proportions of repeaters in each agency have been quantified for the first time and analysis indicated that repeaters within each agency were similar to those across agencies. It is now possible to carry out a more detailed examination of frequent attenders within each agency, in terms of agency-specific data regarding client characteristics such as assessed need and services provided.

The methodology of the Tracking Project and a summary of its results have been given in some detail in this chapter to demonstrate its potential as a means of stimulating and enabling the development of interagency and multidisciplinary working. The potential for exploiting this multi-agency data is examined in more detail in the following chapter on policy and planning issues.

Chapter 3
Planning Comprehensive Care: Assessed Needs Across Populations

INTRODUCTION

The first two chapters of this book have reviewed the recent literature on men and women with complex needs and described a multi-disciplinary database that quantifies the overlap between health and social care agencies in one English county. This database has identified those persons who make heavy use of services and analysed their characteristics. By identifying complex needs clients through their presence at a range of different agencies, we are able to bring together information in these earlier chapters to enable us to see a way forward in policy terms.

In this chapter we explore the policy and planning context within which treatment and other forms of support for individuals with complex needs are located. The nature of social and health care policy and the way in which it is planned and implemented will be outlined, together with an analysis of the constraints and difficulties that have been identified. It will be argued that at present deficiencies in policy-making and in methods of planning make a comprehensive service for persons with complex needs beyond reach. Ways of improving this will be explored.

SOCIAL AND HEALTH CARE POLICY: A BRIEF REVIEW

Given the central importance of policy to the delivery of health and social care in all advanced countries, it may be seen as surprising that there are a number of different, and often conflicting, definitions of policy and equally different accounts of how it is made (Hill 1986). Policy is variously defined as an expression of power, a reflection of 'the public interest', the politics of welfare, formal statements of government intent, and what agencies actually do as distinct from what governments would like them to do. This list is by no means exhaustive. For the purposes of this book, social and health care policy is defined as:

'a set of interrelated decisions taken by a political actor or group of actors concerning the selection of goals and the means of achieving them within a specified situation where these decisions should, in principle, be within the power of these actors to achieve.'

(Jenkins 1978)

This definition directs attention to policy as a set of decisions and to the requirement to specify the situation (for example the time scale) in which the particular policy is set. Seen in this way, policy is about means as well as ends and any policies that are developed are capable of being implemented. This approach to policy also includes the outcome of decisions taken by the state (in the case of social and health care policy) as to what fundamental values underlie social life. Put another way, policy is about 'who gets what, when, where and how' (Weale 1983).

A different view of policy is that of Edelman and others who argued that there are also 'symbolic policies' that are not really intended to be implemented or are not seen as practicable, but serve other purposes (Edelman 1974). It is suggested that health and social care policies are a particularly fruitful area for this. (Ambitious targets for reducing smoking or cancer rates over short time scales are an example.)

Just as there are different definitions of policy, so too are there divergent views on how policy is made. The major confronting perspectives are the rational model and the incremental model of policy-making. The rational model is usually presented as a normative (or idealised) approach to policy that may be of use or value in assessing how closely actual policy-making approximates to an ideal-type process of rationality.

The rational model is best viewed as a series of stages which have to be undertaken if policy-making is to be a logical, informed process. These stages are:

- Clarification of the problem.
- Setting of objectives.
- Identification of alternative policy instruments.
- Evaluation of alternatives.
- Choice.
- Implementation.
- Monitoring.
- Review.

The major criticism of this model is that it is unrealistic insofar as it does not take into account the political and organisational realities of the situation in which policy is made. Moreover, as we shall see later, there may often be conflicting rationalities, rather than one. Policy-makers frequently, of course, claim that they are behaving rationally and objectively.

The incremental model stresses the limitations in the capacities and time resources which policy-makers bring to their task. It emphasises the real life behaviour of organisations, professions and interest groups. Its key elements are:

- Fragmentation of policy-making between and within organisations and professions.
- Existing policy as the starting point.
- Policy as a 'market place' where different groups strive for mutual adjustment.

In this situation, the test of a good policy is typically agreement between all the interested parties, but without their agreement that it is the most appropriate means to an agreed objective. Means and ends are not distinct and important possible outcomes are neglected, as are important potential policies. Selection of goals and the analysis of the needed action are not distinct from one another, but are closely interrelated.

SOCIAL AND HEALTH CARE PLANNING: A BRIEF REVIEW

Planning systems can be considered to be the means whereby policies will be translated into action (Baggott 1994). The planning process can therefore be defined to include policy analysis. A standard definition of planning is usually framed in such terms as 'the process of deciding how the future should be different from the present, what changes are necessary, and how these changes should be brought about'. In social and health care, as in other fields, planning is likely to be concerned with complex situations and with a long time scale; dealing with simple, immediate events ('firefighting') does not demand an elaborate planning process.

Planning, then, embraces the basic assumptions that a deliberate intervention will improve the future and that future events and circumstances can therefore be predicted. It will be clear that planning is usually seen as intrinsically rational, even to the point where it is seen as being a means to overcome ambiguities, uncertainties and inconsistencies in the environment. Rational planning is:

- The specification of objectives.
- The evaluation of outcomes.
- The measurement of present and future costs.
- The evaluation of alternative courses of action.

Planning as a rational activity is the object of repeated criticism. It is often characterised as partial, based on existing situations and therefore incremental. To many it is a form of institutionalised bargaining between groups. Nevertheless, although there is widespread scepticism in most if not all western countries concerning the value of planning, particularly when it is formalised and systematic, it is still seen as a necessary part of social and health care. This appears to be grounded in the belief that planning is a relatively objective means of allocating resources, of establishing priorities in a reasonably equitable way, and of mediating between competing claims and constraining the behaviour of powerful interests who might otherwise dominate. Plans are normally placed in the public domain and can therefore be questioned and criticised and frequently require justification.

The organisational barriers to comprehensive planning of social and health care (as with policy-making) are sufficiently well known to make extended discussion unnecessary. The recent spate of government announcements and exhortations on collaboration, 'joined up working', sharing of resources and so forth reflect the growing realisation of the importance of joint policy-making and planning. (See, for example, the NHS Plan (DoH 2000) and Harrison and Dixon 2000.) To place this in an objective framework, different forms of cooperation in planning can be identified:

- Unconnected planning, where each organisation or profession plans without reference to others.
- Independent planning based on shared information, where each organisation or profession is aware of others' plans but otherwise plans on its own.
- Joint negotiation, where organisations and professions, despite different goals and priorities, recognise the mutual benefit of discussing future plans.
- Joint planning, based on common goals, where organisations and professions collaborate from the outset of planning to implementation.

At present, unconnected and independent planning appear to be dominant, with isolated examples of joint negotiation.

Underlying these varying forms of planning, four principles may be seen at work, influencing what actually happens in real life. The 'aereal' principle is seen in the constitutional and legal arrangements of organisations: the 'client' principle determines that each profession should be more or less responsible for a defined group of the population; the 'process' principle stresses the advantages of concentrating specialised skills and technology within an organisation or profession; and the 'purpose served' principle is normally defined as the driving force for the structure and working of organisations and professions. As we shall see in Part II, both the aereal and the client principles are instrumental in fashioning the way in which professions go about their daily work.

With this framework in mind, we now turn to the realities of care, treatment and support of men and women with complex problems.

SERVICES FOR CLIENTS AND PATIENTS WITH COMPLEX NEEDS

The literature reviewed in Chapter 1 clearly demonstrated that the treatment and support regimes for men and women with complex needs are fragmented and most often confined within organisational and professional boundaries with little regard to cooccurring problems. See, for example, the studies by Drake *et al.* (1998) and Rothschild (1998). Other researchers confirm this. For example, Bearman *et al.* (1997) argue that a comprehensive long-term programme with a case-management focus will produce better outcomes and be more cost-effective than current approaches to women who are afflicted with drug dependency and mental illness. Fuller and Sabatino (1998) point to the 'standard practice' of ignoring comorbidity in client groups where mental illness and learning disabilities are found together. Pyles *et al.* (1997) reinforce this argument and propose a paradigm for integrating treatment interventions.

In a different area, Wolff (1998) examines the challenges posed by specialisation as illustrated by the difficulties of coordinating the roles of mental health and criminal justice agencies working with people with severe mental illness. Dealing with the needs of clients in one system when they are most appropriately served by the other may make both appear ineffective and inefficient. Wolff argues that despite the evident need to manage these issues, conventional methods of coordinating services have failed. The author proposes a model that creates more appropriate incentives for the two systems and bridges the gap between them. Here again, the principles underlying the planning process are significant.

A parallel body of literature is devoted to the cost-effectiveness of services for men and women with complex needs and serves to underline the lack of comprehensive treatment and support. In an atmosphere of cost cutting and moves towards community care, clients with multiple problems may lose access to previous services. Dealing with the needs of clients in an inappropriate system (particularly within the criminal justice agencies) could increase the incidence of disorderly or violent behaviour among this group.

These service users repeatedly use a range of different health and social care services from mental health and drug agencies to accident and emergency departments, homeless hostels, social services and criminal justice facilities. Populations which cross professional boundaries are particularly characterised by a combination of mental health and drug and alcohol problems. In addition, dual diagnosis can also be a reason why non-users cannot benefit from single service provision and continue to contact a range of services without success. It is clear that repeat use and non-compliance are not cost-effective.

Perhaps as a consequence of failure successfully to utilise statutory health services, many non-statutory agencies have high proportions of multiple problems among their clients. The clients may not, for example, be receiving either drug or mental health treatment because of exclusion from single service provision (either because unacceptable in the first place or because of non-compliance or ineffectiveness of previous single treatments). Studies of homeless populations indicate that comorbidity or multiple problems are linked to loss of contact with services. For example, homeless people with complex needs were shown in one survey to be five times more likely to lose contact with caring agencies.

In a literature review, the authors found that loss of contact with caring agencies is related to age, substance dependence, a history of law-breaking or a diagnosis of schizophrenia. They tested these findings through a consecutive series of 71 homeless people with mental disorders, recruited over a period of 18 months. The subjects were new referrals to psychiatrists working in a primary health care clinic for the homeless. The subjects were then followed up for a further 18 months to determine duration of contact with Oxford services for helping the homeless (survival time). Early loss of contact with these services was strongly predicted by substance (mainly alcohol) dependence in the month before first attendance at the clinic. Homeless people with mental disorders who are also alcohol dependent were five times more likely to lose contact with caring agencies than homeless people with mental disorders who were not alcohol dependent (Marshall *et al.* 1994).

This finding may be an indication that clients contact non-statutory services such as night shelters or other low threshold self-referral agencies (such as accident and emergency departments), when other agencies have in effect given up trying to treat or cure them due to repeated failure or non-compliance.

Jerrell and Ridgely (1997) argue that until now few services have been shown to be cost-effective for comorbidity. In a recent clinical trial, standard mental health care augmented by behavioural-skills training was more effective than two other approaches (case management and modified 12-step recovery) for treating dual-diagnosed individuals, in terms of functioning, symptomatology and cost. Regardless of which care-management approach is used to control use (pretreatment authorisation, concurrent utilisation review, efficient providers or others), the care manager needs to know whether the proposed care will be cost-effective. Improvement in utilisation management programmes is likely to result from better targeting and earlier identification of men and women who need specialised treatment, and from development of standardised, clinically effective protocols.

POLICY AND PLANNING IN PRACTICE

It will be clear from this brief analysis that the present situation is far removed from comprehensive policy-making and planning in health and social care. As an example, the modernisation programme of the British Government at the end of the 1990s and early 2000s has recognised the urgent need to confront this problem and is reflected in a series of major statements, notably, *Modernising Social Services* (DoH 1998a), the Crime and Disorder Act 1998 and *The New NHS* (DoH 2000). Their implementation depends crucially on two matters: the availability of accurate, objective and timely data and the recognition of the barriers to interprofessional and interorganisational working.

First, both policy-making and planning for change are directly dependent on a clear specification of the present in order to decide how the future should be different. Chapter 2 illustrated a basic component of establishing a database to begin these activities. It was shown there that the anecdotal evidence of professionals can be substantiated and quantified and that the existence and characteristics of patients and clients with complex needs can be identified precisely. To give three examples:

- Young males who have been in-patients in a mental hospital are very likely to have been in contact with the criminal justice system and other health care agencies. The relevant agencies could use such information to target provision at this group.
- There are high levels of overlap between health, mental health and social services, indicating that community nurses, psychiatric nurses and social workers may well be involved with the same individual clients. Planning and resource allocation for this group can be informed by information concerning gaps and duplication in service provision overall.
- There are high levels of overlap between accident and emergency departments, drug and alcohol and mental health services. Joint needs assessments of these overlapping populations could inform collaborative planning and even common assessment protocols for all three types of agency.

Second, it is evident that many professionals are fully aware of the barriers to comprehensive policy-making and planning. The following quotations, taken from a study of professional ideologies examined in detail in Chapters 4 and 5, illustrate this perspective:

'We are all familiar with the blight of the planning cycle: different agencies trying to collaborate to plan to do something together. For example, two years ago we wanted to do something with the prisons, but they didn't; now they do, and [we] can't provide it. Need to plan together, and have a more immediate response rather than being restricted to the annual purchasing rounds. Most successful ventures have been with 'resource neutral' projects, where resources can just be shifted from elsewhere, for example, so no extra cash is actually needed.'

'A realistic aim would be to get a common consensus of different needs. To get a joint agreement about need, and it's from here that you'd develop joint programmes. Out of that if you can agree what the common need is then you can agree what the common indicators for need are, which means that you can arrive at common indices of health need.'

'We would like to see a shared understanding about the problem, a shared understanding of the way forward.'

'There needs to be a consistency about how professionals work in different agencies, promoting a cohesive, coordinated, planned programme; a strategy which all agencies understand.'

'To give a total picture ... and then for ourselves as a provider service, to have a very clear remit about what our input is and how the other agencies relate. When I say clear remit, I mean realistic objectives from our perspective which is a totally non-clinical service, and a strategy that facilitates working with others; not duplicating, and not leaving gaps because we're both doing similar sorts of things. If the strategy's a continuum, that we can all see where we are in relation to others. We're only just beginning to get a handle on what the other professions do, but probably the situation is different elsewhere in the country. A general clarification of who should be doing what. There will be different attitudes – people who only want to focus on medical problems, not on psychological problems or housing for example, so although one would imagine everybody who's working with these clients would be working towards the same goal, they might not be.'

'From the joint perspective and indicators would come a joint action plan – and the indicators themselves would be an outcome. Also shared targets to aim at.'

'Anything's achievable if you throw enough money at it – well, almost anything ... I would assume that a strategy would have a baseline below which it would not expect its services and its access to services to slip, and that should be the first objective towards which everybody is aiming, and its achievement should be the first outcome. To keep [the agency] independent; to keep it there as an advocate for a very dispossessed section of the community, to work very closely with everybody else who's involved to keep these clients on the agendas of planners and purchasers and to work to target services in areas that they're not being provided at the moment, and to make sure that clients are involved in what we plan to do.'

All these quotations confirm that planning is still independent, that is, it is at the first stage of possible linkages between organisations outlined above.

Equally important, the majority of professions see single diagnosis as the norm. They deploy their professional perspective to define problems and construct a solution without reference to what happens in other settings. Chapter 1 provided many examples. So, while individual practitioners may accept the desirability of a collaborative approach for men and women with complex problems, the reality of their day-to-day working makes this virtually impossible (see Chapter 4).

This fragmentation of support leads to the phenomenon of the 'heavy repeater' identified in Chapter 2. The data collected in the Tracking Project have identified and characterised a small group of clients with complex need and psychosocial problems who are problematic for all professional groups, as they repeatedly re-attend a range of services yet do not appear to benefit from professional expertise. In contrast, they keep failing to be cured or rehabilitated and instead repeatedly use, for their own purposes, a range of services designed to resolve their problems. These clients are revolving through change services because this is their only way of getting support and maintenance for long periods. Some need it all the time, some need it on and off throughout their lives; when they stop needing it, this is often not because they are 'cured', but because perhaps life is less stressful or they have acquired more informal support (relationships/jobs) for periods. In other words, clients have good and bad periods throughout the life course when they will or will not need support.

Therefore, they constitute a repeated drain on resources and these resources are not effective or efficient for this client group. However, before professionals turn repeaters or 'revolving door' clients away on the grounds that they are not a cost-effective use of services, greater understanding is essential to establish why they repeatedly contact a range of professionals and why they repeatedly fail to change as a result.

A WAY FORWARD

It will be clear from the last section that there are severe limitations on the potential for professional perspectives to develop cost-effective services for men and women with complex problems. The most important of these limitations is the case/episode-based view of clients as individuals, which is embedded in the rationales of clinicians and social workers. However powerful this may be in dealing with individual problems, at any one time it makes it impossible to generate a policy which can be used to plan a comprehensive service.

The solution lies in an epidemiological/public health approach. Epidemiology is concerned with the patterns of disease and health in populations and with unravelling etiologic factors. The discipline has moved a long way from its traditional concerns with a single agent producing a specific disease to one 'that encompasses the dynamic influence of social and environmental influences ... in a population' (Levine & Lilienfeld 1987). Stallones (1980) has drawn attention to the common training and experience of the majority of epidemiologists as physicians which 'leave them deeply imprinted and reluctant to accept that most biomedical research is irrelevant to the solution of community health problems'. While this needs to be borne in mind, the essential task of epidemiology in locating problems in subpopulations, combined with a public health perspective, offers an operationally powerful way of developing policies and plans. It is also important to bear in mind that 'epidemiological facts do not speak for themselves but are approached differently by people with different priorities and perspectives' (Levine & Lilienfeld 1987).

The Tracking Project, summarised in Chapter 2, provides an example of this approach. It indicates how this anonymised multiagency database of assessed needs and service provision can be used to inform multiagency service planning. The following discussion considers the potential of the method for future work on both needs assessment in populations and targeting shared client groups. While the study does not examine needs of individuals, the discussion places the results in the context of contemporary research concerning the needs and characteristics of multiagency users.

The project has been successful in enabling the author to specify the proportions of populations which overlap between different agencies and to highlight a group who repeatedly use a range of services. At present purchasers and providers lack such information, making it extremely difficult for the former to plan and develop services and the latter to identify and target shared clients.

This method can be developed to inform policy development and service delivery across agencies, through the addition of needs assessments of populations. This can then be combined to produce an interagency needs assessment profile for the county as a whole. This interagency profile can then be placed alongside service use data in order to inform service planning for interagency populations. This enables identification of duplication of services and gaps in service provision.

A vital part of this development would centre on establishing common priorities and interagency tariffs. The success of the Tracking Project has demonstrated that it is feasible to establish interagency databases in order to identify and define common problems and to plan their solutions, using a bedrock of objective statistical evidence to inform collaborative needs-adaptive policy and practice. However, the development task is a formidable one. Each agency is accustomed to a particular mode of working and defines its role in specific terms and from a professionally defined perspective. To reiterate an earlier example, a man or woman experiencing a serious drug dependency will be treated by a GP as a medical problem, by a drug agency as needing treatment or a harm minimisation programme and by the police as a possible threat to public order. Each agency will assess every patient/client in terms of its perceived remit and allocate them an appropriate priority (a 'tariff'), depending on the agency's conception of the severity of the problems in their specific area. In other words, a tariff is a measure of the level of need necessary to be reached before a service is provided. Little, if any, account is taken of problems presented by the same people to other agencies.

As a consequence, men and women with multiple problems, who make the greatest demands on resources, may often receive a package of support that is inadequate and not cost-effective. Consider, for example, the following:

- *John Smith*. He has a serious mental health problem, is periodically homeless and misuses drugs. His tariff for mental health ensures treatment, whereas those for the other agencies do not result in support. Six months later his mental health has improved but his drug misuse has become chaotic. The balance of tariffs changes. His mental health deteriorates...
- *Mary Evans*. She has multiple and complex problems and is a repeat attender at a number of agencies, all of which assess her needs as of low priority and therefore not requiring any service. Taken together her individual tariffs result in a high score indicating a need for comprehensive help but she does not qualify for a high level of support from any one agency. She continues to be a 'revolving door' client.

In the same way that the project offers the possibility of creating an interagency needs assessment, it also allows the creation of an interagency tariff as a necessary accompaniment. This is required to prioritise services for interagency complex needs clients. One way of doing this would be to marry agency tariffs for this group, but a simpler way would be to develop an interagency tariff by adding additional points for complex needs to each separate agency assessment procedure. Such a general tariff could be placed alongside each agency's specialist tariff, so that practitioners could use it to identify complex needs clients.

The project could also be developed to identify sub-populations of shared clients. These populations can be examined more closely in two ways: as expressions of how agencies work together and to analyse the needs of shared clients themselves. While this type of database cannot identify individuals due to ethical restrictions on data collection, it does provide information regarding particular sub-populations. These data can be used as a foundation for the development of clinical screening instruments, using statistical modelling to identify predictors of multiple service use, which can then be tested by the agency partners themselves. Detailed predictors can be obtained through collection of a much wider range of variables within the project and then from post-sample testing of the findings of the analysis. These results can then be used to design a short screening instrument which will enable professionals to identify repeaters within their agencies, or will enable one agency to predict which clients are likely to be shared with another. For example, it would show which criminal justice system clients are likely to have contact with mental health services or the accident and emergency department. (This screening instrument could consequently be standardised using clinical assessment and tested prospectively against the multiagency database itself.) In this way, this method may have the potential to enable practitioners to recognise patients in common and managers to develop more cost-effective targeting of resources at the particularly resource intensive group.

A screening tool can be used to identify complex needs clients in need of a comprehensive psychosocial assessment. Screening tools can be fairly short additional sections to existing specialist assessments, using actuarial statistics to provide predictors of those likely to have complex needs. These can then be used to screen high-risk populations or for screening normal populations for high-risk clients.

Screening for specialist problems such as mental health or alcohol problems is well advanced in many hospitals and primary health care settings internationally, the appropriate instruments often leading to brief interventions from basic literature to short counselling sessions. (For example the World Health Organisation screening questionnaire AUDIT – see Saunders and Aasland 1987.) This form of intervention has not yet been developed for complex needs clients, although the utility of such schemes seems clear.

Taken together, interagency tariffs and screening instruments could be used for two purposes:

(1) To identify clients who may be low priority in terms of each individual agency (e.g. mild mental health problems, drug problems but no dependency, non-serious crime, homeless but not on the street).

Then to combine the (low) assessment ratings of each agency, to give a (high) overall rating at one time.
(2) To identify clients who may receive a (low) priority at any given time (e.g. not seriously depressed or homeless at present, drug use under control, not in prison). Then to combine their assessment ratings and frequency of service use over a period of time and give a (high) longitudinal rating.

The data analysis so far has already revealed indicators that could contribute significantly to the construction of interagency tariffs. To give three examples:

● Frequent attendance at the accident and emergency department has been statistically identified as the major predictor of complex needs and of multiple agency use. If an agency now includes this measure (frequency of attendance at A&E) in their own assessment, this will help them identify those clients who have complex needs and also those who attend a range of other agencies.
● If clients have problems with both drugs and alcohol they are found to be statistically far more likely to have mental health and general health problems. This might also be used as a criterion for an interagency tariff, indicating that the client should be a priority for that agency which will need to liase closely with mental health and health agencies.
● Self-harm has also been shown to be an indicator of frequent attendance at a wide range of different agencies. This could therefore also be included as part of an interagency tariff.

Such regularities can clearly be used to prioritise within individual agencies and to identify clients that require close interagency working.

It follows that, if these objectives are achieved, the data will provide a basis for ensuring that John Smith will be given a high longitudinal rating and will be supported accordingly, while Mary Evans will be given a high overall rating at one time, with an appropriate pattern of service.

The results obtained so far raise many questions. For example, why do some patients attend a range of agencies? Is it because they are receiving the comprehensive multiprofessional care that they need? Alternatively, is it because they are not receiving all the help they need from one type of agency, or because each agency is attempting to meet differing aspects of their complex needs? It is necessary to explore whether the patients or clients that we have identified as multiple attenders are individuals with complex difficulties or multiple problems. Previous research indicates that patients who repeatedly use low threshold health services may be so, that they are 'difficult', use drugs or alcohol, have psychiatric and/or self-harm histories and may be unemployed (Quinton *et al.* 1995). While it is possible that this group are receiving the best possible care from each of the participating agencies to maintain clients with difficult and intractable disabilities, there are also indications that this group does not use services appropriately and does not benefit so well from specialist service provision (Steel 1995; Woogh 1990). Instead it is often argued that this group need continuity of care but are not receiving it from any source, though different professionals argue about where the responsibility for this care lies (Crinson 1995; Walsh 1995). It is also possible that there are various groups or types of multiple attenders.

The first part of this book has concentrated on people with complex needs. It has to be remembered that they lie at one end of a continuum and that at the other end there are those men and women who have a singular 'simple' need. In between there are many whose needs vary from the relatively straightforward to the much less so. The issue, therefore, for policy-makers and planners is how to design and deliver a service that deals with this great variety.

The answer lies essentially in devising policies that are derived from knowledge of shared client needs that traverse the boundaries of individual agencies, and in producing plans that are population-based and are increasingly directed towards moving from independent planning to joint planning. It is proposed that this goes hand-in-hand with a transition from a perspective that is dominated by the notion of diagnosis and treatment to one that is centred on multidisciplinary assessment and continuing care. Policy and planning will therefore be predicated upon forms of assessment that are both interprofessional and interagency. It follows that policies will be comprehensive, that planning will be collaborative and that service delivery will be needs-based.

At the same time, the transition from diagnosis to assessment will be accompanied by a change in emphasis from treatment to maintenance. The remainder of this book examines the context in which professionals work at present and how this is seen by clients and the professionals themselves. It develops interprofessional practice guidelines that are psychosocial rather than narrowly clinical and that can be evidence-based, using the appropriate epidemiological tools.

Part II

The Limitations of Specialist Perspectives: a Psychosocial Approach to Multidisciplinary Working

This part will examine client and professional attitudes to problem definition and models of care. It will be suggested that there may be a need for new models of both assessment and care in addition to specialist assessment and short-term interventions, in order to provide long-term care for clients with complex psychosocial problems. It will also be argued that, whilst specialist professions should define treatment, clients themselves could play a larger part in defining their own needs in areas where there is less professional expertise such as the psychosocial context of problems and maintenance.

In order to explore in depth the issues raised in Part I concerning the limitations of service provision for clients with complex needs, this part will examine the underlying assumptions in professional philosophies, theories and beliefs which limit *comprehensive* and *ongoing* help for shared clients. It will move away from taken-for-granted professional frameworks and explore, first, how clients understand their complex problems and the service provision available, and second, how professionals understand these issues, together with their views of obstacles and opportunities for more effective interdisciplinary working.

All professions make claims to exclusive understanding and knowledge, based on long-term programmes of training. As part of this training, fundamental assumptions are inculcated which become knowledge that is taken for granted. This knowledge base has a major determining effect on practice and is influential in defining the problems and needs of clients. Different professions working with the same client populations tend to establish boundaries to demarcate their territories and responsibilities, and where rapid change takes place, as in the developments in social and health care provision in many countries, adjustments may be necessary to realign interdisciplinary relationships and definitions. Professions by their nature are conservative and zealously guard their areas of activity and expertise (Macdonald 1995; Dingwall & Lewis 1989). To do this they need a clear view of themselves and also of those professions with which they interact. It follows that, where an area of activity is not clearly defined or is newly defined, ambiguity and unexamined assumptions can lead to duplication and gaps in services as confusion may arise about whose task it is to be responsible and how that responsibility is to be discharged.

It has been seen from Part I that frequency and adverse consequences of problems are higher in the complex needs group where high risk is correlated with frequent service contact and lack of access to some services. Single problem clients often have less contact with services, few adverse consequences and easy access. Different client populations will require specific strategies because of varying patterns of involvement with services. Clients in these populations may also have significantly different patterns of service use and benefit at different times in their lives. There are clear implications in terms of targeting appropriate interventions at different groups of clients; perhaps the most important aspect of this group of complex needs clients is that it must be thoroughly understood in terms of knowledge, attitudes and risk behaviours within the context of its social environment.

Qualitative data are analysed in this section to give insight into the range of different client and professional perspectives and models which inform and determine the practice of each, together with the views of clients themselves. The research findings and analysis in Chapters 4 and 5 are framed within an interpretivist or phenomenological methodology and the methods employed in these chapters therefore give an understanding of the subjective interpretations of all participants and of the process of interacting problems and repeat service use. They are in contrast to scientific and quantitative research that, it will be argued, is not suitable for a complete understanding of complex needs, conceptualised as interacting problems through time.

This section identifies the differences between the 'individual change' philosophies of the helping professions and the 'maintenance and support' philosophies of clients. It also clarifies the limitations of a range of conflicting specialist change practice models. It is suggested that multiple problems need multiple solutions, not just one isolated change model but a range of change models, together with a maintenance approach. It considers the possibility of a generic multiprofessional maintenance practice model. It then highlights the potential within each profession for developing parallel maintenance models for this client group.

Multiprofessional consensus regarding the need for individual client change highlights a significant difference in the perspectives of clients and professionals, where clients see a large gap in service provision in terms of maintenance and support for those who cannot change or maintain change. This is perhaps best reflected in the lack of communication between clients and professional groups as a whole (a relationship often difficult, unconstructive and unpleasant for all concerned).

Whereas specialist models are useful for specialist problems, they are less so for complex problems as they can result in narrow assessments, limited interventions and early termination of support in the light of particular notions of success and failure. It is hardly surprising therefore that there are difficulties in both multidisciplinary and client/professional relationships. Difficulties in the working relationships between clients and professionals can be understood partly in terms of their conflicting perspectives (Mayer & Timms 1970; Rees 1979; Sainsbury *et al.* 1982). In the same way, despite a common change-orientated working philosophy across the helping professions, difficulties in interprofessional working relationships can be understood partly in terms of conflicting practice models. In this way different interpretations of problems and prioritising of resources across professional groups can lead to lack of agreement between professionals themselves.

In order to confront these obstacles there needs to be a recognition that, whilst there is clearly a place for the change-orientated models of the helping professions (whether for treatment, therapy, rehabilitation or reform), there is also a need to take seriously the client view of the importance of maintenance and support and to integrate it with multi-disciplinary professional practice.

A maintenance model would be less constrained by specialist assessments of single problems and not so concerned with conceptualising interventions in terms of success and failure. Therefore comprehensive programmes of help may be able to be provided over long periods without interprofessional discord.

There is a place for interprofessional working with change and maintenance philosophies and practice models. Professional/client and inter-professional working relationships may both be improved through understanding and integration of common, shared, maintenance principles and methods with traditional specialist knowledge and methods. In this way it will be possible to understand and reconcile the differences between the perspectives of professionals and clients, and between professionals themselves which undoubtedly influence whether services are coordinated and whether the client cooperates and benefits.

Chapter 4
Understanding Client and Professional Perspectives: the Need for Psychosocial Care and Maintenance

INTRODUCTION

This chapter analyses the findings of qualitative interviews with clients and professionals. It is concerned with providing a deeper understanding of why clients with complex needs often do not receive the help they need and why professionals have difficulties in working together with this group.

The research review in Chapter 1 involved an overview of studies based on quantitative and experimental method and outcome data. The Tracking Project, described in Chapter 2, used quantitative data concerning predefined assessed need. These methods derive from the particular theories and research methodology of medicine, psychology and the related sciences and are based on a positivist perspective which in effect presupposes that the phenomenon and its treatment can be defined and isolated, all peripheral or 'mediating' variables controlled and experimental comparisons made. There is also a further presupposition that data inaccessible to this approach (concerning subjective interpretations, life course and the helping process itself) are, in effect, largely superfluous.

Positivist studies comparing different outcomes do not, however, help clarify what actually happens during interventions, such as therapeutic change processes, and what happens afterwards. The relative lack of qualitative data in academic research means a dearth of descriptive accounts of the methods used. It is therefore often unclear to academics what clinicians actually do. This has serious implications when drawing conclusions from comparative outcome studies.

Methodological constraints can also be compounded by the limitations of particular theoretical perspectives. Many of the basic underlying theoretical beliefs of a particular discipline are taken for granted; thus the initial definition of a problem or medical condition will influence both how an intervention is undertaken and how it is evaluated (baseline and outcome measures). In contrast, the methodology informing this chapter centres on a phenomenological perspective. That is, phenomena are seen as socially embedded events which take place as a consequence of the reflective capacity of people to create meaning through subjective inter-pretations of the processes and interactions between them. The founda-tions of qualitative interpretive methods challenge the basic assumptions of positivism or scientific research and often its findings.

By using this methodology it was possible to explore how the interac-tions of staff with clients could be understood in terms of their subjective interpretations, and how staff definitions of the problem and its treatment influenced what took place. Over a period of six years and as part of a number of research projects a range of 168 clients and 72 different pro-fessionals were interviewed. The professionals were drawn from a wide variety of agencies in health and social care and the criminal justice sys-tem. As we shall see, in spite of a great variety of respondents there was a striking similarity in the way they saw the issues and possible solutions. The clients were asked how they understood problems, professionals and services. The professionals were asked about their views of shared clients with complex psychosocial problems or their views of the particular client groups identified in Part I as most likely to have complex needs. These included those with dual diagnosis, mental health problems, psychological problems, learning difficulties and drug and alcohol problems, together with offenders, the homeless and other socially excluded groups.

These were exploratory studies and the data present only preliminary findings. Grounded theory was used to systematically analyse the data (Glaser & Strauss 1970) by examining themes and patterns. Themes were identified and refined through open coding and analysis using a strict process of validation against the data, through examination, comparison and categorisation. Data were analysed until the categories were well defined and saturated.

The first section is concerned with the client view of their problems and the services available. The second section will compare client views with professional views of problems and solutions, examining the difference between them and what professionals see as the obstacles to working with this client group. The third section is concerned with the differences in the perspectives of professionals, illustrating how different professional practice beliefs about primary problems and priorities differ and how these differences can obstruct multiprofessional working. This will high-light the limitations of specialist assessments and interventions for com-plex needs clients, illustrating how specialist professional practice models lead to narrow assessments, restricted interventions and time-limited help.

These three sections are followed by a discussion that highlights what professionals have in common; it examines the positive aspects of inter-professional working and professional/client relations and analyses what professionals do that works and what they need to build on this.

CLIENT VIEWS OF THEIR OWN PROBLEMS, PROFESSIONALS AND SERVICES

These interviews were unstructured but included a focus on the types of contact and professionals encountered and the pros and cons of help received. Clients were asked to describe their experience of their problems and their service use over a period of several years, in their own terms. Consumer studies have indicated that clients see their own needs differently to professionals, and that there is disparity between professional assessments and client views (Borsay 1986; Ungerson 1994; Baldock 1997).

It is important to stress that these clients were all using many different services and had a range of different cooccurring problems from health and mental health, substance misuse and psychological problems to relationships and housing problems. These are illustrative of the more severe end of the complex needs continuum, but it is hoped to show that they provide an apt illustration of the types of problems many clients with multiple problems face.

One long detailed case study or client's story is presented to give a picture of the type of patterns of service use. The major themes arising from the total data set are then examined.

Case study of complex needs client's service use

The client has mental health, drug and alcohol, relationship, legal and housing problems.

'Basically because I'd become homeless, what it was, I was on medication and that from the mental health. I mean I'd come out of rehab, I had the bottles of medication from the mental health and I'd been drinking a lot and I was living with my sister and she's got a little girl and she didn't basically want it around her little girl so she chucked me out and I had to go to the hostel basically.

I had my own room to sleep in. I had a downstairs room which was like a little flat. It was all right there, I used it as a place to sleep at night basically. Then because of my drug using and that, she chucked me out. They gave me five minutes' notice which wasn't very fair.

I stopped me medication and was drinking a lot like. I stopped drinking and then I went back to heroin, which I started smoking at first, and then I obviously started injecting and sort of I needed help again. 'Cos that's why I went to rehab in the first place.

Social services had something to do with me. 'B' was my social services worker and then once I came out of rehab he just dropped me basically. He didn't want to know me. He didn't ever write to me or write to see how I was doing or anything so, you know, I don't think they're what they make out to be. I don't think they're too good at their job sort of thing. Really I would have liked him to watch over me and make sure that I was all right and make sure that my housing was all right. Make sure that I was stable and things like that.

Then [housing association] did an assessment and then? Basically I didn't like the medication I was on and I totally lost it and was throwing up and things like that. I'd stopped the medication so I went back to the doctors. To my doctor, my GP, he had put a letter through to the mental health to review my medication. Basically I went up there, spent two hours up there trying to explain to her that I didn't want the medication she was giving me 'cos it was zonking me out too much etc. etc. and at the end of it she just said I don't care what you do with the medication. I don't care whether you throw it in the bin, whatever you do I'm just going to leave you on the same medication. I said well that's no good 'cos I ain't gonna take the medication and she said I don't care what you do, you throw them in the bin, it's up to you.

Did she help me? Basically it went in one ear and straight out the other. Yeah? And she acted like, when I first went in there she acted like she knew me for years. When it was the first time I'd ever seen her in my life. She must have read up on me reports and thought that she'd known me for years. You know? But she never, first time I ever seen her in me life. They've never ever give me a CPN [community psychiatric nurse] all the time I was with them. I've been with them three years roughly now, three and a half years.

After I came out of rehab, they should've give me a CPN, watched me, watched my medication, made sure I was all right, yeah, like they could have give me ... every three months they could have sent me an appointment through to come and see them. Reviewed me, make sure I was all right. If they'd have done that they would have noticed I ain't right. But no, they just ... once I came out of rehab they just left me on the same medication you know? It weren't the right stuff obviously.

She should have waited for me to tell her what I was about, you know. Not come across to me as if she knew me already and she'd known me for years and you know. It chucked me a bit, it made me you know? She relied already on what was in the file and didn't listen to what ... 'Cos I actually went there with my sister and my girlfriend at the time. Like I came out of there fuming and I'm saying she's a *** and things like that which, I was angry that she wouldn't change my medication you know. I thought she'd have give me something what would have stabled me, stabilised me, you know at the time. 'Cos I didn't even have an addiction at that time. And I just thought oh sod it and I just went straight back to it and I started smoking heroin and then banging it up there, you know?

The staff at the [drug rehabilitation centre] were always trying to get into your head and ... trying to change it. But I came out with a worse problem, like with a mental disorder sort of thing. I came out changed, definitely changed.

I go to my GP, but only when I'm ill, you know, when I've got a chest infection or abscess or you know, through banging up or whatever, I go to a GP to get help. And nowadays I don't really want to go there to be honest with you, for help. 'Cos they don't seem to want to help you 'cos you're into drugs and basically I think they just write you off, you're a junkie, you know. That's what I think they do. They talk down to you. You know, you're telling them one thing, that you need help and you want them to help you. They say how do you want me to help and things like that and you say blah blah blah and they say no, we'll help you like this. And you've told them how you want them to help you. When you're into drugs and that, you know roughly how they can help you, and how you can seek help. You know 'cos you've been in there for so many years. So I know it ain't professionally you know, but I know how they can help me and they say to me sometimes, how do you think I can help and I tell them and they say no we'll help you like this and then they give you a load of shit like tablets and that. They don't really help you, you know.

Police are OK, once they get to know you, they treat you alright. He might be a bit arrogant and that at first until he knows ... until you see one of them at the police station and they say all right Jimmy or whatever and they know you by your name or whatever then they might think oh, he is all right, you know what I mean. I've had them where they've threw me on the floor and thrown handcuffs on me and all that. Been violent with me, then when I've got up the police station and they've known that I ain't that sort of, you know. I have got a bit rowdy with them, but I ain't that sort of bloke. That's just showing me up in public but you know, when I'm up the police station and that, they're all right with me 'cos the old police have said he's all right that sort of thing, you know? The ones that know me, you know?

Probation. I've been on two years on probation since last time I went to court I got two years probation. I've been homeless for three months just recently and they haven't even sent me a letter or nothing. They know they can send it to my mum's address care of, they haven't sent me a letter nothing, to see how I'm doing. I haven't been in at all. In the office at all. I haven't seen one probation officer. I've been on it about a year and a half, roughly but like I say, the last three months, they haven't been interested at all. I don't think they were doing their job properly really. Basically making sure that I was all right. That I was happy where I was living and you know. I did like me first probation officer actually, she was like quite a nice woman and we was getting in a relationship where she knew me and I knew her. Then she went and I got another one and he didn't really know me and he was acting like he did through the paperwork and things like that, you know. But he didn't treat me like she did. We didn't build up a relationship where she could say it to me and I could say it to her. This is the last one, he's the one that ain't contacted me at all since I came out of rehab.

There is another woman, I can't think what she is, but she works at something housing any way. So she goes around making sure that people are all right. That's what they're doing at the moment with me. Like now, because I've got a problem and that. You've got to have a problem before they start helping you, yeah?

She basically bugged them and bugged them to death 'til they give me a house. And then just kept ringing them and ringing them and ringing them you know and then got to [other professionals] to get their support. What they'll do now is they're gonna come round and see me every fortnight and make sure I'm all right and make sure me house is tidy and make sure I'm coping all right. Whenever I say to her can you pop around and see me at such a time, she'll come. Basically, they'll help me and that, if I had forms to fill out and didn't know how to do it, they'd help me you know, help me do it.

I haven't seen or heard from mental health, nothing ... when I come off the methadone then they'll be trying to give me some medication to stabilise me but they haven't even bothered writing to me. I think they're a waste of time. I reckon that they couldn't care about me 'cos they haven't give me a CPN, nothing and I've been with them three years. If I had a CPN they could come round, make sure I was all right, if I ever felt that the medication weren't working I could have called ... told him my medication weren't working, he could have gone back and tell it to the team whatever and it could have been sorted without all this shit going back on drugs, you know.

The mental health people were out of order really for the way they left me. You know they just dropped me when I came out of there. You know what I mean, they didn't ever give me the time of day really.

It will be evident from this account that the client has experienced all the problems discussed in Chapter 1 and it is also clear that they interact in a complex and sometimes unpredictable way. We also see that his understanding of professional perspectives and the expectations based on this understanding are a major component of his difficulties. Similar experiences are demonstrated by the extracts from other accounts that follow.

Complex long-term psychological and social problems

The following quotes are not organised as individual case studies but are presented to illustrate the main themes arising from the total dataset. Nine major themes were identified.

Complexity of problems

'There didn't seem to be anybody available then who was interested enough to help or perhaps it's too difficult a story, but it's too difficult a history for somebody to take in quickly. It probably takes two or three years before people start to realise what your problems are. Which is I say that all the people who deal with you get to know you over a period of time. When you need emergency help that doesn't happen.'

'Because I was feeling desperate, I was getting desperate to, I was getting suicidal, I was getting so I just could not cope with my day-to-day living. I couldn't get up in the morning and look forward to dinner time. I was like how am I going to get to dinner time, not look forward to dinner time.'

'I wanted help because I was getting suicidal, I was getting in money problems because of the drugs. I was having trouble working. I've worked for myself and I was having trouble with that, I was having trouble with my relationship with my partner. She had enough really. I don't know, in a way it was like the last resort. Go to the doctor.'

'My past instability of living somewhere because of moving about from place to place and like they also say, I am not capable of stopping in one place for too long. You keep on the move and the (police) can't get you.'

'He referred me to a psychiatrist who really just assessed me as I was at that moment, because I was having all sorts of problems with my mental health, mostly due to the drugs but it actually works both ways I think. When I had problems, I turned to the drugs; when I used the drugs I didn't have problems. It works both ways.'

The need for professional understanding of these problems

'I've only seen him the once, er, and I don't think he really knows, the only thing he knows about me is whatever is down on paper, which is an awful lot by now I'm sure but he doesn't know me as a person at all. But he's probably the most qualified person, I suppose.'

'You want them to listen to you and try to understand what you are going through, but a lot of them don't you know. They want to get you in and out as soon as they can find some reason to, instead of listening to your problems and talking to you and things.'

'I must have been seeing them since I was eighteen and I must have seen four or five different doctors. Each time I see somebody, the next time they've either left or they're not helping me any more, so I have to repeat every single time I see somebody my story and my problems and everything. It's only now that I've got somebody that I know I'll see regularly.'

'Well they seemed like they thought I was trying to rip them off all the time, they didn't realise I needed help.'

The need for psychological counselling and help

'Just someone to come and talk and be friendly. Somebody professional that (actually) helps you more you know, so you know that they are professional and it's not some cowboy doing it.'

'It sounds funny, I could do with sort of like, an answering machine that sort of went on forever, for as long as you spoke, like for a couple of hours, that would be fine, do you know what I mean. I could ring up and blah, blah and then she would come home, play it and then she would ring me up and she'd have it all what had taken me two hours to say, she would have it summed up in three or four lines in one little tiny paragraph. She could sum the whole lot up and that's what's so good with her, she takes the notes.'

The need for a social life and social support

'I like a lot of the people, it is not that. But it's pretty hard to form relationships with people 'cos people aren't around for that length of time. They don't stay like.'

'I always make sure that I am with people, 'cos like you don't get yourself into trouble. Well you could still get into trouble when you are with people, but not in the same sense that you would on your own.'

'But they are familiar friends, safe familiar places.'

'I go to places where there are mates, people who accept me.'

'Some kind of day centre with an emphasis on self-help socially.'

'They are people that I understand, and we all share common experience, they are people who accept me.'

It can be seen how important social life and social support are to vulnerable people with complex needs. While the groups they mix in may be dangerous in some ways, they are less of a risk in social terms. People are not in a vacuum but in a familiar structure. Even if they do not know the people personally, they know who will be there. People return to the night shelter for the company; they want communal living and they are never on their own on the streets.

The limitations of change and rehabilitation services

'I don't want therapy. It was getting too much. I mean looking too much and too deeply into people's past. They didn't believe in looking at the present or future so much but they were trying to be therapists... And looking into people's past history too much. It's not relevant because you are sort of in there basically. As far as I can see to get back to the here and now and into the present and what's happening to your future. And to me my past is irrelevant to anyone's present and future.'

'Well (you leave rehab and you are vulnerable) you don't survive on the streets by giving too much away do you, 'cos the last thing that you want to do is to show a vulnerability do you?'

The need for long-term maintenance support

'Ah well, if I was coming to this the first time again, I'd be confused. I think the first thing that you need when you go to ask for help, or when you ask for help, the first thing you need is stability, you need familiar surroundings, familiar faces. This is not what you get at all.'

'Once I'd started this counselling thing, I realised that wasn't going to be something I just sorted out, that was going to be a life-long thing.'

'Home visits from a nurse are best and to have support on a day-to-day basis from a counsellor when you leave.'

'He was there as often as I wanted him to be. If I didn't think I needed to see him next week then I would say – well say a fortnight and we would make an appointment in a fortnight.'

The need for easy access on an ongoing basis

'I felt that short of doing what I was doing, the only way I can see anybody was to go through accident and emergency by attracting attention in that way, by being taken there as an emergency patient, though actually I wasn't quite that bad.'

'I can only make an appointment to see somebody it seems when I have a crisis, I don't know that I'm going to have a crisis. It's very difficult to actually go to a professional body and get the help there and then when you need it or when you feel you need it.'

'I would like a day centre that is open until 10 PM and at weekends.'

The need for more than one service and good interprofessional communication

'The staff are constrained. They can only provide certain services.'

'I just wanted someone professional to deal with me and [the community psychiatric nurse (CPN)] wasn't there and there didn't seem to be any communication, no line of – well this leads to this, this leads to this – there was nothing. I had to really work and speak to somebody who actually cared about what happened. The CPN wasn't there and I couldn't really trust him to be there when I wanted him to be there.'

'I would think an introduction of 'where to find' and 'who to ring' would be good, but I don't know if it would be as good as [my social worker] actually doing it. But the public need more information about what there is.'

'All these different departments, all these different agencies, are all separate, they don't seem to act as one although they communicate with each other, they only communicate on a part-time basis. There's only certain information that is known to each other. There doesn't seem to be any central information. I can only speak from my point of view but I'm reasonably intelligent, right, I really do wonder what happens to people who aren't or who don't [persevere].'

'He's the only person I've seen connected with that mental health team. I don't know how to contact him apart from ringing up the hospital there. When I've mentioned him in the past to other people, it's not a name that people say, oh yeah we know him. So I'm not sure about what I'm doing there. What I do know is that he's in contact by letter with my doctor and he's advised my doctor that I should change my medication and my doctor is taking notice of him, so there must be something to him.'

Client/professional relationships

Clients often don't know what to expect of services, what will be expected of them and whether they will be able to cope with these expectations

'Oh, I was nervous as hell, I didn't know what I was letting myself in for. Well, I didn't know whether I was going, I had no idea what I was going to at all. I really did not know what to expect at all. My own experience with people really up to this point had been like through my doctor.'

'I've known people who sit on benches around town who have all been in-patients and really that's all I know about them is that they are in and out of hospital and psychiatrists say now and again I think you need to go away for a few weeks and I felt that was where I was and I didn't want that. I didn't want to be locked away. That's how I saw it.'

Clients don't know about professionals: 'It's a strange relationship'

'I've come away from there, furious sometimes. I've actually sat in the room with him and argued with him. He's told me, he's latched on to something that I've said and he's actually told me well you shouldn't have done that, you should do this, this and this and I have argued with him why I didn't. I have ended up actually arguing with him and then the next week I'll go back and he'll say something, like I touched on a nerve there or something and I don't know whether he's doing it deliberate to get me to argue with him or not, but like I say I respect him. I trust him to know what he's doing, but I don't actually know what it is he's trying to do, so it's a bit of a strange relationship.'

'I don't know, I don't know, he, I don't even know what he is really is, what his official title is. I know he works for the mental health team, I know he's qualified at something, I don't know what.'

Being assessed and becoming an 'appropriate' client

'I felt I had to present myself in a particular way because that is what would count.'

'When I first moved [here] and was staying with a friend and this leaflet came through the door saying, 'City Council here to help the homeless'. So I thought, well I will go and question them about it. I even took the leaflet up with me and they said oh no that's not exactly true, you have to be in [city] for at least two years before we can even look at any forms to see if you qualify for housing, and they said we only help mentally disabled people or single families or whatever. I said so what happens to the rest of the people that ain't mentally disabled or homeless or whatever, they says oh they just have to carry on and wait. I thought that, well there goes that lot out of the window.'

'It was like I was performing for them, and I was incapable of performing. I didn't know what I had to present like, even so I didn't know what it was I was trying to do.'

'It's a question of second guessing what they want...'

'I make a show. They want to know I'm committed.'

Different types of professional have different attitudes and offer different things

'One's more on a clinical side [professional CPN] and one's more on you working out how you think about things [non-statutory professional], that's how I see it anyway.'

'Chalk and cheese. She was a real nurse and [the non-statutory worker] is a friend. I think that is the only way I think I can really say it, friendship and trust with [non-statutory worker] is great but with [the nurse] it was medical trust.'

'She got my dole money sorted out and got me a flat and a grant for furniture and then she left and he took over and it has been downhill ever since.'

Health and social care professionals

'I felt very depressed. I felt suicidal and I felt that I needed professional help. I didn't want somebody to say there now never mind, or pull yourself together or stuff like that, I needed somebody to say look we need to have somebody looking after you right now. That's what I wanted.'

'A nurse is indispensable as she deals with my GP and no involvement with the hospital regime is involved.'

'I would expect them to be professional, to keep everything confidential and to be trustworthy. With the psychiatrist I can trust them because of their position. I know what they're there for and so I can trust them.'

Non-statutory practitioners

'I trusted him straight away for some reason as well. I felt he understood me. When I said, like I could talk normally to him, I didn't have to think medically, I could talk normally to him.'

'They don't rush you into anything and all that. They try to talk to you and find out your problems.'

'He didn't judge me, he took me as I was and I felt I was able to be completely honest with him which was very difficult for me to be honest with anyone and he was someone I felt I could be honest with and I wasn't judged. I wasn't feeling relaxed and he was able to give me his honest opinion which was the first time I had had that for a long while.'

'I think it's less professional and more friendship with [non-statutory worker] and the other way round with [statutory worker]. I find it, well, if I met [non-statutory worker] in the street he would stop and talk to me, [the statutory worker] possibly wouldn't. I don't mind, I don't mind. I'm quite happy, I'm quite happy with that like that.'

It will be evident from these brief extracts from the interviews that clients want two things. They want a professional to know them well over time and understand their problems as a whole, and also to know other professionals and have influence; that is, to be able to communicate both with the client himself and with other professionals. These two client needs do not often coincide in the same practitioner but can be found in different people (the non-statutory professional who takes a client-led approach and the statutory professional with credibility and contacts).

DISCUSSION

The quotations above provide a vivid illustration of the client perspective and serve as a context for the understanding of client-professional relationships. These vulnerable men and women do not see themselves as (1) principally ill or sick, (2) socially excluded or (3) criminal; therefore they do not respond to (1) treatment, (2) social rehabilitation or (3) punishment, respectively.

As we have shown, they have little understanding of the differences between doctors, social workers or probation officers, or of the hierarchies in these professions, although they have some awareness of the distinction between health care and other professions and particularly the lack of expertise and influence among non-statutory workers. Clients have little understanding of the variety of professional views of clients, but see that they must please or conform to official expectations. Some see professionals as people who can be manipulated if you play their games to provide food and shelter and who will tolerate you (accept you) and offer you safe haven. At the same time, they are untrustworthy, since if you do not conform to their rules (e.g. if you are seen as non-compliant or a failure) you will be dropped.

To deal with complex problems and difficult circumstances, these men and women have their own lifestyles, routines, structures, communities, etiquette and rules. Their world is one where they are accepted for what they are. This acceptance enables them to cope with personal disorders and maintains them despite their personality characteristics and problems. It provides a milieu in which they are accepted, integrated and supported and without which they may not be able to cope. Seen in this light, therapeutic programmes may 'soften' clients so that they lose street survival skills or become less integrated into their previous social support networks, yet are not acceptable in others. Religion/therapeutic conversion may mean inability to communicate with the street community. Housing may mean social isolation.

At the same time, clients may also not be able to cope without the ongoing support, maintenance and acceptance of the professional network. So non-compliance or failure at any one service or agency means that, in effect, the help will be terminated. Clients may need these services on a fairly consistent or continual basis. They think that professionals need to understand that they have a range of complicated and often unresolveable problems, and that they cannot necessarily change or cope with them at any one time. They consider that professionals often see them inaccurately as having only one specialised short-term problem that can be resolved quickly if the client will only change.

Not surprisingly, therefore, many clients believe that should play a larger part in defining and assessing their own psychosocial and maintenance needs, particularly where professional therapeutic or treatment models are less useful.

It will also be evident from the quotations above that clients have very little information about services and professionals, and have exaggerated or distorted notions of what they can expect, what services are provided and what the professional relationship will be like. However, they think that if they have too many problems, are more difficult to treat or are less likely to improve or become rehabilitated, they are marginalised by both health and social care professionals. These clients expect that, not only should professionals try to understand them, but also should try to listen and comprehend others' expertise. In this way, they could work more closely together in order to gain a full understanding and provide a comprehensive service for clients with more than one type of problem.

For most clients, the non-statutory worker understands all their problems as a whole and does not put them down, but they do not have professional expertise and they cannot get other services. Non-statutory workers are not taken seriously (particularly by health professionals who do not respect their judgements) and therefore cannot refer clients.

The ideal solution is therefore a professional who knows you well, but also has respect and influence among other professional groups and so can obtain services. Clients want both the ongoing maintenance, support and friendship of non-statutory workers, and the expertise, contacts and resources of professionals when necessary. Those clients who cannot communicate with professionals need an interpreter and advocate who can build a bridge between them and different professionals. This is a role they feel can be undertaken by the non-statutory workers who also have the time to offer friendship and ongoing monitoring and support. They believe that at present you need to know at least one professional in order to have access to a range of other professional services, as they realise that the agency system effectively excludes them in terms of self-referral. Ideally, they want easy access care services without professional referral.

Residential services mean hot food, company, safety and someone on hand if things go wrong. This is appreciated but it is more often than not seen as a temporary arrangement, as part of a rehabilitation programme. Some clients cannot ever cope with life on their own without structure and social support. They therefore move from hostel to flat to night shelter to street and go round again (often interspersed with drug or alcohol rehabilitation, probation hostel and prison).

In short, the clients' main questions were concerned with why professionals only provide particular things at particular times on particular conditions. So a 'good doctor' is not seen as trying for a quick cure or having high expectations, but someone who is happy to live and let live, who does not get angry or emotional. The good doctor is in effect defined as one who is using a maintenance model and not necessarily expecting the client to change. A 'bad doctor' is defined as one who uses a treatment philosophy and is therefore ineffective and unhappy when working with problematic patients. Conversely, for a professional perhaps, a 'good client' is defined as one who wants treatment and a 'bad client' as one who wants maintenance. The contrast in views is considered below.

Comparing client and professional views

Data were also collected from in-depth qualitative interviews with a wide range of professionals. These interviews were again largely unstructured but included a focus on the philosophy, practice models and methods of each profession and their views of shared clients with complex psychosocial problems or the particular client groups identified in Part I of this book as most likely to have complex needs. The focus centred on interprofessional working with these clients, what each professional was doing and why, and for whom it was appropriate and inappropriate.

Respondents were asked if they saw multiple problems as a predictor of treatment failure or complex needs clients as more difficult. Interviewers also examined how professionals defined 'inappropriate', 'undeserving', or 'difficult' client groups. The interviews explored whether professionals recognised the difficulties inherent in working with shared complex needs clients, and, if so, how they adapted their practice for this group or if they simply accepted that they were doing something that was less helpful for a minority of clients. If they saw certain client groups as 'inappropriate' for their services, they were asked where they would refer these clients and why.

Professional groups included the following: consultants, general practitioners, nurses, community nurses, health visitors, psychologists, psychiatrists, psychiatric nurses, therapists, counsellors, social workers, care managers, youth and community workers, hostel and housing workers, drug and alcohol workers, police and probation and prison officers.

Specialist models narrow assessment, restrict comprehensive service and time limit interventions.

The major themes arising from this dataset are outlined here.

Professionals assess clients as having a particular primary problem and also the potential to be cured of this problem, before the clients receive help; that is, treatment will be limited to the primary cause and it should be successful and/or cost-effective. It can be seen that much of the disagreement between professionals and clients was concerned predominantly with the need for individual change or maintenance and support respectively.

'Change' philosophies are valuable to professions because they are based on expert knowledge of a particular primary cause and are accessible to the essential outcome evaluations of evidence-based practice. It is suggested that all professions have by their nature a specialist perspective on a narrow range of problems and hold a philosophy that asserts the necessity of client change and that therefore influences all professional practice and is the reason d'être of most professions. While this specialist model and professional philosophy are essential for identifying and intervening with single individualised problems, they are not necessarily appropriate for clients with complex problems without a broader psychosocial perspective and additional maintenance methods.

It is proposed that professional models influence staff definition of problems and therefore also both client assessment and what staff consider to be a successful treatment outcome. It is possible that, as a consequence, theories could serve to limit provision of a comprehensive range of interventions over time.

'Agencies are clear about what they do, but they are not clear about who does what they don't do, so they say "not one of ours" ... if the client is asking for something that the agency does not provide, without consideration of who does provide this, if anyone does.'

'There's a lot of cross-over. I mean the difference is that I'm [CPN] looking at [laughs] giving him drugs and she's [drug worker] looking at stopping them. So to speak.'

'If drugs are mentioned [in a mental health assessment procedure] then the worker will pass them on to the drug team. On the whole referral is difficult in one direction and easy in another.'

'Interventions for problems are not necessarily appropriate in isolation and need to take account of possible interactions. For example, you will need drug treatment and depression treatment together to deal with a depressed addict. The outcome of interventions is often determined by the number of problems, not by severity of one of them, so it is likely that the outcome for both interventions will be dependent on the success of the other.'

'The best way to deal with cases that do not respond to treatment may be to deal with associated problems.'

'Particular professional change models will of course serve a useful therapeutic or clinical purpose, but are of limited use for other associated problems.'

Professional views of the difficulty of working with complex needs clients give an indication of underlying difficulties in working partnerships. This section will examine differences in philosophy, aims and priorities and particularly differences in definitions of problems. It will then consider the practical difficulties of working together and finally consider possible solutions in terms of combining professional 'change' models with client 'maintenance models'.

Differences in client and professional philosophy, aims and priorities

There is a need to examine the concept of help, in order to understand why some clients do not want help and why some professionals do not want to provide help for some clients. Professionals can become frustrated when clients ask for something they do not provide or when clients gain something that is not thought appropriate to their needs. In contrast, clients may be frustrated when the professional is content that the service provided is appropriate, because each has a different idea of what to expect.

It is interesting to consider why some clients do not want to change or do not want professional help at all. It may be because they must accept someone else's definition of the problem and that they see this definition as too narrow or distorting. As a consequence they may not think that the help they are offered is appropriate, or that they are capable of doing what professionals expect of them.

Differences in definitions of problems

'The only way to work with them is not to define the problem. If you define the problem this presents an obstacle to working with a client.'

'There is conflict between what we think is right for him and what he thinks is right.'

'It is partly because of the stigma as they are more visible, but also because they will need to accept someone else's definition of their problems and they may not agree with it.'

'It is only possible to work with some clients if you do not do any form of assessment: initially the assessment process puts people off for some reason. It can work against you. If you have a rigid idea of what they are going to do, then it is less likely to fit with client expectations. Likewise, if a client comes with a very clear idea of what they want, it is very difficult to work with them if you have a different agenda.'

Differences in expectations

'I think [generic] professionals see drug users and people with alcohol addictions being strange people who are dangerous and not workable with and see people with mental health problems as very strange people who they have got no idea how to help.'

'The client wants the professional to behave in certain ways and vice versa.'

'They just want to be cared for, like children, need an adult figure to show them the way and hold their hand.'

The client is expected to change or improve

'It is true that clients are often rejected or marginalised by professionals if they do not improve.'

'Some clients are left in the system but are marginalised by professionals.'

'He's a no-hoper, we can't do anything for him really.'

Clients seen as not wanting any help or not wanting the type of help available

'These people do not want mental health services and didn't choose it. [Clients] with mental health problems hide their problems, they do not admit they have mental health problems and they do not want help.'

'[They] screw professionals for what they can get, instead of what they really need.'

'They see all professionals as policing, until they get a trusting relationship, then they are less policing.'

Reasons why professionals do not provide help

'He's not really ill, it's not serious.'

'It's not that he is an inappropriate client, but we are not the appropriate service.'

'Difficult, uncooperative and untreatable.'

'Taking away the service from those who will make better use of it.'

'There are people far worse off.'

'He doesn't need us, he could look after himself.'

'It won't make any difference.'

These responses give very clear indications of the underlying beliefs and values within the professions. It can be seen, for example, that professionals may not provide help because they think the client does not want it, will not be successful in terms of treatment outcome, or does not deserve it, whether these are seen as medically, morally or socially undeserving clients; that is, whether their medical diagnosis is severe enough, or whether they are needy enough in social terms. Professionals only want to provide their particular specialist help to clients if this help or the clients themselves are considered 'appropriate'. Appropriate help is seen as that for which they are trained and expert. Appropriate clients are those clients who would benefit from this help most because they qualify in terms of their diagnosis or assessment.

Because many complex needs clients were seen as 'untreatable' they could not be understood in terms of success or failure. Professionals had difficulty understanding these clients within their professional frameworks and clients were often described as living in a completely different world to professionals, as they do not understand how professionals see them or their problems. A 'bad client' was described as one that does not accept the diagnosis and treatment at face value and behaves badly, perhaps as a consequence. It is possible that a professional sees the 'good client' as accepting his definition of the problem and the bad client as not accepting it. It is also possibly the mixture of the client accepting the professional definition of the problem and not over-reacting if they disagree or see things differently. In contrast to health care professionals, social care professionals were more likely to think it reasonable to negotiate an agreed definition of the problem, whereas in non-statutory agencies the client is often expected not only to define their own problems, but sometimes the solution as well.

These responses indicate a reliance on particular theoretical interpretations of problems, which can narrow assessments and limit interventions. They also demonstrate the professional reliance on identification and assessment of primary problems in order to deal most efficiently with all problems by allocating resources to the causal problem itself. For example, the notion of 'medically or psychologically deserving' incorporates the belief that there is a primary problem that is causing other problems. If people do not have this medical or psychological problem they should not receive help. If people do have this primary problem, there is no point in giving them help for the secondary (or symptomatic) problems, as the primary problem will only reproduce these problems again.

To be considered 'appropriate' or 'deserving' of any one service the client must reach a certain tariff at any one agency at any one time. The tariffs of different professionals vary. In order to qualify for a tariff the client needs to have a certain level of one specialist problem. So the client with a lower level of tariff for a wide range of different problems will not qualify or reach the tariff of any one agency (see Chapter 3).

In addition, it is clearly important that clients not only have a need, but also are likely to improve and that treatment is successful and cost-effective. However, people with many problems are less likely to benefit from any one intervention whether this is a health, mental health or social problem. So specialist interventions will be more effective for those patients with single problems and professionals may therefore 'cream off' those clients most likely to benefit from therapeutic interventions or support in the community, instead of those with more intractable problems.

Common professional 'change' model contrasted with client 'maintenance' model

It can be seen that much of the disagreement hinges on whether professionals are concerned predominantly with programmes of individual change based on theoretical notions of primary cause and evidence-based treatment intervention on the one hand, or maintenance help and support on the other. It is in the discussion of these concepts that the aims and priorities of professionals and clients can be clarified. If the aims and objectives of any intervention are made explicit and the target audience clearly defined, the skills and priorities of relevant professionals can be matched to the clients. It also becomes easier for different professions to collaborate with clients in providing both change and maintenance support.

Both purchasers and providers need to be aware of the different priorities, content and methods of each profession and conversely of the clients' own perspectives and needs. For example, those most in need of support and maintenance may be less likely to respond to traditional change models, but instead to voluntary services, where, despite having more serious problems, they will receive less expert help.

The beliefs about aims and objectives were reflected in the messages given by different professional groups. Different messages are given by different professions but almost all under the guise of individual change. In contrast, those of clients and some non-statutory workers tended to be less concerned with diagnosis and change and more with the clients' definitions of the problem and ongoing support services.

Professional change philosophy

'For the residential side we use the model of a therapeutic community which has a therapeutic milieu, which is everything that happens needs to be therapeutic or can be used in a therapeutic sense. Even if people relapse or make mistakes, we use it in therapy, so we use group work, sports, one-to-one work, counselling, complementary therapies (shiatsu, reflexology and so on), anything that we feel is helpful and maybe has been tested elsewhere and found successful.'

'The main message is very clearly sent, that inappropriate service use is not acceptable. Either you use services properly and are motivated (to change) or we will not go on providing them.'

'She never meant to give up (drugs), it was a waste of a bed.'

'A strategy has to be multifaceted, multidimensional with a range of interventions and has to have as its aim that people get better.'

'Any strategy has to have as its ultimate aim that people are cured.'

Looking towards the independent voluntary organisations to understand non-theoretical, ongoing helping

It is possible that the apparent dichotomy between professionals and clients is in effect bridged by the traditional non-statutory voluntary organisations. (This is becoming less relevant in the UK as new contracting arrangements require voluntary organisations to take on the aims, staff and evaluative procedures of statutory bodies.)

'If he is stable there is no contact necessary with a professional, the [non-statutory agency] can do that.'

'I think the voluntaries got hijacked to everything to do with contracting. It's almost as if there's a need to bring back the importance of the voluntary aims and priorities, things like client advocacy and social support and help, so that it's recognised again in its own right and not just in relation to a particular group.'

'Providers want a clear statement about where purchasers in the statutory sector want to go, which presumably indicates what they want to buy, but also leaves everyone else with a clear vision about what is not going to be provided, so the non-statutory sector can look towards filling in the gaps.'

Maintenance was often seen as the task of volunteers and voluntary/non-statutory organisations prior to recent contracting arrangements with health, local authorities and the criminal justice system. This was seen partly as an absence of medical, psychiatric and psychological theories which locate the problem in the individual and advocate individual change.

The voluntary agencies had no specialist diagnosis or assessment procedure as they had no professional expertise (were not based within any professional knowledge base). As voluntary agencies are increasingly funded by statutory services, they must accept professional aims and professional notions of success and failure, so that their work can be monitored for cost-effectiveness ('best value'). So, for example, a drug drop-in agency may have provided basic advice, support and practical help (e.g. welfare advice, housing advice, etc.), but on receiving money from probation, social services or health will be expected to demonstrate the ability to change individual clients, to carry out assessments and to monitor success and failure in terms of the aims and outcome measures specified by the funder. These agencies then begin to employ professionals (in the same way as the statutory agencies do) and so change from their original role as atheoretical support and maintenance services, to services designed to change individuals (whether through treatment, therapy and counselling, rehabilitation or reform); that is, their aims and outcome or cost-effectiveness measures must be defined in terms of abstinence, behaviour change, social rehabilitation and reconvictions. They must be evidence-based and evaluate the effectiveness of what they do, rather than simply offering the practical help and support that a client might ask for.

As they take on the task of health, social services and the criminal justice system, the question might be raised of who takes on their old tasks of support and maintenance of the untreatables, the unintegratables and the unreformables? Who provides help, information, sanctuary, asylum, support, maintenance and other potentially life-saving ongoing care despite the lack of individual change or progress?

Professionals identify a need for maintenance methods

This section examines the ways in which different professions work when faced with complex psychosocial problems that they know from experience require more comprehensive approaches than those of their specific profession. It will be seen that most professionals develop a fairly pragmatic approach and use a range of different practical, common-sense methods for dealing with both social and psychological problems.

Need for maintenance after treatment for relapse prevention

'We carry on seeing them after treatment completion if necessary.'

'People often leave treatment for the wrong reasons, not because they have successfully completed the programme. They have dropped out because things have gone wrong in their lives.'

Maintenance for everyday living and coping

'I mean he does, I think he does appreciate having somebody pop in. I mean he's got, he's got friends or acquaintances or, you know, people around him but I think he does appreciate the contact of having someone come in and checking he's OK.'

'I'm not sure what is important to [client], I think he does appreciate having some help with bills because he has mentioned that.'

'I'm sort of there because I have to be there because somebody has to give him an injection, but that I can probably be quite helpful in other areas as well. You know, to have a hand with this because he does feel in such a muddle with things sometimes. So, probably at the moment, that's the major thing. And probably things like helping with the move, it all fell through but he did express that he was appreciative of all the effort and time it spent to organise that, it didn't sort of go unnoticed. He did feel that we were trying to assist him, help him, both of us.'

Maintenance in case of crisis for relapse intervention

'If he was in trouble, he probably wouldn't contact me, he probably wouldn't contact anybody, from what he says. He would just shut himself away and lose contact with people.'

'He's highlighted that you know he's unwell, that he does cut himself off sort of thing and I think he does appreciate that somebody's actually watching out for that and trying to prevent him deteriorating and if he did become unwell that somebody would be there to pick it up or somebody that he has got a relationship with, which is me.'

Maintenance instead of treatment

'The most important thing is straightforward factual information so that people can make up their own minds about what sort of help they need and why. This information needs to start from the basis that people weigh up the pros and cons, and in many cases choose to take the risk of not having 'treatments', 'support' or housing.'

'In a care plan review we wouldn't give him the opportunity to say whether he thinks any things would work differently.'

Common maintenance methods.   A range of maintenance methods are used which are common across a range of different professions. It seems possible that, whilst specialist professionals have different theoretical expertise, they also use a range of practical common-sense methods for maintaining clients.

'Well, for a start he didn't know that the techniques that he was showing me I recognised as techniques from [another agency] so I had already done a lot of this with [another agency]. He didn't recognise that and that confused me a bit.'

'We teach clients to learn how to handle emotions appropriately.'

'Clients are taught to identify situations in which they become angry and aggressive and to learn new ways of coping with these situations.'

'We encourage clients to develop new leisure interests and maintain social support networks, particularly focusing on the client's family. Often also to develop new activities and cut off links with old social groups.'

Some professional views on the importance of maintenance

> 'I suppose everybody having a shared view about the place of their own approach would be very difficult, because everybody would have their own views about it, but we do all agree that these people should receive some help so they are not a danger to themselves and others.'

> 'Health problems and crime are far more of a risk for this group than psychological problems.'

> 'If we prevent someone turning to drugs or getting beaten up, that is a success, because that's reduced the harm.'

> 'We should have safe places and shelters within reach.'

> 'My aims are primarily about damage limitation. I am not concerned so much with curing people, it's the fact that they're putting themselves at risk.'

While many professions were unclear about the aims and objectives of maintenance support, the term 'treatment completion' was a vague and ill-fitting concept for others, as it was not uncommon for complex needs clients to stop attending services for negative rather than positive reasons. Some professionals even felt that treatment intervention itself was not the most significant aspect of the helping process, but that practical methods and social support were often more important to clients than theoretical models. Professionals often used particular methods because those methods worked and not because they were related to a theory.

THE NEED FOR A NEW MAINTENANCE MODEL OF CARE

This chapter has examined the interpretations and understandings of clients and professionals in order to give a clearer view of how each group saw the main obstacles to working together. The main themes emerging focused on the underlying assumptions in professional interventions which limit *comprehensive, ongoing* help for men and women with complex needs.

Client and professional views of problems and solutions were compared, highlighting the limitations of service provision and illustrating how specialist professional models can lead to narrow assessments, restricted interventions and time-limited help. Both clients and professionals identified the usefulness of atheoretical, common maintenance methods and the possible need for broader frameworks of understanding.

Many of these clients need ongoing help, therefore they need a range of interventions which are orientated towards maintenance of those things that cannot be changed, as well as change of those things that can be changed.

This chapter has provided some understanding of why clients with complex needs are often 'difficult' or 'non-compliant'. Professionals may see complex needs clients as people who use services for the wrong reasons, who manipulate professionals for what they can get, instead of what professionals want to give them, as 'untreatable' or non-compliant. Clients see themselves and professionals differently. Those who repeatedly used a range of different services saw themselves as continually going round a circuit. In fact this circuit involved a close-knit social network of similar 'revolving door' clients, many of whom knew each other. They took this for granted and seldom commented on it as a way of life and they did not try to change it. What they could not understand was why the professionals defined and described their progress round this circuit in terms of diagnosis or assessment and success or failure (individual medical, rehabilitative models). These definitions enabled clients to access certain facilities or hostels at certain times for certain reasons and then again served to move them on or out.

Clients seldom understood the professional rationale for giving them access to particular services, nor did they comprehend the reasons for time-limiting help and moving them on. This was equally true whether they were confronted with the medical model of health and mental health services, the therapeutic model of counselling services, the rehabilitative model of social services or the reforming model of criminal justice services.

In all these models the service is seen as ineffective, unsuccessful and not cost-effective if it does not change the person. The clients did not see it this way; rather they saw that they had developed a way of coping with personal disorders and inadequacies, handicaps etc. and that all they needed was some support and structure from professionals in order to keep this up; that is, they needed a model of maintenance, continuing ongoing support, crisis services, safe environments, safe houses, and services that fulfil basic needs of food, shelter, health care and protection.

There remain several questions. The answers below are derived from the interviews with professionals.

Do the definitions/theories of particular professions (while useful for a majority of clients) act as an impediment for dealing with multiproblem clients?

Professional theories/models are of course effective for the great majority of their patients or clients. While much research and practice therefore centre on the successful clients, there is little concern with the failures. The minority will drop to the bottom of the pile in each caseload and will move on through all the professions, dropping to the bottom of the pile in each case before moving on again.

Why don't therapeutic/professional theories work for a minority of people (with multiple problems)?

Professional assessments limit interventions and confuse evaluations of outcome.

Do professionals recognise this?

Qualitative research shows that staff do not see multiple problems as a predictor of treatment failure. Instead, complex needs clients are often seen as beyond help (if they cannot or will not be helped by a particular profession). They may be seen as hopeless cases for various reasons often involving some kind of pathology of client, or as 'difficult' or non-compliant if they are not successful.

Why do professionals not recognise their limitations and adapt?

Professionals and researchers are more concerned with success than the limitations of theories and practice. Professional theories provide inherent rationalisations for when they do not work in terms of individual client failings.

Why do professionals go on doing something that is dysfunctional for a minority of clients?

Because it is functional for the majority of clients. If theories work for some and not others, those they do not work for are seen as 'inappropriate clients' rather than 'inappropriate services'. The question is seldom asked, 'If what I provide is "inappropriate", what would be "appropriate" for this client?'

Why do professionals do what they do? What does their profession take for granted?

Professions have training programmes that socialise and educate into particular ways of working.

Why do non-compliant/complex needs clients fail to use services and what services do they need? (Why are services not cost-effective for these clients and why do specialised services aimed at specific problems not work?)

Notions of success and failure can be counter-productive for this group.

The next chapter considers many of these issues by examining the differences between professionals and the obstacles to interprofessional working.

CONCLUSION

Much research is carried out within the framework of medicine or psychology and in the context of treatment programmes, working with a notion of problems as illnesses, or behavioural disorders, which can be cured (Turk *et al.* 1986). The treatment approaches differ in the language they use to define the problem and in the way in which they define successful treatment. However, all professionals share a common goal of treating or changing clients. It is important to note that while the rhetoric differs, the actual methods used by different professions have much in common. For example, even if using different models, psychologists, health workers and social workers essentially provide much the same kind of therapeutic service; that is, they may be doing the same things but defining them differently (Keene 2000).

It is important to emphasise that research is concerned with how effective treatment is in achieving success in terms of specific treatment outcome aims, not in terms of other objectives, such as long-term effects, relationships, housing, employment, or its effect on other problems. Outcome studies of comorbidity treatments are handicapped by problems in the identification of relevant criteria for baseline, outcome and follow-up measures. There has been much controversy about the identification of predictors of treatment outcome and indeed about the usefulness of treatment outcome as a measure at all. Research indicates that, although specific treatment variables may be significant for immediate health or behaviour change, many other variables 'mediate' treatment effect itself. This is further complicated by variables influencing maintenance of change at follow-up, such as personal and social functioning.

It will be suggested that specialist models of change need to be supplemented by a new generic model of maintenance. While this maintenance approach is not entirely new, it has traditionally remained the area of non-professional voluntary agencies rather than specialist professions. However, professionals are beginning to develop theories and practice methods of prevention and maintenance. So, for example, the theory and research of health psychology informs both psychologists and health workers about teaching clients skills for coping with stress. In addition, practice methods developed for working with chronic illnesses have become widespread, perhaps independently of a theoretical model. In the following section it will be proposed that all professions need to develop a common maintenance model alongside change models for psychosocial clients. This can be used as an alternative to individual client change or used before and after change interventions. Professionals already provide support and maintenance but most do not have a clearly defined specialist professional maintenance model already in place. There is therefore no reason for a newly developed atheoretical model to reflect different types of professional biases as the change practice models do.

While this chapter has suggested that the treatment or change model has limitations for clients with complex needs, it has perhaps also raised the wider question, 'Is a psychosocial maintenance approach an essential addition to a monocausal change perspective, for clients with complex needs?'; that is, for this group, is it useful to see any problem as one of a range of difficulties experienced by clients – not as a cause or consequence of other problems, but as interacting with and exacerbating other problems – to move from monocausal explanations towards an understanding of the complexity of interacting psychological and social variables. If this is the case, there may be a need for a review of solutions and services. Rather than a single treatment or therapeutic episode it may be necessary to implement a range of social and psychological solutions over time in order to maintain and support vulnerable people. This is discussed more fully in the next chapter.

Chapter 5

Understanding Different Professional Perspectives: the Need for a Common Comprehensive Psychosocial Approach

INTRODUCTION

The previous chapter examined differences between clients and professionals as a whole and highlighted two problem areas:

(1) Differences between client maintenance and professional change orientated perspectives.
(2) The limitations of specialist assessment and intervention for complex needs.

This chapter will examine the differences between different professional groups, rather than what they have in common. It will focus on the differences and disagreements between professionals which create obstacles to multiprofessional working with complex needs clients. This chapter also examines the positive aspects of interprofessional working, analysing what professionals do that works and how they can build on it.

PROFESSIONAL VIEWS COMPARED: NEED FOR A SHARED PSYCHOSOCIAL UNDERSTANDING

Professional views of the difficulties of working with other professionals

This section considers the implications of each profession having a different set of expert knowledge and priorities, focusing on a different primary cause and identifying different causal directions between problems. Working with clients with complex needs is difficult because professional perspectives not only differ from the client view but also have differing views from each other. For example, a psychiatrist might find it problematic to work with a social worker if the latter does not use a medical model to assess and prioritise resources for a client. Similarly, a psychiatrist might find it hard to work with a probation officer as they have different aims and priorities, the psychiatrist to treat the patient's clinical needs and the probation officer to reform behaviour and to protect the general public from future risk.

Many professionals who see their own role clearly are aware that their own expertise may not be appropriate or sufficient for any one client. However, it is not part of their professional remit to deal with 'inappropriate' clients appropriately. While they can be clear about what is not their problem, they have more difficulty in determining what is an appropriate service and which professional group is equipped to deal with the variety of other problems. This leads to a situation where 'inappropriate' clients are passed from professional to professional without any one person being able to provide a successful service.

Different professional philosophies, aims and priorities

Different professional aims and priorities

'I used to go to mental health reviews. If you like I acted as the interface. If I use the word interpreter, it's not because the consultant was Greek, it's because doctors are trained to think in a certain way. It's, if you like, an illness, diagnosis, treatment, and cure... Whereas we take a more holistic approach and I found myself forever explaining to the consultant that this is what happens in the real world. I explained to clients that this is the way it works and this is the way the service works so we've got to take things in this order.'

'Enormous difficulties because everyone has different agendas and different philosophies. Trying to coordinate a multidisciplinary approach is for me like trying to ski stylishly. When every agency has different key performance indicators, how on earth can you have a common policy?'

'As I understand it, with "X", you can only work with people who want to work. It has to be client-led, it can't be sort of coming and saying you will do this, this and this. It's not how we work.'

'If it wasn't [appropriate], they might sort of say no, we don't feel it is us, we feel it's you, and then it might be that you need to get further information and an assessment is done to determine what the issues are. I think probably people have different views or different perspectives on it because often you get a situation where people have different ideas but I suppose you're always going to get that, all kinds of different perspectives about whose responsibility it is.'

'Agencies are very territorial. Multidisciplinary working isn't happening either, on the ground.'

'I think if you expect you are all going to think the same thing at the same time and have it as the same priority, that would be extraordinarily unrealistic.'

Different professional perspectives on the same problem

'I think there's a lot of a cross-over because there's a lot of looking at how he's best going to function in his environment.'

'We are focusing on different things, but the whole picture is the same we are concerned about, you know, how stable his illness is that affects both of us, there's a sort of common thing, like the recent plan of moving him to "X". I mean that was something that they [drug agency workers] had talked about as being important because he felt there was a temptation maybe to get back on drugs because of the environment he was in and that was one thing that he wanted to be settled somewhere else, and various other things, that this would generate other activities and interests and meeting people, this sort of thing. So that was something he'd highlighted from the drugs perspective but that was also important for my perspective as well for how he felt, his mental well-being as well. So it was all relevant although it was all stemmed, the reason for going was probably stemmed out of stuff around his drug use. It was still very important, obviously if he's not very happy in his environment that doesn't help his whole picture from the mental health side as well.'

'I think when there's people with quite complex illnesses it's very effective to have joint work because you're getting different people picking up on different things.'

'I've recently had a referral who it would have been beneficial to have a joint assessment for at the time; because of the shortages of staff it wasn't possible to do that, so I'll probably enlist their help further on. I actually got ahead with the assessment, obviously there where it would have probably been helpful to have both of us in from the beginning and I understand that is the protocol for joint assessments. There are times when this doesn't happen and it isn't working. I don't know why this is.'

'A joint assessment can be helpful and appropriate. What's happening now? I imagine – not ever having to do it – is that we then contact a member of the team and come up with a convenient time to do a joint assessment and both meet and interview the client together and then discuss afterwards the findings. So it would be a case of sort of communicating with everyone and then trying to gain access really.'

Inappropriate clients or inappropriate services?

Assessment for appropriate services

'We devised care plans which met the psychiatrist's clinical perspective but which also met the social, psychosocial needs of the client.'

'It is unrealistic to expect that the issue will be held at the same level in every organisation or that you're going to achieve consensus about the overall direction and balance. And you must recognise that for some agencies it will be much more of their core work and for others it is not ... I think if you expect for a strategy that you are all going to think the same thing and have the same priority, that would be extraordinarily unrealistic.'

'Basically people have got to stop being precious and stop saying they are right and they are the people who know what the answer is. What you do is you go and listen to the other guy first and you translate what's being said ... This is not a new technique.'

'We identify a common problem between ourselves and say, "OK how are we going to solve this?"'

'Well, I guess it doesn't matter too much [at the assessment stage] because the point when we do assessments doesn't necessarily mean we're going to take on that person. It's basically going in, seeing what the issues are and bringing it back and then saying, well it looks like these other people need to be involved.'

'You're sort of aware that there is this [multidisciplinary] protocol and you know, we should be doing things ... No it's not something I've sort of discussed in supervision, no. My understanding of the protocol is that ... I got it out earlier and sat it on my desk and haven't read it yet but [laughs] I've, yeah, I know where it is ... in the drawer.'

Appropriate professionals for the appropriate problems?

'There's going to be some overlap because some things like you say are affected by different types of problem. You know, the whole thing is not always clear cut so there's going to be some overlap but basically I would expect if [the client] had an alcohol problem, he may mention something about it to me but he would know that it was something he'd have to bring up with [alcohol services professional] if he wanted, if he had a problem with something. I mean he could approach me and get me in touch with [professional] but I think he would know that it's something that he could take to her himself.'

' It would be discussed within the team as to what appears to be indicated or what appears to be appropriate. If it's felt that it's not an appropriate referral then [we] would then respond by either write back to the GP and say this isn't appropriate because, whatever, because we don't deal with this. Can you give us further information or something like that.'

'We [mental health team] have to take patients on; drug agencies will only work with clients who state that they want to work with their drug problems. If they do not think they are a problem or do not want to work with this problem the agency does not want to know. Therefore there are lots of mental health caseload with drug problems that are not receiving help.'

Practical difficulties in multidisciplinary working

Obstacles to multiprofessional working

'It was made clear more than a decade ago that this [multidisciplinary working] was the way to go. What are we doing? Eleven years on and nobody has moved! What's going on? Why hasn't it moved?'

'There is resistance to the client group itself. "We'd rather buy commodes than treat your people" kind of attitudes. Some of it's very negative and based on prejudice. Attitude problem. Also time; some of these clients are very time intensive, so professionals shy away from them. Professionals feel deskilled by this client group, but often they are deskilling themselves. Could be overcome by training, awareness raising, open days, integration of training into professional courses.'

'Being unable to meet each other's expectations (for example, length of our waiting list) which then skews requests for advice – we start playing games with each other.'

'I feel very much that I'm doing what I do from my small corner, and feeling not very aware of what else is out there or if anything else is out there.'

Records and confidentiality

'But several people I see will also have input from other services, so it's similar in the way that I may be seeing somebody and also a social worker is seeing them or a support worker or there may be access in lots of different services that I'm coordinating their care. And some cases different files are held on people. You know, I'll see somebody and somebody else will see them and they've got their set of notes and the same with ["Y"], we hold different records.'

'It's a secrets sort of thing and there's still the underlying culture ... that you don't talk to other people.'

'There are also issues around confidentiality in working with other agencies.'

'The fact that providers are now in competition with each other is a disincentive to sharing information with each other. Also with lottery grants – any organisation can put in a lottery grant in anybody's area, and possibly get it, and that's just happened here.'

'Confidentiality is another big issue, confidentialities have to change. With community safety now a priority we have to alert other people that we are working with people who may be dangerous. So the communication network is being built up.'

Status and interprofessional working

'There is a real difficulty for us [non-statutory housing workers] making referrals.'

'[Non-statutory] drug workers do not get a response, especially not from health professionals. Professionals in drug teams don't even get a response from other professionals.'

'We're getting a cognitive psychologist [on the non-statutory team]. I think that will actually strengthen relationships with mental health, because it's about professionalism, it's about credibility.'

'The [drug worker] has never talked to the psychiatrist, it is usually only the other way round.'

'Our biggest difficulty (as voluntary agencies) is GPs. In general, the attitude in this area is, I don't want to have anything to do with this group of individuals, and that puts pressure on us, and particularly on the client. Ideally it should be a two-way street; currently it's one-way, with the client losing out.'

'GPs are invited to any reviews we have but don't tend to have the time to attend.'

'I think communication could be improved, yeah communication could be improved, probably on both sides, but in particular I think with GPs communicating with us [CPNs]. To sort of remember to contact us if they do have contact with a patient and not assume that we already know any information that they might have.'

'I think the difference is that I was able to go along [to see psychiatric consultant] with expertise which is transferable between consultants, because consultants do talk to consultants.'

'It's about identifying the key people, using their connections with other people to get introductions.'

Confused roles and responsibilities

'I don't know the job or expertise of other people. I believe she is not trained as a nurse, I think she's an OT is she? Or some different training so I don't know if she's trained to administer and monitor the effects of medication so, that side of it she probably wouldn't do and I don't know enough about the other services really. I mean, I don't know enough about them.'

'The obstacles are that there are two very separate services and we may have limited knowledge of how the other one operates and who to address there. I mean, I've never met Dr "A". I'm sure if I needed to I would but I'm, you know, there can be obstacles in communicating when you've got two different separate services on different sites and you're writing different notes and keeping different records, doing things independently in a way so you've got to make sure that you're communicating enough.'

'We are an enforcement agency, that is our primary role, and putting it very bluntly, that's what people pay their taxes for . . .'

'What I'm hoping is that we can work out where our roles and responsibilities lie . . . if we don't care what health are doing, or they don't care what we are doing . . .'

'I'm not sure that we're all quite clear what our respective roles are, so the difficulty is knowing what each other does and how you fit together.'

'I am very confused as to what social services' role is generally. We try and ensure that (we have not) adopted an exclusion model, because once people get excluded they use the subculture that they've got as a prop and therefore get deeper into it.'

'I'd like to swap the staff round a bit, so that they can see how the culture works in other places and professions.'

Professionals want a common understanding and common priorities

The aims of a broad range of different professionals were vague and sometimes confused. While all attempted to clarify their role as a change agent, some prioritised health, psychological or social changes. Most felt that it would be necessary to agree on common definitions of complex needs, to enable common forms of identification and assessment. Some said this would necessarily have to be based on common understandings of the problems.

> 'There should be a coordinated approach so that everything is enhanced and reinforced by what is going on in other professions, and that would be reinforced by the way each profession responds, rather than these hitting head on because they've got different goals.'

> 'There needs to be a consistency about how professionals work in different agencies, promoting a cohesive, coordinated, planned programme, a strategy which all agencies understand.'

> 'A realistic aim would be to get a common consensus of different needs, to get a joint agreement about need, and it's from here that you'd develop joint programmes. Out of that if you can agree what the common need is then you can agree what the common indicators for need are, which means that you can arrive at common indices of health need.'

> 'We would like to see a shared understanding about the problem, a shared understanding of the way forward.'

The identification of specific obstacles to multidisciplinary work provides a greater understanding of the types of problems that may be common to professionals in a wider context. First, it was found that professionals were often unsure or ambivalent about what their own profession should do, and how to identify or assess complex needs clients. Some professionals felt that their traditional approach needed to be modified to allow them to carry out the appropriate intervention. Second, it was found that respondents often had a lack of knowledge about what other professional groups were doing. For example, respondents either did not know who dealt with complex needs or particular problems or they thought them the responsibility of particular agencies (often non-professional or voluntary). In reality, all professionals were working with this group without realising or defining them as complex needs (partly perhaps because they did not have screening instruments or tariffs or assessments that enabled identification of the complexity of their needs).

Understanding the obstacles: different definitions of the problem

These comments illustrate the problems and difficulties inherent in multidisciplinary working. It is clear that the majority of the professionals interviewed felt that there was a real need for multiprofessional working and they wanted to work together. However, there was confusion about why this was difficult and how it could be resolved. They understood that there were differences in beliefs and priorities concerning complex needs clients, but not why these were so difficult to resolve.

Different professionals had different definitions of the problems of complex needs clients. Each group had elaborate and sometimes contradictory ideas about how to define problems, and a range of different rationales to explain why they were doing what they were doing. In addition, these definitions often differed from those of the clients. However, whereas staff had different conceptualisations of the problem, they shared a common desire for clients and other professionals to accept their definition of the problem.

Different assessments of problems

Professionals have different forms of assessment based on different definitions of the problem. These assessments then inform notions of what counts as a successful outcome (that is after the clients are gauged to have succeeded in terms of the original definition of the problem). Professionals are assessing for treatment or preparatory to a significant change in the client.

'[Between professionals] Communication pathways are not always there, people are not prepared to listen to other people. They've always done it their way and not the other way.'

'Agencies need to be speaking to each other to make sure that they're acting consistently. The first thing is clarity between the agencies about different aims and objectives, and where the common ground is, and a framework that allows professionals to actually communicate and deal with each other. The second is empowerment of staff with skills to actually talk to other professions.'

'Generally service users, I've found over the years, are surprised when you ask them what they need. I think most service users are going to be a touch cynical or a touch amazed at the idea that we're actually going to seek their views on services. [Complex needs, particularly mental health and substance misusers] have always been a disenfranchised group. They've never had a voice. I think that is also quite a scary thing for a lot of service providers. I think that may be a problem.'

Difficulties in agreeing on what is the primary problem

'We need a general clarification of what is really the main problem, what are the priorities for dealing with it and who should be doing what. There will be different attitudes, so although one would imagine everybody would be working towards the same goals, they might not be.'

'Other agencies need to be aware of our agenda and how that fits or doesn't fit with their agenda.'

'My priorities are very specific in that in contracts with people I want to have certain issues integrated and that doesn't go down too well and various agencies may have problems working with particular issues.'

'Gaps in understanding between various agencies lead to misconceptions and misperceptions.'

'Clinical depression is the cause of many problems developing in later life such as relationship problems and employment problems. The answer is to develop early intervention procedures for identification and screening of depression, particularly in adolescents and young people.'

'Serious health problems lead increasingly to social isolation and psychological problems.'

'Poor housing and stress cause a whole range of psychological and eventually health problems.'

'Cognitive and behavioural problems in young people aggravate substance misuse.'

'Drug misuse causes crime.'

Different interpretations of problems and different interpretations of causality

Professionals define problems differently.   The qualitative data indicate that staff theories or understandings of the nature of the problem and its treatment influence how problems are defined, which interventions are considered necessary, how success is perceived and when treatment is terminated.

Professionals may then often assume that the client will accept that this single problem is the most serious or primary one and recognise that it causes other problems. Consequently, clients may be required to change their individual behaviour and other aspects of their lifestyle in order to improve this one aspect, with little consideration of the costs or consequences in other areas of their life. Professionals therefore also had differing definitions of successful outcome. It became clear during the course of the research that professional definitions of the problem were relevant in determining what was considered a successful outcome. This was often seen only in terms of completion of the programme of help or of changes in personal lifestyle.

It seems that professionals may be focusing on those characteristics of the client which they define as problematic and attempting to achieve particular changes in these areas only. It should be remembered that the translation of the language and nature of treatment for clients takes place in a context where, whatever the model and the methods of treatment, it is largely professionals who decide what the problem to be treated is.

Professionals find it difficult to agree about priorities because they cannot agree on what the primary problem actually is. Different professionals saw different problems as causal or primary, usually defining the problems in their own field of expertise as contributing significantly to the development of other problems. That is they saw 'their own' problems as the primary or causal problems.

Although many professionals understood various problems as contributing to each other, they often adhered to a model which was based on the premise that one particular problem or set of problems caused or contributed to all others. So, for example, mental health workers might see clinical depression as the cause of social problems, whereas a social worker might see the social situation as the cause of the problems. The causal direction would then determine which services should be prioritised and which professional group take responsibility for a particular client. This was particularly clear for dual diagnosis patients where a psychiatrist or psychologist might feel that cognitive and behavioural problems caused substance misuse, whereas a substance misuse worker might feel the opposite, that the substance misuse itself caused the psychological problems.

These 'chicken and egg' arguments about causality have very significant implications for practice, not only for which profession takes responsibility, but also for the type of service provided, if any. The research literature in Chapter 1 indicates that usually only one type of service is provided for one problem or that no service at all is provided.

Similarly, even if a particular profession does take responsibility for more than one problem (and some professionals were in effect using similar methods to deal with a range of problems), they were likely to vary the sequence in which those methods or interventions were provided, depending on their notion of causal direction. So, for example, a psychiatrist or psychologist might insist on establishing a prescribed drugs or a therapeutic programme before providing practical help for social problems, whereas a social worker may feel that finding supported accommodation was an essential first step.

It can be seen then that different professionals have different views of complex needs, in which the reasons for change, the type of change and the ways of evaluating that change are defined differently. This gives rise to much misunderstanding or argument over priorities, interventions and resources. It provides obstacles to multiprofessional practice that may seem unresolvable. However, the best way forward would seem to be to clarify differences and understand other professionals' perspectives, rather than to try to pretend they are all the same or try to become all the same. They are different because they are designed to deal effectively with different problems. When working together, professionals need to agree on how the client's different problems will be understood in order to be able to agree what to do about it.

Doing the same things, but defining them differently?

Professionals have different theories, which determine who they provide help for and when they provide it and terminate it, but they often use the same practical maintenance methods.

At first sight, the differences between professionals and their respective theories are clear cut and distinct. It was therefore surprising that the data derived from observation and interviews with professionals also demonstrate clearly that many used similar maintenance methods, and suggest that there is no necessary relationship between the maintenance methods used and treatment theories. However, it appears that although staff's actions to help maintain complex needs clients were essentially the same, their definition of problems and their understanding of solutions and successful treatment outcome were very different. These findings are reflected in the work of Baronet and Gerber (1998) and Keene (2000). Baronet and Gerber reviewed four rehabilitation programmes and Keene reviewed the theories and methods of two treatment and rehabilitation programmes. Both conclude that clients are able to develop similar psychological and social skills, independently of the rehabilitation model. Outcome effects were not related to theoretical approach or model, but to client characteristics and multiple problems.

Common maintenance methods but different theories

Interviews with professionals indicated that despite differing models of intervention, they were using the same methods. For example, health, mental health care, social workers and probation officers all used initial motivational strategies, cognitive and behavioural methods, relaxation, stress management and anger control, task-centred and client-centred counselling methods, skills training, social support, practical help and life skills training. There was, however, often a difference in the timing and rationale for using them. If there are similarities of methods, despite a variety of theories and types of assessment, perhaps this also helps explain why various professionals may be equally effective with complex needs clients. It may also explain why these clients often could not tell the difference between different types of professional.

It can be seen that professionals themselves felt that practical methods and social support were often more important to clients than theoretical expertise. Professionals often used particular methods because these methods work and not because they are related to a theory.

This strange coexistence of conflicting theories and common methods is better understood when it is seen that many professionals from social, health care, criminal justice and voluntary agencies have an eclectic approach to complex needs clients, using a range of different methods. The service these clients receive and the methods used are therefore very similar whichever agency they attend, although most professionals encourage the client to identify one thing as a serious or primary problem and to recognise that it causes other problems.

The actual models and methods used are discussed in more detail in Part III of this book, but it is relevant to mention here that methods which form part of the training and procedures of many social, health care and criminal justice professions included:

- Examining the problems associated with the primary problem (whether they are seen as underlying or perpetuating this problem).
- Encouraging clients to change their individual behaviour and other aspects of their lifestyle.
- Using recognised counselling and therapeutic techniques.
- Designing structured programmes involving the setting of a series of concrete goals.
- Using cognitive behavioural techniques to change attitudes and beliefs and modify behaviours.
- Providing practical help and support concerning housing, welfare rights, employment and training.
- Teaching life and social skills.
- Encouraging clients to develop new leisure interests, occupations, social contacts and support networks.
- Providing some kind of ongoing support, easy access or crisis service after treatment.

It is possible that all such forms of ongoing professional help use methods which have an unrecognised positive effect, such as providing a socialising process with successful socialisation as an integral (necessary if not sufficient) part of each approach. Socialisation is just one of many factors treated only as a mediating variable or ignored altogether in treatment research.

In addition, many professionals mentioned a sequential process model of change. This is discussed in more detail in Part III, but it should be noted here that client-centred, non-directive counselling methods and skills of unconditional positive regard, understanding and empathy are used within many models as the initial stage of a sequence. This is commonly followed by more structured and directive counselling, including cognitive techniques such as awareness raising, information, decisional balances, re-evaluation of life events and drug-related problems. Client-centred and task-orientated counselling techniques, useful for motivating people to change, are also used within most models, including giving feedback to the client, taking a non-confrontational stance and providing pragmatic alternatives (Miller *et al.* 1988). These methods of interviewing and counselling in the field were developed in the 1980s using notions of individual change processes, apparently in the absence of any coherent theory or testable hypotheses, yet they were tremendously popular among practitioners and spread rapidly in the early 1990s.

Despite a common core of methods and techniques, it should be remembered that different professional theories and consequent assessments are extremely influential in determining whether the client receives a service, which services they receive and when these services are terminated.

Theories which clarify problems through an understanding of etiology enable accurate assessment and determine appropriate treatment solutions and definitions of success. However, with complex needs clients it is possible that, because theories can narrow problem definitions and exclude a range of possible interacting problems, they effectively limit appropriate interventions and may terminate help prematurely. So some therapeutically useful theories may do more harm than good with multi-problem clients.

AN EXAMPLE OF PROFESSIONAL DIFFERENCES AND PRACTICE SOLUTIONS: THE ISSUE OF DUAL DIAGNOSIS

Expanding theories of single and dual diagnosis to include multiple assessment of interacting psychosocial problems

The difficulty in multidisciplinary working with complex needs clients is well illustrated by perhaps the most common of all cooccurring problems – mental illness and substance misuse. This issue is therefore examined in detail here in order to illustrate the problems and solutions of working with this group.

As mentioned earlier, the difficulty when assessing clients with complex needs or multiple problems is that one of these problems, such as depression, may be a consequence of another, such as unemployment, or vice versa. Moreover, the relationship between them may itself exacerbate both. The greater the depression, the less chance of employment, and the less chance of employment, the greater the depression. The problem of deciding whether depression has caused certain disabilities or whether certain disabilities have led to and aggravated the effect of other psychological and social problems is very difficult, if not impossible, as there are no simple objective criteria for assessing it, for professionals and clients alike. The causal direction attributed often depends, not on research but on the initial theoretical structure and beliefs of the observer. An observer working with psychological theories would understand the client's problems in terms of clinical depression and seeing this as the primary problem would assess it using psychological criteria and tests such as the Beck Depression Inventory. They would therefore be more likely to define social problems as a sign or symptom of depression. In contrast, a social worker or probation officer might be more likely to see the depression as a sign of social and relationship problems.

Dual diagnosis

In order to examine these problems more closely it is useful to examine the difficulties involved in assessing or diagnosing two problems at the same time. As we saw in Chapter 1, 'dual diagnosis' is generally understood to mean a mental health problem and a substance misuse problem together. For example, it is possible that drugs prescribed for mental health reasons can lead to dependency problems. Landry *et al.* (1991) suggest that patients attending treatment for anxiety disorders are commonly prescribed psychoactive drugs which can lead to dependency if not carefully monitored.

In the same way, illicit drug misusers may be self-medicating (knowingly or unknowingly) for problems of anxiety or depression. Khantzian (1985) suggested that individuals misuse drugs adaptively to cope with intensive adolescent-like anxiety. He formulated a self-medication hypothesis, proposing that drug misusers will select drugs which will 'medicate' their dominant painful feelings. It is also possible that illicit drug misusers may be self-medicating for behavioural problems such as aggressive and/or violent behaviour. Again there are problems in determining whether behavioural problems are an effect of drug misuse and withdrawals or whether these predate them. Powell and Taylor (1992) showed that hostility and anger were common among opiate misusers after withdrawal; they suggested that anger management would be a useful intervention at this stage.

It is perhaps the relationship between depression and substance misuse that is most significant to practitioners (Paton *et al.* 1977; Deakin *et al.* 1987). Many clients would say that they used drugs (or alcohol) because they were depressed, and that therefore it is the underlying depression that needs to be treated; whereas others would see depression as a consequence of their drug misuse. It is, of course, likely that each contributes to the other in a worsening spiral of problems, but in terms of practical assessment it is very important to distinguish between the two, as the type of problem will determine the type of intervention.

Although there are difficulties in determining the causal relationship, many professionals are concerned at the incidence of 'comorbidity' (Kandel 1982) and the increased incidence of depression. Deykin *et al.* (1992) have shown that among adolescents in drug treatment the rate of depression is three times higher than in a similar population and that this is linked to a very high incidence of physical and sexual abuse and neglect in the histories of depressive drug misusers. They have demonstrated that the high rate of depression among substance misusers can be explained in terms of two distinct groups: those with primary depression and those with depression subsequent to dependence. The authors suggest that these different types of development of depression require two different types of treatment approach:

'Patients with primary depression who are chemically dependent might well profit from treatment directed at their depression rather than their chemical dependence. Conversely, those who become depressed after they have developed chemical dependence might show greater improvement when treatment is targeted at their alcohol and drug misuse rather than their depression.'

Deykin *et al.* also found that males were twice as likely to have depression follow drug misuse than vice versa, while females were more likely to be self-medicating.

Magruder-Habib *et al.* (1992) have shown that those at highest risk of suicide were women misusing a range of non-narcotic drugs. The researchers found that if clients felt suicidal tendencies soon after treatment they were more likely to attempt suicide a year later and that this was related to relapse.

Saxon and Caslyn (1995) examined treatment outcomes for substance dependence in a clinic that made psychiatric care readily available. Psychotropic medications were prescribed for four-fifths of the dual diagnosis subjects. The authors concluded that dual diagnosis patients may initially perform more poorly than substance-only diagnosis patients in substance dependence treatment. However, in the presence of psychiatric care they eventually exhibit comparable success. Fisher and Bentley (1996) compared the relative effectiveness of two types of group therapy – the disease and recovery model and the cognitive behavioural model – in a public in-patient and out-patient setting. Outcomes for dual diagnosis patients in four areas of problem severity were measured:

alcohol use, drug use, social and family relationships and psychological functioning. The authors found that in the out-patient setting cognitive behavioural therapy was more successful than other forms of treatment and for in-patients both forms of group therapy were more effective than other forms of treatment.

Bellack and Gearon (1998) and Drake *et al.* (1998) are recent examples of the many studies that are critical of the state of treatment for dual diagnosis. The former, while asserting that there is widespread agreement on the need to integrate psychiatric and substance abuse treatment, observe there are at present no programmes based on reliable empirical findings. Drake and colleagues argue that dual diagnosis patients traditionally received care from two different sets of physicians in parallel treatment systems and criticise this. The authors review 36 research studies of a new integrated approach and find that the majority of them (26) have produced disappointing results and the remaining ten have varied levels of success. Rothschild (1998) discusses similar problems.

In the UK, papers by Smith and Hucker (1993), Hall and Farrell (1997) and Holland (1999) examine possible future developments. Holland proposes special teams following the example of the USA. The other two papers argue in favour of continuing with existing mental health services, Hall and Farrell referring to section 1 (3) of the Mental Health Act 1983, which excludes those 'suffering from a mental disorder purely by reason of ... dependence on alcohol or drugs'. The problems raised by the Act are discussed by Macpherson (1996) and the Act is currently under review by the Scoping Study Committee which has recommended that 'the express exclusion be removed on the basis that in the absence of any underlying mental disorder substance misuse on its own could not meet the eventual criteria for compulsion' (Scoping Study Committee 1999).

Dual diagnosis therefore has practical implications in terms of therapeutic intervention, as what is believed to be good practice for dealing with dependence may be at odds with treatment of depression and other mental health problems where prescribed drugs are considered beneficial. There are also particular treatment issues concerned with the psychiatric models of care and the disease/abstinence approach to dependency. Dermott and Pyett (1994) recommend that conflicts over conceptualisation should be resolved; while this is most improbable, it is important to recognise the likely conflicts between psychiatrists and disease model adherents and negotiate working relationships that take the differences in belief and practice into account. In addition to these problems, Kofoed (1993) outlines the difficulty of working with these complex needs patients over time, suggesting that different types of treatment intervention should be planned in a structured way through the treatment and recovery process.

Relevant here are those shared methods used for substance misuse and for psychological and mental health problems (Keene *et al.* 1999). For example, the methods used for treating drug addiction are very similar to those used for depression, anxiety and obsessive compulsive behaviours (Bandura 1977; Beck 1989). These common methods are discussed in detail in Part III.

Fresh complications are also introduced by those clients who misuse a variety of different drugs (polydrug misuse). Although it is clearly the case that some clients will prefer certain types of drugs, there is also an increasing number of polydrug misusers. The problems of dependency are then compounded. For example, it is fairly common for certain drugs such as depressants to be misused interchangeably e.g. heroin, methadone and alcohol. Work by Carrol *et al.* (1993) indicates that heavy alcohol use is not uncommon among opiate and cocaine misusers. A longitudinal study of heroin misusers 12 years after treatment shows that a quarter of a group of 298 were classified as heavy drinkers, indicating a form of substitute drug taking (Lehman *et al.* 1990). Iguchi *et al.* (1993) have also identified illicit benzodiazepine and sedative misuse among methadone maintenance clients. San *et al.* (1993a) found that benzodiazepine misuse (particularly flunitrazepam) was common among heroin addicts. However, these authors report elsewhere (San *et al.* 1993b) that clients on a drug-free programme consumed more of a variety of illicit substances than those on methadone maintenance.

It seems likely that certain types or combinations of drugs are preferred by different people. Other researchers have also identified this phenomenon. For example, Kidorf and Stitzer (1993) found that patients had preferences for particular groups of drugs and not others, e.g. patients using methadone did not particularly like cocaine. Craig and Olson (1990) compared cocaine and heroin misusers and found that the latter were more likely to have anxious personalities and evidence somatic distress, whereas cocaine misusers demonstrated antisocial personality traits. The authors conclude that there were clear personality differences between the two groups. Unfortunately, it is difficult to determine causal direction, that is to distinguish between the effects of long-term misuse and the reasons for misusing.

A COMMON PSYCHOSOCIAL PERSPECTIVE AND MAINTENANCE METHODS

This chapter has examined the differences and conflicts between clients and professionals and between professionals themselves, particularly in terms of diagnosis and assessment. It has also highlighted what professionals have in common and the positive aspects of interprofessional working and professional–client relations. It examines what professionals do that works and what they need to build on this, from maintenance methods to a broader psychosocial model to inform comprehensive assessment.

Themes arising from these data

Differences between professionals and clients: understandings and care models

Professionals have similar philosophies or models of care in which individual problems become the focus of professional activity and individual change is essential. This differs from the views of clients, who often see professional assessments as unhelpful, and professional interventions as inappropriate, restricted and time-limited. This disparity forms the main obstacle to effective intervention.

Differences between professionals: understandings of primary problems and priorities

The second theme is concerned with the differences in the perspectives of professionals, illustrating how beliefs about primary problems and priorities differ and how this obstructs multiprofessional working. Professionals have different specialist theories and therefore also different definitions of problems, different assessments, different reasons for starting and stopping help, and different definitions of success and failure.

The need for a common comprehensive psychosocial perspective and an additional maintenance model of care

Although it is clear that professionals may have specialist change theories and these differ, they also have similar maintenance methods.

Professionals have much in common in terms of practical understandings of clients' needs for maintenance or ongoing support and it is possible to build on this through the addition of two extra factors: additional psychosocial theoretical context and maintenance methods. These are not alternatives to specialist theory and methods, but additions that may be necessary when working with complex needs clients.

It appears that clients are working with a maintenance philosophy, often in direct opposition to professional change philosophies. The professional change-orientated approach underpins much of the basic professional assumptions to do with client motivation and success; it also time limits any form of help (whether the client is seen as a failure or a success).

In addition, professionals are using different models of change to carry out restricted assessments and intervention of complex needs clients, each profession focusing on its own area of expertise (whether this is health, mental health, substance misuse or crime) and ignoring the cooccurring problems. So if, for example, a person is assessed as having a drug problem, she/he may be considered successful even though they finish with untreated depression and alcohol problems.

A possible way forward may be to avoid these two obstacles, both professional change philosophies and professional specialist assessments, in the first instance, though both are essential at a later stage in the process.

Implications for practice

The research review indicated that there is little evidence to show differences in outcome in relation to which problem is dealt with first. It is more likely that variations in outcomes can be understood in terms of numbers and severity of problems, many services being (as might be expected) more successful with clients who have not only less serious levels of any one problem, but also fewer other problems. It is apparent that many variables are likely to influence client progress in resolving a range of complex interacting problems. There is therefore a need to consider not only a range of possible client problems and their interactive effects, but also the range of services and their interactive effectiveness.

It may also be useful to include a focus on methods common to a range of professions, before and after specialist interventions (together with explanatory theories of aetiology and treatment outcome); that is, to concentrate on factors which promote and maintain general well-being or post-treatment recovery. This chapter has highlighted the limitations of focusing on particular specialist problems to the exclusion of other potentially influential factors. Non-treatment factors are seldom considered in specialist literature, often being relegated to the status of 'mediating' variables. In order to introduce a new perspective on unresolved issues of problem definition and outcome measures in the area of complex needs, it is clear that major research is necessary to explore the comprehensive understandings and effective methods of maintenance that all professionals have in common, and the limitations of theoretical differences.

While professional models differed in some respects, all perceived complex needs clients in the following ways:

- Conceptualisation of a heterogeneous population as homogeneous (in terms of their shared possession of one common problem).
- Conceptualisation of multiple interacting problems as a single problem or a single cause (differential diagnosis or assessment).
- Conceptualisation of success or failure in terms of short-term outcome and often also in terms of a single treatment goal.

However, it should be emphasised that complex needs clients form a small proportion of most specialist caseloads (except perhaps for homeless hostels, prison, probation, and substance misuse and mental health agencies). For the majority of clients, professional theories and models are clearly of benefit and professionals derive their expertise and effectiveness from specialist knowledge and skills. There is therefore a dilemma for specialist professionals working with complex needs clients: while specialist treatment models are essential for most clients or patients, they also appear to distort both diagnosis and definition of success for complex needs clients. If this is so, it is possible that specialist models may have more costs than benefits and may be counter-productive for clients with a range of problems among this essentially heterogeneous population. Instead of a single diagnosis, a single treatment and a single goal, there should be multiple diagnoses or assessments, multiple interventions and multiple goals.

There has been very little work concerning the assessments, methods or goals that might prove more effective for those clients with multiple problems. As we have seen earlier in this chapter there is, however, already a wide literature examining the concept of dual diagnosis in the relationship between mental health and substance dependency. This has led to the development of the understanding and treatment of comorbid, or cooccurring, substance misuse and psychiatric problems, enabling the initiation of an integrated approach to treatment (McLellan *et al.* 1996). It has contributed much to a field where clinicians using differential diagnosis had previously prioritised presenting symptoms in terms of a single cause. It is possible, however, that the dual diagnosis approach itself may be too limited as it excludes cooccurring problems that are not classified in psychiatric terms or in terms of dependency; for example, unemployment and social problems (Kozarickovacic *et al.* 1995), homelessness and forensic history (Lambert & Caces 1995) and non-dependent drug problems (Keene 1997). The heterogeneity of this population and their multiple treatment needs has been highlighted by Mowbray *et al.* (1997).

While the concept of dual diagnosis is itself limited, this literature has provided the foundation for developing a broader concept of 'multiple diagnosis' as part of assessment, in order to identify more intractable clients and to provide indicators of extra need. In addition, work needs to be done to examine the indications and contra-indications for the use of particular methods in the context of complex needs; for example, therapeutic change methods may be contra-indicated for those with housing and mental health problems.

A useful way forward might be to examine how the diagnostic limitations of specialist models could be reduced without removing the treatment or other benefits. For example, early identification of single problems and early intervention programmes may help prevent the development of complex psychosocial needs. It may be useful to treat depression early before further psychological, relationship and social problems develop, rather than deal with complex psychosocial problems at a later date. Many agencies may also fail to reach some at-risk clients who may be irregular attenders. It is possible that there should be direct intensive interventions for the minority of clients who are particularly susceptible to complex psychosocial problems at any one time. It is possible that professionals could be trained to identify this type of client.

Multiprofessional working: practical issues

It can be argued that the premises on which policy are based are not appropriate for people with complex psychosocial problems and that therefore it is not surprising that the solutions, while well-meaning, are ineffectual. Before outlining possible solutions and alternative professional roles, it has been necessary to seriously reconsider the nature of the problem itself. It can be seen that an emphasis on psychosocial factors would, in effect, balance the focus on treatment and rehabilitation with that of social support and maintenance.

The difficulties are compounded by the difficulties of collaboration between members of the health, social care, criminal justice and psychological professions. These professions have differing perspectives, defining different aspects as problematic and developing their own solutions which combine their priorities with their particular skills and expertise. So, for example, health professionals are concerned with treatment and cure, social care professions with the extent of social need, police and prison officers with preventing crime, and psychologists or therapists with therapeutic or behaviour change. These aims can be incompatible in some circumstances.

There are many difficulties inherent in multidisciplinary working, not least those of establishing shared objectives and reaching consensus in developing coherent multidisciplinary strategies. This is partly due to conflicting professional aims and priorities ranging from health and public health to community safety.

It can be seen that contemporary solutions fail to take into account differences in type of professional. If, as has been suggested, an additional solution is seen in terms of maintenance it becomes possible to resolve these issues. Despite traditional differences in the values and priorities of different professional groups, if the most effective way to help complex needs clients was through an additional model of maintenance care, this would provide an area of common ground between all professional groups. At present, the solutions to this problem are complicated by the desire to achieve distinct professional aims such as treatment and rehabilitation. If the solutions were also seen in terms of prevention of harm and maintenance, these can be achieved equally well, if not better, by working together to provide a long-term supportive environment.

Whilst this solution would need to be based on a reconsideration of the roles and responsibilities of different professional groups, there is far more potential for joint working when at least some aims and priorities are similar.

The groups traditionally responsible for providing non-professional maintenance services are the independent or non-statutory sector. However, this sector is also traditionally of low status and less qualified and yet complex needs clients are probably among the most serious and difficult men and women with whom to work. This provides a dilemma. At present generic or multidisciplinary training is often limited to very basic levels. The way forward may be to increase the status and training necessary to work with these vulnerable people, without involving a particular specialist professional approach.

In addition, it might be possible to keep the traditional philosophy and methods of the non-independent, statutory services in place, but simply add a range of different expertise by enabling these agencies to employ a variety of qualified professionals under their traditional remit. This is already happening in many countries and may help resolve the problem of the need for highly skilled professionals who can work together without imposing specialist models of change on a particular client group. This might involve giving a pre-eminent role to prevention, early intervention and maintenance as opposed to treatment, rehabilitation and reform. In parallel with these changes, multidisciplinary teams could be formed specifically to deal with this group of complex needs or non-compliant clients and raise their profile as skilled professionals in this area. If these teams were to take a large part of this responsibility, it would free up other professionals to concentrate on the priorities of their own profession and more importantly to use their skills and expertise in an appropriate way. These practical issues are discussed in more detail in Part III.

CONCLUSION

The scientific base of medicine is not broad enough to encompass the psychological; and the psychological approach is not broad enough to encompass social influences. Not only do health care workers focus on individual models of health and treatment but, together with social workers and probation officers, they also use individualistic models of change. Nurses focus more on psychological factors than doctors do, and this is reflected in their training, where there is an emphasis on the holistic approach to patients' health and psychological needs. However, this approach also remains individualistic. As Sheppard (1990) points out, the nursing profession understands problems in terms of physical and psychological characteristics and not social or environmental factors. It is suggested that all health professionals need to add a psychosocial perspective, broadening out from individualist approaches that focus on medical conceptions of treatment and change to include psychosocial perspectives incorporating additional options for intervention which focus on social as well as psychological factors through time.

In contrast to the health care professions, the areas of social work and probation have histories of attempting to integrate psychological theories and counselling methods with an emphasis on social justice and equality. However, while the training programmes for these two professions often provide an understanding of the political and social policy context, there is less emphasis on the immediate social environment in the adult care field, in terms of assessment and intervention. Most social work and probation remains firmly casework-orientated; that is, focused on the individual and individual change.

In contrast, complex needs cannot be understood as purely medical or psychological, that is as a consequence of individual pathology or individual failing alone, but are part of a range of interacting psychological and social problems.

In addition, clients with complex needs are often seen as difficult, inappropriate and/or morally or medically undeserving. There are frequently moral issues of child care and crime which are the specific remit of social workers and probation. Unfortunately, the moral and control issues often become confused with social and health care tasks. If a client is not seen as appropriate or deserving by a particular profession or agency, they are unlikely to be given help, in spite of high levels of need which may be 'inappropriate'.

This has implications for development of services. The trend has been towards ensuring that the care-givers who make first contact have the skills and knowledge to identify and respond effectively to complex needs clients. In some cases this intervention will be sufficient but others will require specialist support or consultation. Such an approach implies a local support network of adequately trained specialists including perhaps a specialist consultant. Essentially this would be a service that would function on two levels, firstly, providing a service for the population which either experiences minor problems or is seen to be developing more than one problem, and secondly, dealing with those individuals who have developed multiple problems, some of which are serious.

A METHODOLOGICAL POSTSCRIPT

Methodological issues: different kinds of knowledge, evidence and understanding

Research methods in the medical and psychological fields are not the equivalent of clinical or practitioner methods. Although quantitative methods are essential for health and social researchers to attain scientific status, they are less essential or useful to clinicians.

Clinicians may in effect be more dependent than academics on in-depth or qualitative data derived from individual case studies. Assessment, diagnosis and treatment are often based as much on individual clinical casework experience as on research findings. So many clinicians may view both diagnosis and treatment as professional crafts, rather than scientific procedures. Psychological therapies are often based on phenomenological philosophies, for example psychodynamic models, and cognitive psychology is based on notions of the significance of subjective interpretation. There is little academic research in this field based on phenomenological methodology.

It can be seen therefore that separate bodies of knowledge exist: that based on scientific research and that based on practitioner experience. These different types of knowledge have resulted in the formation of different beliefs and practice. The programmes derived from these theories are radically different and as might be expected neither can be 'proved' to be superior to the other. The relative assessment of 'goodness of fit' and usefulness of these theories varies depending on the theoretical orientation and job of the professional concerned. There are many traditional differences between researchers and practitioners, indicating that neither group can necessarily see the relevance or credibility of the other's knowledge base.

Two examples will be used to illustrate these differences: behavioural methods and 'motivational interviewing' methods (Prochaska & DiClemente 1982, 1994). Both methods are discussed in detail in Part III. The practitioner theories underlying motivational interviewing are often poorly understood and difficult to demonstrate with positivist outcome studies. In contrast there is a great deal of scientific research demonstrating the effectiveness of behaviourism. However this research is not necessarily so useful for practitioners, unless they are sure at the outset of two points: that their client's problems are behaviour problems and cause associated problems, and that these can be dealt with without reference to processes or interpretations. These assumptions are often taken for granted by a behavioural psychologist.

Predefined problems and interpretations

It is possible that any profession's theories incorporate a set of assumptions parallel to those of any other. Each respective definition often has as an underlying premise that a particular problem or history is the cause of all other problems and, as such, there will never be a case of these problems which is not underpinned by that problem. It is these built-in assumptions about etiological processes that undermine attempts at objective independent research, as each profession often takes one interpretation or one etiological explanation for granted and dismisses all consideration of any others. (It should be emphasised that the inability to produce experimentally testable hypotheses within a positivist framework does not of course preclude the ability to form hypotheses and gather data within structured theoretical frameworks based on interpretive or phenomenological methodologies.)

For example, a great deal of research has now been completed into behavioural problems and interventions, which sheds some light not only on the effectiveness of behavioural techniques in dealing with behavioural disorders, but also on the usefulness of defining a range of different problems in behavioural terms. So the psychological approach in effect offers a common set of principles to enable definition of problems in behavioural terms and then the application of behavioural methods for dealing with these problems. However, the critics of this approach would suggest that while psychological social learning theories and methods of treatment are useful in dealing with behaviour, they have not yet been shown to be effective for many different problems, particularly where social problems interact with behavioural problems.

Many of the professional groups interviewed had accepted a psychological interpretation of particular problems and to a greater or lesser extent adapted psychology to the particular issues with which they were dealing. So different professional theorists will take account of social (or biological) factors but still place them within the context of the social learning paradigm and cognitive psychology. For example, probation officers and others working in the criminal justice system may be well aware of the social and mental health problems of their client caseload, yet interpret and assess problems in behavioural terms and so advocate general cognitive and behavioural techniques as solutions.

It is interesting however that different therapies can be effective and that contradictory theories can exist side by side. In order to understand how conflicting theories can coexist it is necessary to examine the differences between the kind of methodology and knowledge of researchers and practitioners.

Positivist methodology

The behaviourist methods are derived from positivist methodologies which can be seen as limited, as process and interpretation cannot be studied within this scientific framework (see, for example, Nachmias & Nachmias 2000). Much of the research in the field is undertaken within the confines of the medical and psychological (behavioural) sciences. These essentially positivist approaches presuppose that the problem can be defined and isolated, all peripheral variables controlled and experimental comparisons made. This approach is seen as both necessary and sufficient for understanding and responding. The question is not whether the experimental approach is necessary, simply whether it is sufficient, as the methods derived from this approach tend to ignore subjective interpretations and the therapeutic change process. Methodological constraints can also be compounded by the limitations of particular theoretical perspectives. For example, attempts by 'outsiders' to explain and understand another's approach are often made within the context of their own theoretical framework, which will in turn be limited by its basic premises.

Positivist studies comparing outcome statistics do not help clarify what practitioners actually do and what happens before, during or after interventions. They do little to explain why non-statutory or voluntary approaches at odds with contemporary professional consensus should survive and flourish alongside their scientifically credible and professional opponents. Such approaches based on a positivist methodology assume an objectively measurable reality, which is difficult to reconcile with the various differing subjective interpretations. The data gained from empirical evaluations are also limited in that they do not convey information concerning the individual change process within therapeutic change programmes.

Interpretive methodology: the importance of subjective interpretation and process

Individual change process and subjective interpretation are the subject area of the interpretive or phenomenological methodologies, using qualitative methods (Berg 1995; Burgess 1988). It is not possible to measure either process or interpretation in positivist terms. Both the medical and behavioural disciplines are based on explanatory theories developed from experimental research designs. It is difficult for these disciplines to integrate notions of qualitative data for interpretive theory.

It can perhaps be suggested that the limitations of positivist research are more apparent to practitioners than academics, and in order to study areas of interest to practitioners it may be necessary to utilise methods derived from phenomenology rather than positivism. This issue is of particular importance in this study, as the focus is on the need to study individual subjective interpretations of the therapeutic change process.

This decline of the importance of the 'clinical reality' can perhaps be correlated with a similar reduction in the importance of case study data for research purposes. As data collection became more 'scientific', individual change processes and client interpretation became less important as they could not be measured or researched in a 'scientific' way.

The phenomenologist perhaps voices the same complaint in different language about research data. However, although the complaint may be the same (that most of the research in the field is undertaken within the narrow confines of the medical and behavioural sciences), these two disciplines have little else in common. Though both approaches are interested in understanding individuals as separate entities, there are important differences between the old clinical case study methods of doctors and psychiatrists and those of the phenomenologist.

It is clear then that the narrow limitations of scientific theories and scientific data obtained by controlled studies of human behaviour are not necessarily acceptable to clinicians. It is possible that, while scientific data are useful to researchers, in the area of clinical practice the quantitative data of the positivist social sciences are less useful than the qualitative data derived from individual case studies.

The difference between the preferred knowledge base of researchers and practitioners is probably best illustrated by the recent growth of the idea of 'stages of change' and of motivational interviewing. The popularity of these methods among practitioners spread rapidly in the early part of the 1990s. These ideas now form a base for much specialist and non-specialist training in the UK. However, its relevance to practitioners can easily be understood in terms of the importance of individual differences and individual change processes to clinicians. Data concerning individual change process cannot be gained using positivist methods, therefore scientifically orientated research can do little to provide the practitioner with guidance for work with individual clients. The motivational interviewing method offered a means of integrating notions of long-term individual change with more general theories of aetiology and treatment.

The notion of the importance of individual change processes was publicised by Prochaska in *Systems of Psychotherapy: A Transtheoretical Perspective* (Prochaska 1979). He then worked with DiClemente to develop the idea of transtheoretical therapy (Prochaska and DiClemente 1982) and in 1983 they produced their much quoted paper *Stages and processes of self-change of smoking: toward an integrated model of change* (Prochaska & DiClemente 1983). This work was paralleled by Miller's development of the concept of motivational interviewing (Miller *et al.* 1988).

The ideas of change process and motivational interviewing have been subject to criticism on the grounds that they have no underpinning theory and that they are not testable. Academics from the psychological and medical fields have expressed surprise at the widespread popularity of the approach among practitioners. It is therefore interesting to examine the enthusiasm for clinical methods not accessible to positivist-based research.

The practitioners' perspective: advantages and disadvantages of different methodologies

As highlighted previously, research methods in the medical and psychological fields are not the equivalent of clinical or professional practitioner methods. Although quantitative methods are essential for social researchers to attain scientific status, they are less essential or useful to clinicians and other professionals. Donald Schon (1990) argues that practitioners themselves do not utilise scientific knowledge as it is seen as less useful than task-based, experiential 'knowledge in action'.

Although professionals may find scientific research less useful, they may be more dependent than academics on qualitative data derived from individual case studies; for example, interpretive and interactive processes between client and professional are not accessible to scientific experiment. Yet if they are discarded, it would be difficult for the clinician or the client to interpret and communicate, that is to 'recognise' or make sense of certain phenomena or experiences.

The lack of qualitative data in academic research means a lack of descriptive accounts of the methods used within treatment process. It is therefore often unclear to academics what professionals actually do. This has serious implications when drawing conclusions from comparative outcome studies. It is also probable that professionals use a wide range of practical support methods without these being researched, as it is often taken for granted that professionals will be applying theories taught during their training.

The practitioners' perspective: advantages and disadvantages of using any one model

It is possible that a clinician or practitioner will prefer to work with only one approach. There is evidence that it is important that counsellors believe in the particular approach within which they are working. However, again it cannot be taken for granted that professionals use one consistent theory for all stages of the helping process. It may be that they can select several different theories for each client, describing the development of the problem in terms of a particular theoretical perspective and then, perhaps, independently of this initial understanding of the etiology of the problem, choose a particular treatment process to structure their practical response. While it is no doubt true that academics would require some degree of 'fit' between a theory of aetiology and one of treatment, it is not necessarily true for either clinicians or clients. It seems possible for clients to work both with therapists who take a cognitive behavioural approach and those who work with the medical or social perspective; it is also possible for 'eclectic' clinicians to use both. The cognitive dissonance which would be generated in many academics is also problematic for some clinicians and clients, but for many people these discrepancies are not of any importance, if they are recognised at all.

The limitations of particular theoretical perspectives on academic research are reflected in their limitations on professional practice. The disadvantages of using one particular theoretical perspective are of course the constraints that each places on alternative options. The basic premise of any one specialist approach may rule out possible courses of action which theoretically may be equally viable and perhaps have a greater 'fit' for some groups of problems. If, for example, psychosocial problems are seen as physiologically-based, this may exclude methods which involve teaching individuals to control and modify their own behaviour or provide social support networks. The same is true for the behavioural approach. If clients accept the initial premise that they can control their own behaviour, they cannot then admit the need for medication or social support. It should, however, be noted that, while logical contradictions present obstacles for academics, this may, again, not be the case for clients themselves, some of whom seem quite happy combining different perspectives such as cognitive behavioural, medication and social support.

Part III

Comprehensive Practice: a Psychosocial Approach to Change and Maintenance

INTRODUCTION

Most social, health care and criminal justice professionals are likely to have clients with complex psychosocial problems on their caseload. Complex needs clients who present at agencies often do so for brief periods in their lives when a range of different problems become unmanageable. Professionals are therefore likely to become involved at different stages in the client's life, for a range of different reasons. Part III will consider the practical implications of this for helping these clients. It will examine how individual professionals can use a multi-disciplinary psychosocial approach to assessments, interventions and ongoing maintenance care in order to provide a better service for complex needs clients.

The psychosocial approach emphasises the significance of both psychological and social problems in interaction with health and other needs and the importance of taking it into account when making an assessment and offering help. This third part of the book examines the usefulness and limitations of a purely psychological approach to individual change and proposes an additional model of psychosocial maintenance, offering alternative models to both psychological methods and individual change.

The proposed psychosocial approach is not focused on individual pathology or even on personal change, because as soon as complex needs are understood within a psychosocial conceptual framework, it becomes apparent that definitions are not limited to individual problems or individual need to change. Therefore assessments should concern not only individual needs and abilities but also social needs and constraints. In addition, solutions should not be limited to short-term, change-orientated interventions but also include long-term maintenance support options.

It will be suggested that there is a need for new models of comprehensive long-term care for psychosocial problems, whatever types of specialist problems with which they are associated. So, for example, a health care problem could be assessed within its psychosocial context and an additional maintenance care model used in addition to the traditional short-term acute health care model. Clients should play a larger part in defining their own maintenance needs (with or without change interventions) and also in determining if they have the ability to change and maintain it (that is, what they can and cannot cope with over time.)

As a consequence of these changes, professionals will need to develop collaborative skills based on a common overview of assessed needs in shared populations (discussed in Part I) and a clearer understanding of the different perspectives of client and professionals (discussed in Part II). This has implications for professional education and training.

Finally, whereas most social and health care professionals are familiar with psychological and social helping skills, some practical guidance is necessary concerning the introduction of two new elements into practice: psychosocial assessment and ongoing maintenance or relapse prevention. These elements are critical when working with clients with complex needs as both address the issue of high failure rates in this field. Clients are unlikely to respond if specialist change interventions take place when they are unable to confront the specific problem or are unable to succeed without additional help for other problems and ongoing support. They are also likely to deteriorate or relapse if there is no maintenance or relapse prevention.

In summary, although many of the methods and skills necessary for working with clients with complex needs are similar to those used in all health, social care and criminal justice work, the client group is different for the following reasons:

- Clients have more than one type of problem and these problems may exacerbate each other and reduce the clients' abilities to achieve personal psychological change in any one area.
- Clients may not have the capacity to change or maintain individual change in any one area.
- Clients may not want to change or resolve particular psychological problems; their priorities may be different to those of professionals.
- Clients may be difficult to communicate and work with, often disagreeing with professional assessments and not using specialist interventions appropriately.
- Clients often relapse within a short period.

It can be seen therefore that complex problems need multiple solutions. For both assessments and interventions there is a need for comprehensive psychosocial assessment together with specialist psychological and health assessments and a range of both maintenance and change methods for clients. This presents two problems. First, there is a need for a wide range of change methods from different professions; therefore there is a need for specialist professionals to work with others with different (perhaps conflicting) beliefs and priorities, to provide continuity of care. Second, there is a need for an additional range of maintenance methods. Because these are not clearly outlined within any one professional context it may be possible to develop a set of methods that is common to all professional groups. This shared approach would make multidisciplinary working easier when using a maintenance approach.

Because of the complexity of problems and needs in this group, it is necessary to use a range of interventions derived from both change and maintenance methods. It will be seen that, while maintenance methods are essential without change, or before, during and after change, change methods may not be appropriate for all psychosocial clients (or only appropriate at particular times in their lives).

A PSYCHOSOCIAL APPROACH TO PROBLEM DEFINITION AND INTERVENTION

It has been argued in Part II that the scientific base of the health care and psychological professions is not wide enough to take account of interacting psychological and social factors. Also that health care workers such as general practitioners, nurses and those in the paramedical professions, together with social workers and probation officers, use individualistic models of change. These professions understand problems in terms of physical and psychological characteristics and not social or environmental factors.

A psychosocial approach in effect broadens the conceptual framework for understanding and defining problems, to include psychological and social factors. If all professional groups utilise similar understandings of the psychological and social context of problems this will provide invaluable common ground for interprofessional working.

It is clearly necessary to have a range of different kinds of professional expertise in assessing need and allocating resources, but it is useful to draw a distinction between what should be provided by a specialist professional and what could be provided collaboratively. Developing skills across professions or multidisciplinary teams which focus specifically on complex needs could provide for this common or collaborative element. However, it may be necessary to go further than this and consider the development of a new type of generic professional who specialises in complex needs clients. Whichever policy path is followed, there is a clear need for individual professionals to develop new skills for working with complex needs clients on their caseloads:

(1)   Psychosocial, interdisciplinary assessment.
(2)   Psychological change methods.
(3)   Psychosocial maintenance methods.

Psychosocial, interdisciplinary assessment

There is a need to base understandings of health in the context of psychological change and then base psychological change in a psychosocial context. It can be seen that it is essential to take account of psychological factors and social context when doing assessments. There is also a need for ongoing assessments and for each assessment to take account of the history of problems through time.

Psychological change methods

There is a need to develop the ability to teach clients personal life skills including social skills. Basic psychological techniques for motivating clients to change, and cognitive behavioural methods for achieving individual change, include dealing with the stress, anxiety and depression that are associated with a range of other health and social problems.

Psychosocial maintenance methods

If problems are assessed as part of a psychosocial picture, this reconstructed definition has implications for solutions, most significantly that if the problem is not defined in terms of a single individual dysfunction, then the answer is not necessarily a single treatment intervention with the aim of individual change. In addition, there is a need for any model to recognise both individual and social change throughout the life cycle, rather than a single acute illness or crime episode; that is, a model that shows changes in a person's life circumstances and consequent ability to cope and survive. If problems are seen from these perspectives the solutions might include a programme of psychosocial maintenance and support services through time and a more comprehensive range of services.

New forms of assessment, new models and new methods will require new skills. The previous chapters have examined the opportunities and obstacles to multiagency and multiprofessional working. This part will be concerned with providing practice guidelines for individual practitioners (independent of their professional affiliations) for work with complex needs clients.

Part I identified the types of client groups most likely to have complex needs and indicated that there is inappropriate, inadequate and inefficient service provision for this group. Part II examined why this is so and identified two major obstacles to service provision. First, there is only one, common, limited, helping philosophy based on the desirability of individual change, and second, there is a range of conflicting specialist practice methods. The implications are that, first, there is a need to develop an additional common maintenance philosophy with common practice methods to facilitate future multidisciplinary working in this area. Second, there is a need to develop an understanding of the specialist methods of other professions so that it is possible to work together to provide a range of different methods for different (often interacting) problems.

As can be seen from Part II and the following chapters, each professional group is aware that some of their specialist caseload also have complex psychosocial problems, and they have developed practical common-sense methods of dealing with this. Recognition that particular specialist client groups are more likely to have complex needs is also evident in the increasing complexity and comprehensiveness of assessments, particularly for the following groups where there is a very high incidence of multiple problems: criminals on probation; substance misusers; people with mental health or alcohol problems; and older people with health problems.

Psychological and social methods are an integral part of the training of most professionals, although they may be defined in different ways and used as means to different ends. It is not unusual for a similar solution to be effective for a range of apparently very different problems; for example, developing social skills or building social support networks.

As a consequence professionals, though they might not be aware of it, have often developed a range of (non-specialist), practical methods for helping these complex needs clients. Psychological methods can be used for motivating clients, particularly those in the criminal justice system and those with substance misuse problems; behavioural techniques can be used to help clients manage anxiety, aggression and risky behaviour; and cognitive techniques can be used to prevent relapse or depression. In addition, social skills training can be used to help clients build supportive relationships. Social interventions can be deployed to change the client's environment and reduce stressful situations in an appropriate community setting, together with housing and with training programmes.

The actual mix of methods will vary from one client to another, depending on the mixture of complex needs. It is not suggested that all these techniques or methods will be useful for all complex needs clients, but many will be useful at some time.

These methods which have been developed by one group of professionals are often appropriated by another, often without recourse to research evidence or theoretical coherence. For example, the motivational interviewing method, developed initially for people with smoking and drinking problems, has been used effectively for people with behavioural problems in the criminal justice system. The cognitive behavioural techniques developed to deal with depression and anxiety have been successful in the prevention of relapse among people with substance misuse problems. The rehabilitative methods developed for the mentally ill and the maintenance methods developed for the chronically ill are being introduced for those complex needs clients who cannot cope with personal change and those who need maintenance and ongoing social support structures.

In some cases it may even be unclear whether particular psychological techniques are actually acting on the problem identified or on a different problem. So psychotherapy aimed at aggressive or violent behaviour may be affecting social isolation or relationship problems, and cognitive behavioural techniques directed at preventing relapse to drugs or alcohol may be dealing effectively with depression. Similarly, motivational interviewing techniques for cigarette smokers may be raising awareness about a range of other risky behaviours, while social skills training for relationship problems may be changing the social environment and reducing stressful situations.

Chapter 6 will describe comprehensive psychosocial assessment. It has already been emphasised how important it is to carry out multi-professional or multidisciplinary assessments combining the skills and specialist expertise of a range of professionals in order to give a comprehensive account of a range of different types of problem. It is also essential that any assessment should take account of the psychosocial context of problems, for example the social and psychological difficulties associated with illness or criminal behaviour. This chapter illustrates the important factors involved in carrying out a comprehensive assessment of psychosocial problems and maintenance and change needs. It includes an overview of the progress of psychosocial problems through time, rather than a single snapshot. This 'life course' approach enables comprehensive and coherent history of interacting patterns of problems and services provision.

Chapter 7 will describe a range of psychological change methods. Psychological methods can enhance the effectiveness of other interventions for problems, whether health or social. Individual process models are used in order to examine the client's motivation to change and, more importantly perhaps, the client's own views of their problems. Psychological methods are designed primarily for change-orientated interventions, but have also been appropriated for the maintenance methods discussed in Chapter 8.

Chapter 8 will describe a range of maintenance methods. This chapter emphasises the need to develop an additional common maintenance philosophy with common practice methods. This may also contribute to shared multiprofessional understandings of the wider psychosocial context of a variety of specialist problems. This chapter will draw on a broad range of fragmented maintenance techniques from a range of professions. It will be concerned with the development of a common complementary maintenance model to be used in conjunction with specialist change models. As will become clear, professionals, clients and non-professional workers have between them the knowledge necessary for ongoing maintenance support and the experience of the problems and the practical skills necessary for working with this approach.

In this way Part III highlights the practical implications of the findings in Parts I and II, examining how professionals can identify the limitations of specialist approaches and change models and develop parallel maintenance models and methods when working with complex needs clients. It provides a simple framework integrating both change and maintenance philosophies and methods for psychosocial problems.

This can then be placed in the context of the guidelines in Part I for developing interagency population studies of assessed need and the development of interagency planning for complex needs clients in shared populations.

Chapter 6
Comprehensive Psychosocial Assessment

INTRODUCTION

This chapter will provide guidelines for making a comprehensive assessment of maintenance and change needs. It will be concerned not only with the clients' *need* for individual psychological change, but also their *ability* to change and the personal resources they have to maintain that change. It will also be concerned with assessments of the clients' needs for maintenance support.

Complex needs clients often have health and mental health problems. It is not possible to include here the range of specialist assessments of each type of problem. These, of course, remain the remit of each professional group, needing to be diagnosed and assessed by qualified specialists. In contrast, the psychosocial assessment procedure is designed to be used in conjunction with traditional specialist single diagnoses and assessments, to provide the psychosocial context of the health and other problems.

Whilst it is necessary to bring several professionals together for a comprehensive assessment of, for example, dual diagnosis, it is also important for any one professional to assess the psychosocial context of problems. This chapter provides guidelines for assessing the social and psychological needs associated with many different specialist problems. This psychosocial assessment can be added to each specialist assessment in order to identify complex psychosocial needs for maintenance and/or change, and multidisciplinary working.

Assessments of need and client capabilities and resources require knowledge of both psychological and social problems. Psychosocial assessment includes social factors such as stress, unemployment, poverty, housing etc. and psychological factors such as depression and anxiety.

This chapter also emphasises the progress of psychosocial problems through time, rather than a single snapshot. This 'life course' approach makes possible an understanding of the history of interacting patterns of problems and services provision. Assessments can be used to evaluate a client's need for maintenance and/or change-orientated help. If they are used for change-orientated interventions they should include assessments of ability to change and maintain change.

It is often thought that professionals should only provide main-tenance services as a last resort, if it is appropriate at all; that is, main-tenance is only provided for those who have already changed or who fail to change. It is suggested here that it may be more appropriate for complex needs clients to consider the maintenance option first, or at least alongside the change option. For example, rather than providing maintenance for those who fail or those who succeed, it may be more effective to provide maintenance for those who are assessed as likely to fail a psychological change-orientated programme or unable to maintain treatment gains.

SOCIAL AND PSYCHOLOGICAL PROBLEMS, INTERACTING THROUGH TIME

Many agencies employ social workers and psychologists to work with the relevant clients. The relevant professionals may wish to deal with these problems themselves, refer clients, or work together with social workers or psychologists if they identify problems in these areas.

Social and psychological problems may be associated with a range of other problems including health and mental health issues.

Social problems

Social problems can include financial problems, debts and, perhaps more significantly, violence and intimidation for non-payment of debt, and accommodation, employment, child care and legal problems.

Financial problems may be resolved by debt counselling, welfare rights advice or the provision of assistance with benefits or employment training. There may also be a need for support with accommodation. The social environment in which a client lives may determine the level of risky behaviour that is normal. Help with new accommodation may avoid unhealthy, miserable conditions. Risk is increased among the homeless. Clients with legal problems often require support in the form of court reports. Attending a treatment service for mental health prob-lems can be seen as a real alternative to custody. It is therefore valuable for other professionals to work closely with probation officers if neces-sary.

In addition, social isolation and loneliness are significant areas of dif-ficulty. Lack of social support or involvement with social activities and the community may constitute greater problems than more practical environmental issues.

Psychological problems

Psychological problems can include depression, anxiety, anger and aggression. Complex needs clients who present at agencies often do so for brief periods when they seem to lose control of their lives. (Professionals are therefore likely to become involved at this stage.) Life-saving interventions include health care and social support such as accommodation and benefits, but basic cognitive behavioural interventions can also be useful. Cognitive behavioural techniques are particularly appropriate for aftercare maintenance, helping those clients who have received treatment for some kind of individual and lifestyle change, to help them maintain this change and not to relapse back into old behaviour patterns. In addition, the most common of psychological problems in the general population, such as depression, anxiety and anger, can all be associated with substance misuse, either as direct effects, withdrawal effects of drugs (Trinder & Keene 1997), or as precipitating factors leading to self-medication (see Chapter 8).

Methods derived from cognitive behavioural psychology can be used for general problems of depression and anxiety, substance misuse problems and behavioural and mood control, such as compulsive behaviour and loss of control.

Understanding the interaction of problems through time

In order for both professional and client to gain greater understanding of complex psychosocial problems, it is necessary first to gain an awareness of the range of problems and interaction between problems that characterise this client group. The information from the Tracking Project and review of the research literature in Part I, together with the views of clients and professionals in Part II, give a greater understanding of the types of problems that characterise complex need clients who repeatedly use agencies. It becomes clear that substance misuse, mental health, mild learning difficulties and psychological problems characterise this group (Tucker 1999) together with more health problems and a greater incidence of accidents.

Different problems at different stages in the lifecycle

It is possible that not only do clients have different types of problem simultaneously, but also they are more than likely to have different problems at different periods in their lives. This is an important concept as it emphasises that complex needs change over time. In the long term this may mean that a small proportion of clients with complex needs move along a continuum and that quite serious health and mental problems vary across the life course. Also, that particular combinations of problems may temporarily amplify symptoms as a whole (Ries *et al.* 2000). It may be much more common for certain types of problem to be temporary phenomena or to change at various times in a person's life. The notion of shifting symptom patterns challenges the concept that these categories need be immutable within individuals (Ries *et al.* 1998).

Substance misuse provides an apt illustration of this: variations in patterns of problems may mean that one person may misuse drugs in chaotic, risky ways for short periods of time, gaining and losing control in response to different circumstances. A young mother may respond to the stress of a broken relationship by misusing drugs in a chaotic way but will quickly get her drug misuse back under control if she receives support and help at the right time. Whilst it is possible that complex needs get worse as more drugs are misused in a more uncontrolled manner, it is probably more accurate to say that individuals will have short periods of problematic misuse at different times in their lives.

Causes, correlations, coincidence or common cause

It is useful to identify causal direction in the development of any problem as this too will often determine the type of intervention. However, a recurring question when dealing with complex needs is, which problem came first? So to extend the previous example, substance misuse can be functional, providing a solution to certain needs or problems, or it can cause problems itself, or more commonly, it can be both. Problems are often dealt with by misusing drugs as a remedy and it is also true that drugs cause problems of their own. Therefore it is useful to discover if the client is 'self-medicating' for serious underlying psychological problems such as clinical depression. If so, they will need to be dealt with separately from the drug misuse. This situation can call for two distinct assessments and two different interventions.

While it is necessary to determine the existence of underlying problems, it is often less than constructive to spend time consistently trying to disentangle cause and effect. Ill health can lead to psychological problems and social problems, which remain long after the initial difficulties have been resolved. In contrast, social problems such as unemployment can lead to psychological and health problems.

It is questioned in Chapter 5 whether it is possible to deal with these issues at all or whether the matter is largely redundant with clients with ongoing multiple problems. Causal direction will not be significant if a range of different problems have developed by the time any one type of professional becomes involved. All problems will need solutions if they are serious enough, irrespective of which came first. It is only in terms of preventing recurrence of problems that the primary cause needs to be identified, if indeed there is a primary cause.

In addition, assessments and diagnosis can cause conflict between professionals and between professionals and clients. The question of cause and effect is often a source of controversy and can cause insurmountable obstacles to the helping process. Clients may see their psychological problems as a consequence of social problems and they may see medication or substance misuse as a solution or remedy for various matters ranging from boredom and depression to social deprivation; whereas professionals tend to see social problems as a consequence of psychological or mental health problems and drug misuse as the cause of unemployment and social deprivation.

These disagreements can become a serious block to communication between clients and professionals and between professionals themselves. Causal arguments may be as unresolveable as the proverbial chicken and egg. While an etiological theory of cause is useful in health care, it is often not realistically achievable in understanding mental health, psychological or social problems and becomes even less achievable and unclear when problems interact. Here the phenomenon is perhaps most usefully understood as a circular self-perpetuating process.

THE RELEVANCE OF THE THEORIES OF DIFFERENT PROFESSIONAL GROUPS

Part II described the problems and obstacles to helping clients with complex needs. The professional should be aware of the limitations, not only in their own specialist assessment and intervention models, but also in those of other professions. They must then decide whether to work alone with the client's complex needs or to collaborate with other agencies. If the former, professionals can use a range of methods to maintain and support clients and to help the client to change behaviours and lifestyle. These methods and the relevant skills are part of the basic training of most social and health care professionals.

However, there is a need to understand the perspectives and specialist practice models of other professional groups, first, in order to communicate and negotiate about resource allocation, clinical priorities, risk assessment etc., and second, in order to know what they provide and what they do not provide (that is, how different perspectives limit different professional interventions).

There is also a need to know when it is necessary to work with other professionals and what other practice change models and specialist skills are necessary and available from other professional and non-professional groups to counter the limitations of any one profession. So, for example, if a particular professional is working to maintain a client and prevent relapse to mental health problems, they will need to be aware of the therapeutic change models used by cognitive behavioural psychologists and/or alcohol treatment rehabilitation workers.

It should be emphasised that there are limitations for professionals who adhere to any one specialist approach. As can be seen from the earlier chapters, many clients with complex needs are unlikely to respond successfully if one problem is dealt with in isolation.

The status of a particular theory in clinical practice is, in effect, dependent on its usefulness. It should be remembered that competing theories can be useful for the same therapeutic purpose and different methods may be useful for a range of different purposes. It may be unnecessary to argue about the premises of different theoretical approaches, if the methods used and outcomes are similar. However, the theory may determine the aims of an intervention and the theoretical premises are likely to have serious implications in assessing whether a client is justified in receiving resources, for how long they should receive them and whether they are successful.

If a particular method is helpful or a particular theoretical interpretation 'fits' with the beliefs and aims of the client themselves, it can be counter-productive for professionals to limit their clients' choices to their own theoretical orientation.

Once armed with a basic understanding of complex needs, the professional can use a range of different professionals and agencies as a source of additional specialist expertise and advice, rather than a means of referral. Specialist professionals can help by providing additional specialist assessments and help.

PURPOSES OF A PSYCHOSOCIAL ASSESSMENT

The aim of an intervention will be determined from an initial assessment procedure, but it is necessary to decide if maintenance or change are more appropriate before detailed specialist assessments are undertaken; that is, whether the client is capable of changing and maintaining change or whether it is more practical and effective to provide maintenance.

It may then be necessary to assess different factors depending on whether the initial aim is maintenance or change. For example, those initially assessed as changeable would need a more detailed assessment of their ability to bring about and maintain change and what they need to do it. Those assessed as needing maintenance would need an assessment of their abilities, resources and needs in order to prevention deterioration and/or risk taking.

The factor most likely to account for the lack of successful outcomes in change-orientated methods is the inadequacy of accurate assessments prior to clients making demanding life changes. The amount of support and the length of time required are often underestimated as a consequence of incomplete assessments.

The clients' view

It is also important to find out the clients' own understanding of their problems and more importantly their own assessment of their ability to change. This can be clarified using motivational interviewing described in Chapter 7.

Before assessing the various problems that clients with complex needs face, it is worth asking why they seek help. The qualitative research examining their perceptions of the process of help-seeking indicates that clients looked for help following a growing accumulation or escalation of problems and dissatisfaction with their lifestyles. Many saw their problems in terms of needs for practical help or financial support and therefore saw therapeutic solutions as unnecessary. Help is often sought in a period of crisis and/or as part of a pattern of long-term recurring problems. These data highlight the relevance of a wide range of physical, psychological and social problems, but perhaps more importantly they demonstrate that the reasons why people seek help are related to how they perceive agencies and what type of help they think is available. For example, clients may be less likely to seek help for health problems or depression if they expect to be diagnosed as mentally ill.

Many clients will not want to make major changes, or at least do not want to make these at the same time as the professional. Part of the assessment process should be concerned with determining whether change is likely (does the client want to change) and whether it is sensible (is the client capable of changing and does she/he have ability and resources to cope after therapy or change-orientated methods). It is only when there is a likelihood or immediate necessity for change and when clients are assessed as capable of maintaining change that a therapeutic change process should be undertaken. Even then, it is pointless to undertake this change process without an aftercare programme. Assessment for aftercare should include assessment of the need for aftercare support, particularly the type of relapse prevention and intervention necessary.

It is important to emphasise that, whereas specialist expert knowledge is better informed than that of most clients, the clients themselves may have greater understanding of their own ability to cope and their maintenance support needs.

Type of assessment: maintenance, change or aftercare

The overall purpose of assessment is to determine what help and which interventions are appropriate.

General initial assessment

A general initial assessment of client problems, needs and resources (skills and social support) allows the professional to identify whether or not a client has multiple problems and if so, whether there is a need for a further comprehensive assessment. This assessment is designed to determine not only which interventions are necessary, but also which interventions are likely to be useful or lasting. It also clarifies the physical, psychological and social problems that need to be addressed. This enables the professional to determine the range of support needed and the type of intervention and the length of time for which it is likely to be needed.

Motivational interviewing

A motivational interviewing assessment enables the professional to determine how clients see their own problems and whether or not they want to change or are 'ready for change' in their own terms. This form of assessment is dealt with in detail in Chapter 7.

Maintenance

Assessment for maintenance informs the professional whether the client is capable of maintaining their present lifestyle without further deterioration or risk-taking behaviour, and what support she/he will need to do so. This assessment includes ongoing needs such as stabilisation, support and maintenance of clients. The aim is to reduce risks to this group and to reduce deterioration in social situation and health.

This intervention may be the most realistic response for some clients with complex needs. Whereas traditional crisis intervention strategies suggest individual change is possible at periods when the client is most stressed, it is possible that the most chaotic or stressful episodes in a person's life may not be the best time to induce personal changes. It may be more pragmatic to provide more general social and financial support to maintain the client through particularly chaotic periods.

Change and aftercare

Assessment for change and aftercare not only informs the professional of the client's need to change, but also their ability to change and maintain change, that is, whether the client is capable of making individual change, in terms of motivation, ability and social support networks and consequently what support she/he will need to do so.

When assessing the client potential to make and maintain change, it is important to be aware of the psychological interventions available for personal change or growth. It is also necessary to recognise the limitations of these models for clients needing social support and/or ongoing help. These interventions vary from cognitive behavioural programmes to non-directive therapies based on a client-therapist relationship and to interpretive therapies.

Relapse prevention and intervention

Assessment for relapse prevention and relapse intervention informs the professional what skills and social support the client needs in order to prevent relapse and what support they will need in the event of a relapse.

Appropriateness of terminating help

Assessment for appropriateness of terminating help involves more than the usual assessment of success or failure. Rather than informing the professional whether the client has successfully completed a treatment programme or not, this is concerned with the client's own resources in terms of skills and support and their ability to maintain themselves (and/or their treatment gains) without additional help. Assessment of problems in the context of the life course establishes a history of problems, needs and service use in order to see what has caused present problems, what might cause relapse and how to prevent this situation happening again.

This should be seen as part of a continuous monitoring programme. Assessment of complex needs clients is often an ongoing process, whether for maintenance management or change-orientated methods where clients are working towards changes in behaviour and lifestyle. If a client is changing behaviour or working towards practical short-term goals, monitoring of progress on a regular basis allows for the identification of client readiness for decisions and action; and also the renegotiation of short-term goals on the basis of progress made or of failure to achieve these goals.

PSYCHOSOCIAL ASSESSMENT

Comprehensive psychosocial assessment of need and ability to change, or maintain present lifestyle

What is important?

The following factors should be considered in developing comprehensive multidisciplinary assessments of complex psychosocial needs. The assessor should:

(1) Decide which psychological and/or social theories are appropriate.

(2) Decide which theories are inappropriate at any one time (i.e. those that limit interventions and ongoing support).

(3) Carry out a comprehensive overview, including psychological and social needs and resources.

(4) Include a range of professional assessments but also step outside them and include a non-professional assessment as well.

(5) Take into account the perspective and priorities of different professional disciplines and non-professional perspectives in order to achieve cooperative and effective working relationships between professionals and between professionals and non-professionals.

(6) Take into account the perspective and priorities of the client in order to achieve cooperative and effective working relationships between professionals and client.

(7) Ensure as far as possible that the assessment is needs-led rather than resources-led. It is resource-led interagency working that causes most problems, as each profession and agency is only able to prioritise resources in terms of particular criteria into which the complex psychosocial needs client does not easily fit (though this may be partially resolved by planners through the development of interagency tariffs and screening instruments described in Chapter 3).

Problems vary over time within the social context of other life events and individual resources. A useful assessment attempts to understand an individual's problems over time within the social context of other life events. This helps clarify what type of problems the client has now, what precipitated these problems and what might lead to relapse after they have been dealt with.

What information should be recorded?

(1) The clients' own view of their problems, including present coping mechanisms and support systems and needs for maintenance support.

(2) History of problems.

(3) The problems leading to and/or arising from others.

(4) Medical history.

(5) Mental health history, including psychological problems such as anxiety and depression.

(6) Social environment, problems and resources – present social situation, relationships, dependants, accommodation, employment, legal status.

(7) Relationships – amount of emotional support available including

the level of family support and involvement and support from partner or spouse.

(8) Interrelationships between crises and life circumstances and events in life history (particularly focusing on periods of well-being and periods of crisis or relapse).

(9) Present interrelationships between health, social and psychological problems and other social/emotional life patterns.

(10) History of help-seeking, interventions used and outcomes.

(11) History of previous interventions and consequences.

Implementing assessments

Plans for intervention and support involve utilising the initial assessment of individual needs together with an assessment of individual potential and resource, to decide on what support is necessary. They are therefore concerned with a consideration of the client's needs, alongside his/her personal resources, followed by the provision of agency and professional resources where appropriate. The plan can be designed to ensure that the client's situation does not get worse, they do not take unnecessary risks and/or that the client can change and maintain change; also, if change is to take place, the resources available during and after change.

The plan prioritises needs and sets practical goals within the resources available and should include the following information:

- Client's needs for maintenance, change and aftercare.
- Client's resources in the short term (personal coping strategies and skills).
- Client's resources in the long term (skills and social support networks).
- Agency resources for maintenance, intervention and aftercare.

The role of professionals. The plan can also coordinate a range of specialist responses, concurrently or consecutively, within the constraints of differing priorities and budgets discussed earlier. If possible it should also implement the interagency tariffs described in Chapter 3.

The role of clients. Assessment is concerned both with estimating the extent of problems and the resources already available to clients. Clients will probably have the best view of their ability to cope and their ongoing support needs. Even if this is not so, it is still important to listen to the client's viewpoint as this may be the only information available to the professional about the social and psychological context of their lives.

When the plan is drawn up and a service is offered to a client, the terms and conditions should be made clear, including the extent of support available, the time it will be available and penalties for non-compliance.

Professional agreements with clients should include the negotiation of short- and long-term goals. While all practitioners have a responsibility to help clients make informed decisions, there are often situations where the client and professional (and indeed different professionals) may have different priorities; it is necessary to clarify them when agreeing and defining goals for therapy or change-orientated methods. (See the section on counselling skills in the following chapter.)

MONITORING AND EVALUATION

Monitoring is an essential part of assessment and intervention. It is important to keep notes to monitor progress and reassess where necessary. The aim is to maintain regular assessments which will determine the type of intervention appropriate at each new stage.

Monitoring

Monitoring can involve:

(1) Self-monitoring and self-assessment by the client. Clients can be asked to complete diaries, record feelings and behaviours, for example, to identify the antecedents and consequences of risky behaviour or relapse.
(2) Professional monitoring of the client's progress can be used to modify interventions, change goals and increase support where appropriate. (This will include reassessments for therapy or change-orientated methods and aftercare maintenance where necessary.)
(3) Monitoring of aftercare maintenance is also necessary to enable identification of danger signs and to facilitate early intervention if the client's situation deteriorates.
(4) Professional monitoring and evaluation of their own input (with individual clients, with the agency population and with the targeted population as a whole).

Evaluation

It is important to clarify the aims and objectives of any intervention before deciding what to measure and how to measure it. The understanding of the problem and its solution will influence what is counted as success. Events such as short lapses can be seen as failures or as part of the process of change itself. Successful change-orientated methods outcome can be seen as success, or the long-term maintenance of therapy or change-orientated methods gains can be assessed in follow-up several years later.

Evaluation of maintenance

Professional monitoring and evaluation of work must take account of the aims and purposes of each intervention. If the aim is maintenance, outcome studies are inappropriate as the effects are often only visible in total populations over long periods of time. Epidemiological measures give an indication of outcome in terms of changes of prevalence and incidence of problems. Longitudinal studies of changes in attitudes and behaviour over time can be useful. Process measures at least give an indication of what has been done, if not what has been achieved.

Ongoing maintenance precautions can only be evaluated as an absence of harm over periods of time. Many professionals will feel that any client ending contact without personal change is in effect a failure. If the aim is personal change, outcome measures have more significance, but here again it is the two or three years following change-orientated methods which are crucial indicators of 'success' or 'failure' for clients with complex needs. The question here is whether success at treatment end should be relevant, rather than the long-term maintenance of treatment gains, which can only be assessed through time.

It is possible that severity of a particular problem is not related to risk or accentuation of other problems. Severity of a particular problem may only be relevant to harm if correlated with other problems and circumstances; that is, the adverse consequences of certain problems may be higher in particular high risk groups. If this is the case, different populations will require different strategies. These different populations may also have significantly different patterns of change over time. These issues have important implications in terms of targeting appropriate interventions at different groups of people and underline the importance of understanding the target group in terms of knowledge, attitudes and risk behaviours within the context of their social environment.

CONCLUSION

Comprehensive psychosocial assessment is necessary, in addition to traditional specialist assessments. It can be used to assess the extent and interaction of a range of different psychological and social problems and to determine if a maintenance approach alone is appropriate or whether a maintenance and change approach should be used in combination, and which practice methods are most appropriate in each case.

An assessment must determine the client's needs and capability to cope and include assessment of a range of different social and psychological problems and resources. It should include whether or not the client has the ability to change, wants to change and is ready to change at this time. It should also include what is needed to prepare for change and to maintain change. So, an assessment before change must include the capabilities of the client to make and maintain the change and what services they will need to both make and maintain the change.

While some methods can be used to achieve different ends, it is essential to clarify what the aims of any intervention are, as this will influence resource allocation and length of time of intervention. These aims will also affect definitions of success/failure and evaluations of effectiveness. It is possible that the same method or service may be given for different reasons; these reasons are reflected in the content of the professional assessment. This does not affect the actual service provision, but does affect who receives the service and when it is terminated. So if someone is assessed as having a psychological problem they may receive cognitive behavioural counselling. However, this will not be provided for someone who is not assessed as having a treatable psychological problem. Even if a client is assessed as having such a problem, help will soon be terminated both for those who are seen as resolving their problem and for those seen as failing to comply or succeed.

The discussion of the need for a comprehensive assessment has highlighted the problems of specialist professional assessments of all kinds. These problems not only constrain and distort professional understanding of problems, but also alienate clients. It is easier to understand why complex needs clients become 'difficult' when faced with assessments which are biased or incomplete and delimit the type and amount of help available.

The professional and client should be aware of two possible aims, either maintenance (maintenance management) or change (therapy or change-orientated methods). Assessment should reflect these aims and take into account not only the needs of clients but also their capacities. A comprehensive assessment will include the client's problems, skills and resources. It should include assessment of the client's ability to change (or not) and also his/her ability to maintain any changes in behaviour. The assessment will determine the need for change when appropriate, achievable and maintainable, and the need for ongoing maintenance for those who do not change and aftercare maintenance for those who do; that is, maintenance management and/or change-orientated methods and this forms the basis for agreement of goals and the development of a plan of action. The plan will include the basic treatment and rehabilitation methods described in Chapter 7, together with the maintenance methods described in Chapter 8.

If all professional groups utilise similar understandings of the importance of the psychological and social context of problems and the need for long-term psychosocial help, this may also contribute to a firm common foundation for multi-disciplinary training and inter-agency working.

Chapter 7
Psychological Change-orientated Methods

INTRODUCTION

This chapter will examine a range of different psychological change-orientated models, including cognitive behavioural or therapeutic programmes with the aim of individual client change. It will examine the effectiveness of cognitive, behavioural and counselling techniques. It will then consider the limitations of focusing on individual cognitive behavioural or therapeutic change for clients with complex psychosocial needs.

Many health, social care and criminal justice professionals acquire knowledge of individual counselling, group work, therapy and/or cognitive behavioural change techniques as part of their professional training. This chapter explains how these skills can be used for work with complex needs clients, but only as one part of a broader set of psychosocial change and maintenance-orientated tools.

Chapter 8 examines the second half of this tool set – psychosocial methods of maintenance. Psychological methods provide clients with cognitive-behavioural frameworks in which they can understand their problems. They can use these to cope and maintain present lifestyles or they can be taught new cognitions and behaviours enabling them to develop new lifestyles. Social and community work methods can maintain or change (improve) stressful relationships, develop social support systems and modify community and environmental factors to make social environments less stressful. The psychological change-orientated methods in this chapter must therefore be seen in the context of this wider remit. Before attempting to treat, provide therapy, rehabilitate or reform a client with complex needs, it will be necessary to consider the option of not changing the client at all, but of maintaining his or her present lifestyle and instead preventing further harm or risk and/or dealing with social rather than psychological problems.

It should also be noted here that while most psychological techniques have been developed for individual change-orientated programmes, they may be equally effective for maintenance purposes.

PSYCHOLOGICAL THEORIES OF CHANGE AND PROCESSES OF CHANGE

This chapter provides information about both psychological methods and effective sequences of methods. It explains how the knowledge and skills of the health and social care professions can be used for working with clients with psychological problems. It is however important to stress that whilst all professionals have the same overall aim of individual change, they are interested in different types of change for different reasons. They are likely to use the same psychological techniques, but may employ different priorities, objectives and outcome measures.

This chapter will demonstrate how particular psychological methods can be used effectively for different purposes. It will show how methods used by professionals for particular specialised problems are transferable to other problems. There are many texts outlining cognitive behavioural methods and psychotherapeutic counselling techniques for both clinical psychologists and generic professionals. The following may be useful: Goldfried and Bergin (1986), Kanfer and Goldstein (1986), Egan (1990), Trower *et al.* (1991), Wilkinson and Campbell (1997) and Snyder (1999). Those particularly concerned with the psychological context of a range of different problems include Stone *et al.* (1979), Gentry (1984), Steptoe and Matthews (1984), Weinmann (1987) and Pitts and Phillips (1991), and those concerned with the role of psychology in assessment of these problems include Mittler (1973) and Lawson (1986).

Methods traditionally developed for work with a particular client group (e.g. learning difficulties or substance misuse) may have been effective because that group has complex needs and these methods in effect deal with a range of complex problems rather than a single one (Moos 1984). There is no doubt that methods developed for one group of clients with complex needs can be equally effective with others.

CHANGE-ORIENTATED METHODS AND THE FOUR PERSPECTIVES

Most training in the helping professions is based solidly on scientific, medical and psychological theory and on the corresponding focus on individual change and treatment outcome research. The psychological approaches can all be criticised for too narrow a focus on the individual and individual change when dealing with complex psychosocial problems. However it is equally viable to criticise the social approaches discussed in the following chapter for not taking account of the individual.

The helping professions encompass four change-orientated perspectives:

(1)   Treatment, by the health care professions.
(2)   Therapy, by the psychological professions.
(3)   Rehabilitation, by the psychological and social work professions.
(4)   Reform, by the criminal justice professions.

Each of the four perspectives understands client problems (treatment, therapeutic, psychological or crimogenic) in terms of individual needs which can be resolved through changes in that individual. The theory and methods of these four approaches share a psychological perspective on problems, which results in a focus on the individual in assessment and also in aims similar to those of the clinical psychologist, that is short-term individual change. This tends to exclude possible social definitions of the problem and long-term social solutions.

However, as mentioned above, the different professions which use a common change approach also have differences in how they define and prioritise problems and how they specify success and failure. These differences are very important as they influence and delimit the kind of help provided and the period for which it is provided; that is, assistance can be provided by a range of professionals, but it will be made available and terminated for different reasons, depending on professional definitions of problems and successful outcomes.

PSYCHOLOGICAL THEORIES OF INDIVIDUAL CHANGE

Specialist problems and needs in health, mental illness and criminal behaviour are not discussed in this book, as the focus is on their psychosocial context rather than the specialist issues themselves. However, this chapter provides information about the psychological context of specialist problems, including the psychological theories and methods underlying both health psychology and health promotion.

Many psychological methods are based on cognitive/behavioural methods together with a more general psychodynamic approach to the client–therapist relationship. This can involve non-directional counselling where relationships with the therapist are often integral to change.

Cognitive behavioural theories

Cognitive and behavioural change methods derive from social learning theory (see Kim *et al.* 1989) and cognitive psychology. They can be very effective for certain conditions ranging from depression to phobias and for obsessive/compulsive behaviours (Bandura 1977; Ellis 1987; Beck 1989).

This approach sees cognitive and behavioural problems as lying on a continuum, rather than being divided into either/or categories as in mental health diagnosis. Social learning theory is a general theory offering an explanation of behaviour formation and maintenance. It assumes that behaviour can be either positively or negatively reinforced and that the sooner the reinforcement occurs the more effective it will be. The development of behavioural habits can also be influenced by 'modelling' and other social factors such as the need to conform (Bergin & Garfield 1978; Bandura 1977; Bolles 1979; Catania & Harnad 1988).

An emphasis on the influence of cognition on behaviour led to the development of cognitive psychology (Ellis 1962; Beck 1989). One of the early models derived from this source was the health belief model (Becker 1974) which emphasises the relevance of individual beliefs to the consequences of an action (for example, heavy alcohol consumption), risky activities leading to increased likelihood of getting a disease and the perceived costs and inconvenience. However, Leventhal and Nerenz (1985) point out the limitations of both social learning theory and the health belief model in that both assume that people react to events such as illness in specific ways (e.g. in terms of perceived seriousness and vulnerability). They argue that ordinary people do not function in the same way as scientists and statisticians using abstract and general notions and suggest that people think and react to situations in a specific rather than generic way, in concrete rather than abstract terms; they do not react to the world as scientists do. An abstract or generalised intention does not therefore necessarily lead to a concrete or specific behaviour.

Although psychological models can be useful, it is important to understand their limitations. Another model of health behaviour derived from this psychological base is the theory of reasoned action. This explains how cognitions are linked to health behaviour but it does not account for the very small variance in outcome studies and serves no real predictive function (Silver & Wortman 1980; Turk *et al.* 1986). There is little evidence to show that cognitions actually influence behaviour change and some psychologists have themselves come to doubt the usefulness of these theories.

Cognitive behavioural theories derived from social learning theory also ignore the contemporary importance of advertising and the media, which are a major feature of most people's lives, and perhaps more importantly, they underestimate the importance of social factors (Cartwright 1979). For example, cigarettes perform a 'social' function for the young and provide a means of social barter and bonding. Young people are often aware of the hazards of smoking, yet they perceive that benefits in social terms outweigh the perceived potential problems. As far as smoking is concerned then, ensuring the establishment of non-smoking as a social norm appears to be crucial to the prevention of smoking in the longer term (Royal College of Physicians 1992). The theory of reasoned action mentioned in the last paragraph is used in health promotion and prevention work, but places more emphasis on the socioenvironment. The key components are intention (the beliefs and evaluation of consequences) and the socioenvironmental component (the individual's perception of how peers or friends react to that person's smoking in general). The theory stresses the importance of an individual's beliefs about the personal consequences of a particular course of action (Sutton 1992). It leads to an analysis of what is seen as rational behaviour in terms of the individual beliefs and social/cultural context of subjects.

Alternative theories have been developed from the interpretive or phenomenological methodologies and research discussed in Part II. These focus on social interactions and interpretations and indicate that a 'situated' rationality located in the socially constructed context should take the place of the 'single' individualised rationality of psychology (Kane 1991; Rhodes *et al.* 1996).

Behavioural methods

Behavioural interventions set out to provide an accurate description of behavioural problems and change in the specific behaviours identified. The approach normally involves close monitoring of concrete changes in behaviour.

General behavioural techniques teach clients to monitor and understand specific behaviours in terms of what causes or motivates each action (antecedents and consequences). They can then learn to modify their behaviour patterns by changing the controlling factors and testing out new behaviours and coping strategies. The major methods are:

- Assessment of antecedents and consequences.
- Behavioural monitoring.
- Schedules of reinforcement and punishment.
- Stimulus control and generalisation.
- Deconditioning and desensitisation (cue exposure).
- Modelling and imitation.

Initial assessment

A first step is to find out which variables are significant in creating a problematic behaviour, such as aggression, but it is even more necessary to identify those important in continuing this reinforcement.

Positive and negative reinforcement

Assessment should be followed by changing the reinforcing properties of the aggressive behaviour, either by offering positive reinforcement for alternative behaviours or negative reinforcement for the problematic behaviour.

Cue exposure or extinction

The typical cues for problem behaviours are generated without the reinforcing antecedents. The client is gradually and then repeatedly exposed to these cues, but without feeling positively reinforcing effects.

Self-monitoring and self-control training

The terms self-monitoring and self-control apply to the basic behavioural techniques of identifying the antecedents and consequences of any problem behaviour and learning to alter it by changing either or both. The client is taught to identify situations and cues that are likely to stimulate problematic behaviour and to respond either by avoidance and/or by developing alternative coping strategies.

Cognitive behavioural methods

Most contemporary behavioural psychologists also include a cognitive element in both their theory and practice. The way persons define or interpret their experience is considered to have a strong influence on their behaviour (Ellis 1962; Weinmann 1987; Beck 1989).

As with behavioural interventions, cognitive interventions are based on an accurate description of cognitions and beliefs, leading to identification of maladaptive beliefs and consequent changes to more constructive alternatives. Accurate initial descriptions are therefore essential, followed by continuing assessment, self-monitoring and feedback. The first step in the helping process is to examine the beliefs and thinking processes which lead to problematic behaviours.

This is followed by demonstration of inaccuracies in beliefs and by identification of inconsistencies in personal belief and value systems. Thus a client may believe that she/he is inherently depressive or anxious, without realising that it is a consequence of a recent loss. It is also useful to highlight any inconsistencies and conflicts between clients, short- and long-term aims and priorities and help them to consider the evidence for the advantages and disadvantages of change in behaviour. This in turn may be employed to demonstrate the ways in which beliefs are linked to emotional and behavioural consequences and alternative beliefs.

The methods used in this approach include cognitive restructuring, self-instruction training, stress inoculation, thought stopping and basic self-control, self-talk methods and relaxation tapes. These methods are in widespread use for reducing anxiety and promoting relaxation etc. Tapes and instruction booklets are usually available from psychology and health promotion departments in health authorities. Clients can also be taught new skills and coping strategies, including a decision matrix, reminder cards and self-talk or cognitive restructuring.

These techniques can also be effective for the maintenance strategies discussed in the following chapter to develop new coping strategies and alternative activities (Moos 1984). Changes in lifestyle can also help · reduce stress and anxiety. Engaging in new occupations may provide new forms of interest and social life that militate against the re-emergence of old problems.

Generic counselling skills

In the field of psychotherapy, the actual methods used by different types of therapist are often similar, though the interpretations may be diverse. For example, any 'behavioural' technique can also be seen to incorporate other therapeutic elements, resulting from a therapeutic relationship, and any therapeutic programme could be seen to involve cognitive and behavioural elements in terms of restructuring cognitions and reinforcing behaviours. This section will not consider the several hundred therapeutic models, but instead focus on the common counselling skills shared by most effective counsellors.

The basic training and experience of most social and health care professionals incorporates various types of counselling skills. The term 'counselling' is often ill-defined and can vary from chatting to a client to a carefully structured programme of behavioural change or intensive psychotherapy. Such programmes deploy a mixture of psychodynamic client-centred methods with cognitive behavioural techniques. The skills developed from these programmes are outlined below, but for practical guidebooks and exercises the following are useful: Truax and Carhuff (1967); Kanfer and Goldstein (1986); Egan (1990); Wilkinson and Campbell (1997); Snyder (1999).

The distinction between different kinds of counselling is important. Many are designed to achieve therapeutic change, such as cognitive behavioural and therapeutic programmes. It is therefore necessary to distinguish between those counselling techniques aimed at change and those simply designed to build constructive helping relationships and to clarify problems.

There is a substantial literature on non-directive, client-centred counselling (Egan 1990). This counselling can be important for building relationships before offering support and practical help and may also result in changing the clients' attitudes and in their desire to change their behaviour. However, if significant changes in behaviour are desired through counselling, these particular measures are not sufficient.

There is much less information concerning the translation of changes in attitudes into changes in behaviour. Therapeutic programmes address this problem by offering specific cognitive behavioural programmes. Such programmes have a specific definition of problems and practical solutions in common, that help the client to understand the problem and the possible solutions and also assists the client to understand the ways of achieving the solutions. The essence of goal setting is to define clearly the sequence of steps necessary to achieve the aims; that is, to define exactly *how* a goal will be achieved.

Much research has been undertaken to identify what effective factors counselling sessions have in common. The most significant is the counsellor. The qualities of a good counsellor have been variously listed as: warmth, genuineness, empathy, respect and caring, together with the use of feedback, confrontation, self-disclosure, commitment and careful listening. Carl Rogers (1967) has suggested that warmth, empathy and unconditional positive regard lead to a more genuine and authentic relationship; however he was not convinced that these qualities could be learned. Gerald Egan (1990) has suggested that, while certain personal qualities produce a more effective working relationship, this can be largely achieved by using skills that can be learned and practised. Particular emphasis is placed on empathy and the ability to communicate understanding of the client's feelings and point of view, followed by a stress on genuineness, unconditional positive regard, respect and a non-judgemental attitude.

An essential part of counselling is accurate empathetic feedback. This centres on the ability to paraphrase what the client has said (rephrasing or active listening) and to be specific and pinpoint significant issues. The object of paraphrasing is to avoid misunderstandings and clarify issues. It also serves as clear indication to the client that the counsellor is listening and taking seriously what is said. Feedback also includes empathetic responses in terms of attempting to understand what the client may have felt in certain situations and asking specific questions about emotional states. Positive comments and questions are an integral part of feedback but brevity is most important. Summarising is similar to paraphrasing but can be used specifically to clarify what has occurred so far and to determine what issue or direction should be explored next.

The initial stages of listening and feedback in most counselling programmes are followed by the challenging of a client's point of view. This can be introduced by establishing a new perspective on the client's problem or situation, usually taken from the counsellor's own frame of reference or that of a significant other. It incorporates possible new patterns or themes and the pointing out of discrepancies. Confrontation often requires self-disclosure or giving the client information. Information giving is a skill in itself. To be effective, simple words, short sentences and explicit categorisations should be used. It is necessary to be concrete and specific, avoid jargon, summarise and ask for feedback from the client.

The counsellor should clarify the practical means of achieving change goals, step-by-step, so the clients not only know what they are going to do, but how they are going to do it. They need to know who will do what, what will happen when each stage is completed, what will happen if a goal is not achieved and what will happen in the event of relapses. The more specific and concrete each step, the better.

Counselling skills have many purposes and benefits:

(1) For motivation, when attempting to understand the client and develop a working relationship.
(2) During assessment when understanding problems and needs.
(3) When helping the client to work out what choices are available, make decisions about which to choose and develop strategies for achieving these goals.
(4) For therapeutic change.

Client-centred listening skills are the essence of motivation and assessment, whereas more directive and confrontational skills are an integral part of therapeutic change. Cognitive behavioural interventions are useful for both therapeutic change and relapse prevention.

Initial client-centred, reflective and non-directive counselling often precedes the more change-orientated later stages. If there is a need for therapeutic change, the therapeutic component (whether cognitive behavioural or psychodynamic) follows initial non-directive listening. Finally, the emphasis on maintenance of change and relapse prevention requires further cognitive behavioural counselling skills. This is discussed in the following chapter.

PSYCHOLOGICAL PROCESS THEORIES: PREPARATION FOR CHANGE AND MAINTENANCE OF CHANGE

As can be seen, psychologists have tended to focus on outcome studies of particular interventions. However, a recent model of change processes has highlighted the limitations of this approach.

In recent years the use of a change model developed by Prochaska and DiClemente (see next section) and of motivational interviewing (Miller 1983) have become widespread. These models of attitude and behaviour change were developed from work with smokers and later modified for practical motivational counselling methods with drug and alcohol misusers. This process model is now used widely for working with a range of different client groups, particularly those who are ambivalent or have multiple problems, and who may find changes difficult to make or maintain. It is therefore particularly useful when working with clients with complex needs. It is suggested that for these clients, interventions will be more effective at particular stages, for example when an individual is contemplating change or has reached a decision to change.

The change process

Prochaska first published *Systems of Psychotherapy: A Transtheoretical Perspective* in 1979 and with DiClemente built on the ideas in this seminal work (Prochaska & DiClemente 1982, 1983, 1986, 1994). The authors present the model as transtheoretical, and therefore usable in parallel with a range of different theories, but it can be seen to be most closely aligned with a cognitive behavioural approach and the interventions suggested are concerned with cognitive and behavioural change. The authors developed this model of change processes from their work with smokers and drinkers respectively, incorporating the notion of a sequential change process approach. They then modified it to develop a practical motivational counselling method for work with offenders and alcohol users.

The stages of change model

Pre-contemplation

The model predicts that people in this first stage of the change process will respond less well to information and advice than people in the following contemplation stage. It therefore follows that counselling for clients in this stage will be more effective if it is designed simply to raise awareness of problems (rather than attempting to offer information and advice or to move the client towards premature change), in order to prepare clients for the next stage. Intervention at the pre-contemplation stage is seen as less constructive than intervention when clients are at the contemplation stage.

Contemplation

It is at this stage that information and advice are more likely to be assimilated and used. Suggested interventions include cognitive techniques such as awareness raising, information, decisional balances, re-evaluation of life events and problems. Clients at this stage are more receptive to alternative observations, interpretations and direct confrontation. Behavioural assessments and analysis of the problems and coping strategies can also be useful here.

Action

This stage is sometimes divided into the 'decision' stage, including a firm commitment to change, which can be of very short duration, followed rapidly by the 'action' stage, where therapy or change-orientated methods are most effective.

Maintenance of change

This stage follows therapy or change-orientated methods and indicates that achieving change requires maintenance.

Relapse

As this model was initially developed for smokers, the concept of relapse is focused on return to substance-using behaviours. It is now also used for a range of risky or dangerous behaviours such as offending.

The authors have demonstrated that smokers progress through this whole cycle on average about three times. They have therefore incorporated a relapse phase into the overall model. Although the later stages of maintenance and relapse are integral parts of the model, the emphasis is on the pre-contemplation and contemplation stages and the later stages are less well developed. The model is therefore particularly useful for initial assessments and appropriately timed therapy or change-orientated methods interventions, but perhaps less useful for working in the maintenance and relapse stages.

Motivational interviewing

Miller *et al.* (1988) developed the idea of motivational interviewing in parallel with the work of Prochaska and DiClemente, focusing on change processes and stages of change. The basic underlying premise to the motivational interviewing approach is that change is a process with clearly definable sequential stages. The helper can be more effective if she/he identifies which stage the client is at and makes the appropriate intervention for that stage. As emphasised earlier, whilst the motivational approach is useful, it should be remembered that it is based on the premise that change is the best way forward. There are, of course, many reasons why this might not be the case.

This approach has the following key principles:

- The client must be accepted in a complete and unconditional way.
- The client is a responsible person.
- The client must be ready for change and not forced into it by the counsellor.

- The goals and the forms of therapy or change-orientated methods must be negotiated.

The stages are:

- Assessment, to determine if a client wants to change, or is 'ready' for change.
- Increasing motivation by encouraging the client to recognise the problem.
- Helping the client to weigh up the advantages and disadvantages.
- Monitoring progress through the cycle of change from pre-contemplation.
- Contemplation, decision, action and maintenance of change.

Miller developed his model through work with clients with alcohol problems. He proposed that it was possible to increase motivation and reduce denial among them by emphasising the 'decisional balance', or helping clients to weigh up the advantages and disadvantages of their drinking. This was to be achieved by clarifying the range of choices open to them and by highlighting the discrepancies between their beliefs and behaviour.

Why a process model is useful for complex needs clients

Motivational interviewing and the change model are very useful as assessment tools, allowing professionals to determine if the client is 'ready' and 'contemplating change' or not, and determining which interventions are likely to be most effective at the pre-contemplation and contemplation stages. While motivating the client is seen as the first step of a sequence leading the clients to make change (rather than an ongoing supportive programme of maintenance), it helps provide the crucial distinction between those who need maintenance management alone and those who are more likely to respond to change-orientated methods.

Although motivation is only one of a range of possible factors to be taken into account in assessment of clients with complex needs, it is a useful starting point. The importance of motivation has long been understood by professionals working with clients with complex needs (Davidson *et al.* 1991). There is little research in this area, as the phenomenon is difficult to measure, but lack of motivation is often cited as a primary reason for breakdown in professional client-relationships, attrition and change-orientated methods failure.

This approach places a great deal of emphasis on the need to develop a working relationship and 'link the client in' to the helping process. This is expected to take place before assessment in order to ensure cooperation, because the client's view of their problems may be different to the professional's view (and this is often a reason for the breakdown of a working relationship). This is particularly significant for clients with complex needs who may expect to be judged adversely (and perhaps treated badly) because they are often seen as 'difficult' or 'inappropriate' and as presenting particularly difficult and intractable problems.

Motivational assessment has been developed for those with behavioural problems and only for those clients who need to change: it effectively selects from this group those who want to change. This model has been shown to be useful for specialists working with heavy drinkers (Davidson *et al.* 1991) and for smokers. However, both heavy drinkers and smokers are concerned with the long-term health consequences of heavy use. 'Readiness to change' is therefore a useful concept and change in drinking or smoking is the logical step. When these concepts are transferred to clients with complex needs the same is not necessarily true. The client's 'readiness to change' may not be a useful measure, if the client is not in a position to maintain that change, or if the client does not even have the capacity to make the change.

So, while the model is useful for clarifying the client's view of their problems and identifying those clients who do not want to change, it is less useful for identifying those clients who cannot change or cannot maintain change. It does not include assessment of the practical constraints on change but limits itself to the client's own motivation. It takes no account of external constraints outside the individual's control.

The importance of preparation for change and maintenance of change

Despite the limitations of using motivational interviewing and the change model for clients for whom short-term personal change is not appropriate, the model is very useful for those complex needs clients who do want to change and have the ability to do so.

It is interesting to examine why a process model of motivation and change should achieve such popularity among professionals in the absence of research evidence as to its effectiveness. It might be because the model of change enables professionals to understand that clients do not necessarily see their problems in the same way as professionals and that this will affect motivation. However, a more significant factor for complex needs clients is perhaps the recognition of the need for clients to be prepared before they make major changes and to be provided with ongoing help and support to maintain these changes.

In practical terms this approach may simply be identifying those clients who are actually able and ready to change because they feel they have enough support to maintain change; that is, it is possible that clients' motivation to change is a reflection of their ability and resources. If so, motivational interviewing is very helpful because, in effect, it allows professionals to provide a maintenance service before and after change interventions, and after relapse. However, this approach does not take account of the possibility that motivation to change may not be correlated with ability to change; in fact the inverse may be the case. When the client feels most distraught or has most problems, this may be the time when they have least resources.

Alternatively, it is possible that this model has introduced professionals (perhaps for the first time) to the possibility that a fairly large proportion of clients do not want to change (for whatever reason) and that if they do not want to change, then interventions are likely to be ineffective. Perhaps the 'change' model may not really be a change model at all but a maintenance model in disguise!

LIMITATIONS OF TRADITIONAL AND PROCESS PSYCHOLOGICAL THEORIES: THE NEED FOR A PSYCHOSOCIAL PERSPECTIVE

The limitations of both traditional psychological methods and contemporary process models include the lack of an interactional or social context and an emphasis on individual change and individual change methods. There is a real need for a process model that shows both psychological and social ongoing changes in an individual's life, without indicating that the person themselves needs to change.

As discussed in Chapter 5, the advantage of social learning theory and behavioural methods is that they are empirically testable and can be disproved. Thus if the maladaptive behaviour is not changed after 'treatment' in a controlled setting, then the chosen method can be shown to be of no use in dealing with the phenomenon in question. A great deal of research has now been completed in this area, which sheds some light, not only on the effectiveness of behavioural techniques in dealing with behavioural disorders, but also on the usefulness of defining various problems in behavioural terms. Whilst psychological theories and methods of treatment are useful in dealing with psychological problems, they have not yet been shown to be effective in serious cases of physical problems or combined physiological and psychological problems.

The behavioural approach can be criticised because of the limitations of its theoretical base and cognitive psychology can be criticised for its lack of scientific testing. It is also problematic that it is only possible objectively to measure observed behaviour change, and not so easy to measure the many possible factors that may underlie or mediate that behaviour change. In addition, outcome is only measured at one point and in particular controlled circumstances. There is much controversy, not concerning whether cognitive behavioural methods are useful for behavioural problems as a whole, but regarding how far the methods are effective when dealing with complex psychosocial (or medical) problems.

The limitations in research in this field are partly due to the inherent constraints within the psychological discipline itself. As its subject matter is restricted to individuals and small groups, psychology tends to ignore the complexity of social context. Similarly, because its methods are largely scientific outcome studies, the relevance of process in individual change is disregarded. Despite these considerations, the theories of health behaviour help to interpret the complex interactions of cognition and behaviour. Although research cannot demonstrate that changes in cognition will produce corresponding changes in behaviour, it does not necessarily follow that they are not related. It is equally possible that cognitions are related to behaviour but that other factors are also influential. Unfortunately, there is much less research about such influences.

Whilst there seems little doubt from the accumulated evidence that psychology has a good deal to offer, there are the difficulties in problem definition. Many different professional groups may accept that problems are complex and multifaceted; however there is little consensus regarding which is considered the primary problem. Whether, for example, psychological problems such as depression have caused the social problems, or whether the social problems have caused depression. These issues were discussed in Chapter 5, but it is useful to highlight here the lack of agreement concerning the interactive relationships between physical, psychological and social problems.

At present, research is limited in two main ways. First, there is little evidence of individual differences among clients affecting outcome. As might be expected, therefore, psychological researchers have looked not at social factors but at individual differences between therapists. So while there is much evidence identifying the characteristics of the most effective counsellors (Egan 1990), little work has been done to assess the influence of social variables. Second, treatment gains are often lost at follow-up. Yet researchers have not succeeded in explaining the reasons for relapse following treatment. This again suggests that maintenance of treatment gains may be correlated with social factors rather than treatment variables (again, there is little research in these areas). While the distinction between treatment change processes and long-term maintenance of change is useful, much research indicates that social variables may not only be important in long-term maintenance of change but also for within-treatment change.

Recent reviews suggest that social programmes focusing on individual functioning, such as social skills, family relationships etc., seem more successful than other programmes (Azrin *et al.* 1982; Becker & Thornicroft, 1998; Bogenschutz & Siegfreid 1998). Similarly community reinforcement programmes seem fruitful (Dhooper 1991; Gordon 1998; Dillon & Dollieslager 2000). Relapse prevention and intervention are perhaps most appropriate in psychological terms in the mental health and substance/alcohol field, though these methods have been extended to all problem behaviours from crime and sex offending to phobias and obsessive compulsive behaviours.

In the light of these findings, it seems clear that research into psycho-social factors in treatment and post-treatment recovery processes is essential in order to develop practice in this area.

Chapter 8
Psychosocial Maintenance Methods

INTRODUCTION

This chapter provides a psychosocial maintenance model that is an alternative to that of individual psychological change discussed in the previous chapter. It can also be used in conjunction with the psychological change-orientated methods. It describes different means of long-term support and preventive working methods and incorporates a psychological focus on developing individual coping skills and methods of community and social support.

The methods used for maintenance can also be used for maintaining treatment gains. Similarly, relapse prevention methods can be used not only to help maintain treatment gains, but also to reduce risk taking and help prevent clients' lifestyles deteriorating further.

Professionals, non-statutory workers and clients have between them accumulated a great deal of practical experience of the problems and the practical skills necessary for working with this approach. It is now only necessary to build on this common experience and broaden all specialist models in order to incorporate an additional common maintenance model. This may also help avoid interprofessional conflict and engender good multidisciplinary working by developing a common approach with shared client groups.

Maintenance methods have often been established and adopted for a range of different client groups with complex psychological and social problems. Many were developed as part of a pragmatic response to clients with intractable or 'untreatable' problems such as mental health or chronic illnesses, rather than as an integral part of contemporary treatment perspectives. These maintenance approaches therefore tend to be atheoretical and seen in parallel with treatment interventions or alternatively provided within a change-orientated rationale such as 'rehabilitation'. So in much of health and social care the term rehabilitation has become practically synonymous with maintenance; and support is often provided under the category of 'prevention', or long-term 'rehabilitation' or 'intermediate care' but in effect offers ongoing care.

There is a need to draw on this wide range of fragmented maintenance techniques in order to understand and develop a new comprehensive approach which can be shared by all professions. This chapter will therefore give a brief overview of research on maintenance methods used by different professionals for different client groups. It will then examine how maintenance methods can be used as an alternative to change-orientated methods or as a complementary part of post-treatment programmes and will provide guidelines for practice.

A psychosocial approach to maintenance

It has been shown that a psychosocial approach is not purely focused on individual pathology or even on individual change. As soon as complex needs are understood within a psychosocial conceptual framework, it becomes apparent that problem definitions are not confined to individuals. So assessments should not only concern individual needs and abilities, but also social context and constraints. Complex needs are therefore not seen as purely medical or psychological, in fact they are not seen as a consequence of individual pathology or individual failing alone, but also of a range of interacting psychological and social problems.

The implications of this approach for helping clients with complex needs are not simply to offer a range of different change-orientated interventions. It is essential to consider that individual change is not necessarily the only, or indeed the most appropriate, response at all. In contrast, it may be more effective and efficient to provide ongoing maintenance support, including both social support and psychological skills training.

The term maintenance management is used here to include all strategies where the aim is not change in terms of therapy, rehabilitation or reform, but to reduce the physical, psychological and social harm, limit damage or prevent deterioration. It includes both risk and relapse intervention.

Some methods used for maintenance management can also be used for change, but it is important to remember that the aims of each approach are different and consequently assessments and interventions and definitions of successful outcomes will not be the same. This is particularly important where, for example, the aims of a treatment approach will require the client to succeed (or fail) within a specified period. Either way this aim will involve termination of help.

Maintenance is an alternative or additional approach to change-orientated methods for clients with complex needs, which does not time-limit help. While most professionals working with complex needs clients have developed practical methods of helping these clients by offering a range of social and psychological assistance, it is often difficult for them to justify ongoing support. As a consequence, these clients will need to constantly recontact or reregister with professionals in order to receive an ongoing support service.

Maintenance management is useful for those who cannot or do not want to change and those who would not be able to maintain change (treatment gains) after an intervention. In addition, it is also useful for the high proportion of clients with complex needs who are at risk of relapse after change-orientated interventions. It is therefore necessary with this client group to spend a good deal of time and effort on the aftercare period. This involves completing assessments and plans for the post-therapy period as an integral part of that therapy or change-orientated methods process. These plans should contain clear-cut procedures in the event of crisis or relapse.

A REVIEW OF PROFESSIONAL MAINTENANCE METHODS

The relevance of clinical and practitioner experience to the development of maintenance methods

There are two kinds of knowledge and therefore two ways for professionals to learn: by using academic research and from professional and clinical experience (as discussed in Chapter 5). Despite their different theoretical persuasions, many methods used by professionals in the field are in effect very similar. The sequence in which problems are dealt with may vary and the theoretical interpretations are clearly different.

The following psychological and social methods can be utilised by health and social care professions to treat complex problems; many of these methods and skills are part of their own professional training and experience and they will find themselves already equipped with the basic skills necessary. As with all problems, particular professions may need to consult each other for specialist expertise. For example, probation and health care professionals would need to consult social workers about implications for child care, and social workers will need to consult doctors about health risks.

There is also a need to use the methods of non-statutory groups which provide support and maintenance. Methods will be selected from a range of approaches to 'untreatable' or 'unchangeable' clients such as those with chronic illnesses such as Alzheimer's, drug misuse or cancer.

Common methods include, for example, client-centred and task-centred counselling, cognitive behavioural techniques for behaviour change and maintenance, and the development of new social skills and social networks. It will be seen that while many of the methods and skills involved in working with people with psychosocial problems are part of the everyday work of most social and health care professionals, these methods are often understood within theories and models of change or rehabilitation.

An overview of professional maintenance methods

As highlighted earlier, most professional training is largely concerned with individual change-orientated methods, whether treatment, therapy, rehabilitation or reform. However, much everyday practice is concerned with the management of intractable problems and social interventions.

As might be expected, therefore, much of the work with non-acute patients or long-term interventions in any one field is defined within the context of eventual change or long-term gains. So in the mental health field 'rehabilitation' can be used to refer to long-term service provision; similarly 'intermediate care' for the elderly disabled can last until death, and both 'maintenance treatment' or 'secondary prevention' in the drugs field can refer to ongoing maintenance support.

Despite a lack of comprehensive texts on the subject or a clear exposition of theory and practice, many professions and specialisms can contribute to a common base of knowledge about effective maintenance methods, whatever the ultimate aims or philosophy of the interventions:

(1)   The mental health field.
(2)   The substance misuse field.
(3)   Disability and social work.
(4)   Psychology, health psychology and public health.
(5)   The contribution of the voluntary and non-statutory services.

The contribution of mental health practice to maintenance methods for complex needs clients

Psychiatric rehabilitation, which is aimed at helping people who have long-term mental illness to develop their capacities to the fullest possible extent, has been an integral part of psychiatric treatment for several hundred years. It includes family care, the day hospital, social skills training, psychoeducation and vocational rehabilitation (Lamb 1994). Treatment and rehabilitation are often seen as two sides of the same coin (Dillon & Dollieslager 2000), and Anthony (1996) argues that the absence of psychiatric rehabilitation services in a managed care system is logically, empirically and ethically unacceptable.

Wallace (1993) and Prendergast (1995) have carried out extensive reviews of the literature on psychiatric rehabilitation. Both authors conclude that severely mentally ill individuals can usefully learn skills if their training is embedded in a comprehensive system of care that addresses all their needs and disabilities. Wallace stresses that this should include a carefully prepared environment to provide occasions and rewards for using the skills, and to unify the elements of care to a few caregivers who have the expertise to cope with the unpredictable, individualised course of the illness. He also emphasises that individuals' cognitive impairments make the training more time-consuming and labour-intensive than teaching skills to individuals with physical disabilities. Difficulties are exacerbated by the individual-to-individual, time-to-time, and disorder-to-disorder variations in these impairments and disabilities.

Rehabilitation for mental health problems is used in conjunction with medication to achieve more effective outcomes. Specific programmes are implemented for various diagnostic groups, especially schizophrenic psychosis, mental retardation, substance dependence and organic brain damage (Uchtenhagen 1996). Mentally ill patients have a wide range of impairments and disabilities which vary throughout the life course. These include reduced motivation to participate in community life, and deficits in the cognitive processes of attention, memory and abstraction, which limit individuals' abilities to perform life skills and function in major societal roles. Psychiatric rehabilitation, in effect therefore, continues throughout a person's life, with the types of services adapted to different needs at different times, for example, during periods of relapse (Dillon & Dollieslager 2000). The emphasis of support is often on clarifying the person's own goals, whether these be self-control, freedom of choice, privacy and time with friends and family. In addition it is felt important to educate the patient, not only about their problems but also about the possible solutions, such as effects of medication and behavioural techniques of self-control and self-monitoring. There is a strong emphasis on links with the family or other natural supports that the person has in the community with a focus on continuing treatment needs after discharge from in-patient services (Dillon & Dollieslager 2000).

This is confirmed by Lambie *et al.* (1997) who found that mental health clients in the community had additional needs often overlooked in conventional programmes. These included the need for groups to provide ongoing support in the community itself.

Whilst it is recognised that integrating traditional psychiatric rehabilitation approaches with targeted cognitive interventions is necessary, Silverstein *et al.* (1998) point out that there are problems with developing rehabilitative skills for this group. Many mentally ill patients have cognitive deficits that limit their ability to benefit from psychiatric rehabilitation interventions. The authors suggest that more needs to be known about which cognitive deficits interfere with which aspects of outcome and functioning before effective interventions are developed. Tsang and Pearson (1999) have attempted to work with these limitations in developing a conceptual framework for work-related social skills. This is a three-tier framework comprising basic skills, core skills and the results subsequent to the possession of these skills. Another example of a successful integrated model is the in-patient psychosocial rehabilitation model called PRISM (The Psychiatric Rehabilitation Integrated Service

Model). This emphasises skill development and patient participation and has been shown to improve quality of life, decrease relapse, and increase the efficiency and responsiveness to patient needs (Starkey & Leadholm 1997).

Before leaving the mental health field it is important to mention the criminal justice aspects of mental health work. Rehabilitation for criminal mental health patients has important additional problems in terms of the risks to the patient and public safety. The extent to which forensic psychiatric rehabilitation alters an individual's level of risk is unclear, but Lindqvist and Skipworth (2000) state that it is necessary to discuss risk assessment in psychiatric rehabilitation for offenders and to create a conceptual framework for risk research and practice. They review the literature in this area and argue that current risk research has limited application to rehabilitation and that any studies in this area will be hampered by the complexity of the treatment systems and the number of relevant methodological issues. These findings may be equally true for a range of offenders with complex psychosocial problems, whether these are defined as 'crimogenic' or not.

Finally, it is important to mention that there are concerns in the field of mental health regarding the oversimplification of contemporary research findings and the overuse of terms such as 'rehabilitation' and 'recovery', where there is no real long-term progress or cure (Lamb 1994). There are few terms for ongoing life-time maintenance care, though this is often provided under the guise of treatment or rehabilitation.

This research has implications for developing services for complex needs clients, particularly those with mental health problems and/or cognitive deficits, but also more widely for those with ongoing psychosocial problems.

The contribution of the substance misuse field

The substance misuse field has developed substantially in the past decade, moving from medical and disease models of addiction towards the inclusion of psychological and social understandings of use and misuse throughout the life course. Attention is consequently directed towards cognitive behavioural and social methods of controlled use and harm minimisation over time. Many of the issues in this field, like those in the mental health field, are therefore particularly relevant for clients with complex needs and, not surprisingly, many maintenance methods that have been developed are useful models for use with complex needs clients as a whole.

Practitioners and researchers in this field emphasise the importance of both individual cognitive behavioural skills (Marlatt & Gordon 1985) and the creation of social support networks together with social skills training (Catalano & Hawkins 1985). The importance of a psychosocial approach, together with an emphasis on both harm minimisation and aftercare and relapse prevention, have resulted in the development of a wide range of different methods for supporting and maintaining clients. These can form part of harm minimisation or HIV prevention programmes, long-term rehabilitation or aftercare and relapse prevention initiatives.

Treatment effects in both drug and alcohol programmes appear to be only short-term. However, while within-treatment processes are qualitatively different to maintenance of change processes, Maisto and Carey (1987) found that staying in treatment seems to be associated with benefits that may be maintained for some time. In the drug field, pre-treatment and during-treatment variables do not predict post-treatment functioning; this suggests that other variables may have a significant effect on post-treatment functioning (Cronkite & Moos (1980); Finney *et al.* (1980); Simpson & Sells 1982; Catalano *et al.* (1990–91). The factors seen as particularly important in relapse are lack of involvement in active leisure and in education and an inability of treatment clients to establish non-drug using contacts in work and educational settings. Rounsaville (1986) argues that professionals should explicitly encourage re-entry into treatment after relapse. Clients should be taught to anticipate and cope with feelings and conditions that predict relapse and there should be continuing contact after treatment, together with a crisis intervention service.

Researchers have shown that there is more chance of success the sooner the re-intervention after the relapse (Brown 1979; Brown & Ashery 1979; Hawkins & Catalano 1985). There is also evidence that self-help groups, networking and skills training help minimise relapse (Nurco *et al.* 1983; Hawkins & Catalano 1985). In the area of smoking, research indicates that individual relapse prevention skills and social and life skills (Marlatt & George 1984; Leukefeld & Tims 1989) together with improved social support networks, are the most effective means of preventing relapse (Brown 1979; Ravndal & Vaglum 1994). The work of Marlatt has been developed in other areas where self-control techniques are useful.

Marlatt and Gordon (1985), Marlatt (1985) and Wilson (1992) found that the main precursors of relapse are identified as negative emotional states, interpersonal conflict and social pressure. This again suggests that maintenance of treatment gains may be correlated with psychological and social factors rather than treatment variables themselves (Moos *et al.* 1990; Lindstrom 1992). Saunders and Kershaw (1979), Valliant (1983) and Nordstrom and Burglund (1986) indicate that social relations are a major precondition for the persistence of whatever the severely dependent client may have gained from treatment.

Perhaps the most influential research on environmental stressors and social supports is that of Rudolph Moos and his colleagues (Cronkite &

Moos 1980; Moos *et al*. 1981; Billings & Moos 1983; Moos *et al*. 1990). This research found that relapsed alcoholics had more negative experiences and fewer positive life events than those who had not relapsed. They also discovered that those who retained therapy or change-orientated methods gains had significantly improved their quality of life and had developed social support networks and cohesion. They exhibited low levels of conflict in family relationships and low time-urgency and pressure in work settings. The work of Moos has also been developed to encompass a range of physical problems (Moos 1984).

It is clear that the researchers and practitioners in this field recognise that it is not possible to develop effective interventions without reference to the wider society in which the individual lives. There has been an attempt in this field to take account of social context and, particularly for many clients, the absence of contact with everyday social networks and therefore lack of social skills. Catalano and Hawkins (1985) describe a project involving cognitive behavioural skills training and social network development using volunteer partners for each client, to act as a bridge to the non-drug-using world. The authors proposed that this programme would reduce the factors associated with relapse and strengthen those associated with the maintenance of (in this case) abstinence. These factors included the absence of strong prosocial interpersonal networks, isolation, lack of productive work or school roles or recreational activities, negative emotional states and physical discomfort. As a consequence of these findings they developed informal social supports in the community and facilitated social and recreational activities. In addition they developed cognitive behavioural skills programmes to maintain treatment gains including becoming involved in social and leisure activities, coping with stress and 'negative emotional states', recognising and avoiding situations with high risk of relapse and coping with slips without having a full blown relapse.

Work in the area of community reinforcement is limited, but early evidence suggests that it may be very effective (Hunt & Azrin 1973; Azrin *et al*. 1982; Mallams *et al*. 1982; Sisson & Azrin 1986). The community reinforcement approach centres on modifying the client's social environment. This is achieved by making an assessment of social resources or 'reinforcement contingencies' available and using them, rather than taking the individual out of their environment to treat them. Hunt and Azrin (1973) designed and implemented a community-orientated programme to improve the quality of life. They systematically programmed reinforcement schedules into areas of social, family and vocational activities by employing social reinforcers, such as marital and family counselling, social clubs, driver's licence, telephone service and newspaper subscription. They discovered that those who remained abstinent spent more time gainfully employed and with their families and participated more in socially accepted recreational activities.

Unfortunately, there has been little more work to date directed towards helping clients with complex needs modify their social environments either by developing less stressful lifestyles or more supportive networks. The need for such work is now clear in this field.

The contribution of social work and work with the elderly, chronic long-term illness and disability

Long-term care and case management has been the major form of intervention for chronic illness (Kane & Kane 1987) and work with the elderly (Applebaum & Austin 1990). Home care is seen as an ongoing process (Balinsky 1994). However, much ongoing care is often seen within the conceptual and administrative framework of 'rehabilitation'.

Rehabilitation or intermediate care for individuals with physical disabilities is based on the premise that illness produces impairments that make men and women less able to perform basic life skills. Rehabilitation teaches individuals to perform these basic skills using methods that compensate for the impairments, and modifying the environment so that the new methods are successful or the skills are not required (Wallace 1993). This approach is usually connected with chronic and intractable illness (e.g. diabetes, back pain), long-term mental health problems and work with the elderly. It is also associated with work in palliative care and terminal care.

These methods are firmly grounded in individual models but do not focus on individual change and change-orientated methods; rather they move away from traditional medical approaches and examine the practical steps that can be used to support and to reduce harm or deterioration. Such methods often involve changes to the environment and supporting the individual through time.

Social work has traditionally concentrated on the chronically ill, elderly and disabled. It is therefore not surprising that this profession has developed a range of methods less constrained by the medical approach to acute problems and their treatment. The links between poverty, stress, violence and crime and psychological and health problems are well established in the social work field (Reed 1985; Reder *et al.* 1993).

Social work in the UK in common with the USA, has focused largely on individual problems and the need for individual change and rehabilitation, though social work theory in the UK has perhaps more recently been replaced by a more pragmatic care management rather than case management approach. Policy changes in the UK following the *NHS Plan* have resulted in the development of three types of intermediate care service: for those who will recover quickly and need little help with rehabilitation, for those who will take much more time and need a lot more help, and for those whose recovery will be limited and who will need palliative or continuing care (Rickford 2000). Methods proposed for implementing intermediate and rehabilitative care for the elderly and physically disabled include community rehabilitation teams, rapid response teams, and hospital-at-home services.

Whilst the goals of these approaches are often rehabilitation and recovery rather than ongoing support (Salaman 1986), they do enable the development of alternative professional roles and methods in the social work field. These include sustaining family relationships (Greene 1982; Solomon 1983; Dhooper *et al.* 1993) and maintaining and developing community support networks (Trocchio 1993).

The goals of child protection in social work are also clearly rooted in preventive approaches, where prevention, management and maintenance are already part of the philosophy (Cohen 1989; Kearney & Norman-Bruce 1993).

A range of studies indicates that rehabilitation practice is extremely variable across geographical areas, agencies and individual professionals. For example, a study of current post-stroke rehabilitation practice in the USA found that it varies substantially across different regions (Lee *et al.* 1996). A similar study of cognitive rehabilitation services identified confusion about who should provide such services and what is entailed (Johnstone *et al.* 1997).

It is clearly necessary in this field for professionals to become more knowledgeable, not only about the maintenance or rehabilitation needs of particular groups but also about the services that can be provided for which type of client; for example, work with the elderly is still limited. Hanks and Lichtenberg (1996) carried out a study to investigate different types of rehabilitative or maintenance need among the elderly, examining the social, cognitive, psychological and medical factors in geriatric rehabilitation in different decades of life. Their findings suggest that the younger old and the older geriatric patients represent two different rehabilitation groups. The younger had higher alcohol abuse and comorbid physical disease, while the older had poorer cognitive skills and more dependent social status. As might be expected, the younger groups recovered more quickly. There are clearly implications here for tailoring psychosocial care.

The contribution of health psychology and public health

The relatively new field of health psychology has contributed much to our understanding of stress, anxiety, and coping and dealing with long-term physical problems. The following models of health psychology offer theoretical interpretations of human attitude and behaviour change which can be applied to maintenance practice: the health belief model (Rosenstock 1966; Becker & Maiman 1975), the theory of reasoned action

(Fishbein & Ajzen 1975) and the self-regulation model of illness (Leventhal & Cameron 1987). These models conceptualise the individual as actively solving problems and see his/her behaviour as the result of a reasoned attempt to achieve a sensible goal. The models emphasise the importance of the individual's cognitions or subjective understanding of the health implications of their behaviour and the efficacy of their own actions in avoiding harm.

The maintenance approach and methods can also be found in preventive public health work in terms of major initiatives such as the prevention of HIV and also in targeted health promotion programmes (concerned with maintaining health rather than treating illness). The theories underlying public health and health promotion work are also based on psychological theories of cognition and behavioural change. The methodologies of this approach are also useful for developing prevention and harm minimisation or maintenance policies.

Models of public health are concerned with all aspects of the prevention of disease and promotion of health. They include social and environmental factors as much as the provision of health promotion and health care. 'Public health' has been defined in different ways. The WHO definition is 'science and art of preventing disease, prolonging life and promoting health through organised efforts of society'. It involves research into the prevalence, incidence and etiology of conditions of significant morbidity and/or mortality, and the evaluation of population-based interventions aimed at preventing disease or promoting health and well-being.

The main aim of such definitions is to extend the concept of public health research into corporate activity across organisational boundaries, at the level of populations rather than individuals. So it extends its remit to cross-environmental, social care and housing issues as well as health within these populations. This approach underpins the discussion of assessed needs across populations dealt with in Part I. In addition, recent research has focused on the epidemiology of social phenomena and constructions of social life (Rhodes 1995).

The contribution of voluntary and non-statutory services

It has traditionally been the role of voluntary and non-statutory services to deal with those clients that could not be treated or rehabilitated. In order to understand the type of work involved in maintenance and management of problems, it is therefore useful to look towards the voluntary or non-statutory organisations.

Services for people with complex needs are still often provided by non-statutory organisations. They are staffed by people who are often not professionally trained and who view clients' needs differently to the medical profession. These workers may see psychological and health problems as related to other social problems and not necessarily their cause at all, simply part of a wider social malaise. They therefore try to deal with these social problems rather than change the individuals with whom they come into contact.

These workers respond to problems such as homelessness and unemployment. This form of maintenance is not health-orientated, but directed towards the individual's social needs. Newly developing non-statutory agencies in some countries are largely non-professional and until recently this implied lack of status, influence and funding. One of the consequences is that the beliefs, values and priorities of these agencies differ from the change-orientated methods centres. Clients are not referred by other professionals, or diagnosed and treated; in contrast they are often seen as being as knowledgeable or 'expert' as the staff and therefore as capable of defining their own problems and determining their own needs. Self-referral as opposed to professional referral is a common form of entry to these 'low threshold' agencies and clients are helped or enabled to make their own decisions.

This philosophy of client participation and enablement does not increase the professional standing of the agencies as it becomes difficult to define clearly the expertise of the staff and the theories underlying their work. Staff qualifications and training vary from nurses and social workers to unqualified workers and former clients. Experience becomes an important component of this pragmatic approach, together with practical common-sense. Where the maintenance approach has developed from this type of agency, it has evolved from a pragmatic approach to a range of problems, rather than from coherent theoretical models of etiology.

In the UK new contracting arrangements with local authorities, health authorities, primary care and care trusts, police and probation have often radically changed the working practices of these organisations. As their aims and priorities change to become closer to those of their new contractors, so do the staff they employ (who often have professional qualifications) and therefore also the methods used. It is perhaps important to ask who or what organisations will provide the services traditionally provided by the voluntaries if this practice becomes widespread.

Overview of contemporary maintenance methods

It can be seen that the research focus in each of the areas described above has moved away from the change-orientated methods of therapy, rehabilitation and reform models towards models of long-term rehabilitation, coping and damage limitation, relapse prevention and managed decline. This often involves integrating treatment or change models with maintenance and long-term rehabilitation approaches (Dillon & Dollie-slager 2000).

Whilst traditional models still influence the definition of both problems and service provision, the rationale of many of these different approaches is simply to prevent clients or patients sinking lower and becoming more resource intensive. Agencies and professionals using any of these approaches may use terms such as 'rehabilitation' and 'intermediate care' but, in effect, change-orientated methods often become a secondary issue, dealt with after the client has been supported and helped in practical ways and so 'stabilised'.

While many professions have attempted to evaluate their interventions, research findings in the area of maintenance and rehabilitation are difficult to assess. Research is often inconclusive and differing outcome criteria make comparisons problematic. There are clear indications across a range of different disciplines that, not only should future models of care be altered, but also that future research should include different measures so that the benefits of the new maintenance or rehabilitative care can be evaluated in terms of the psychosocial objectives of these programmes (e.g. Evans *et al.* 1995).

PSYCHOSOCIAL MAINTENANCE METHODS FOR ONGOING MAINTENANCE AND MAINTENANCE OF CHANGE

It will be clear that the methods used to help maintain clients' lifestyles safely, with little risk or harm, are similar whether the professionals' aim is to provide simple maintenance or to maintain treatment gains. This chapter has concentrated on the theoretical and research implications for process, social factors and aftercare. These have been neglected areas in the treatment literature. However, as emphasised in Part II, while the work of professionals refers to theories, scientific research and textbook methods, methods are also developed from personal experience, accumulated practice wisdom and common-sense. So professionals make assessments of health needs and health risks and they offer health care and medication for underlying mental health problems. They will appraise psychological deficits and provide relaxation techniques and cognitive behavioural methods for psychological problems, perhaps also social skills or assertiveness training. They will make assessments of social needs and then provide welfare rights advice, housing, and other forms of social work help. They will also offer individual counselling and support groups.

While general practitioners and other professionals can provide access to psychological support and/or prescribe for anxiety and depression, most social and health care professionals are also trained to provide basic counselling and some provide cognitive behavioural support. It is possible to use cognitive and behavioural methods, irrespective of the theoretical interpretation of the problem. This is true for ongoing risk prevention work and aftercare relapse prevention whatever the diagnosis or treatment. In the same way it is possible to give social and life skills training and help in developing social support networks independently of any theoretical beliefs about the etiology of an illness or nature of problems. This can be provided alongside practical social support such as advice about finances, housing etc.

General improvement of confidence and coping skills is an important part of maintenance. It is also necessary to teach clients about risk and risk management and/or relapse and relapse management. There are two main methods: to help clients to modify their own cognitions and activities that may lead them closer to risky behaviours or relapse, and to help them identify and modify their high risk environments. In addition, any maintenance service should provide rapid, easy-access support in the event of a crisis or relapse.

The provision of information about problems and resources

Problems

It is essential to provide clients with information about their problems and perhaps also a cognitive behavioural framework, so that they can understand their difficulties and behaviour patterns.

Resources

The first step is to accumulate as much information as possible about available services and ensure that clients have easy access to it. Agency staff can find out from health authorities and local authorities which facilities are available and where. This information should be made available to clients.

Removing obstacles to service provision

Many clients with complex needs have negative experiences of service use (see Chapter 5) and may find it difficult to obtain health care services as health professionals have often had negative experiences of this 'difficult' or 'inappropriate' group in the past. It is therefore useful for professionals to mediate on behalf of their clients with the relevant service providers. This may also include a professional identifying all the other workers involved with a particular client and maintaining contact with this network as a whole.

Improve general individual coping skills

Perhaps the most useful maintenance method is to teach new cognitions and behaviours to clients in order to help them develop new confidence, coping skills and self-control.

After potentially dangerous risky or relapse situations have been identified, the client and professional can decide on coping or avoidance strategies. These can incorporate individual skills such as learning to recognise and avoid high risk situations, increasing personal confidence and developing coping skills, together with changes in the environment, from improving stressful relationships to developing new supportive circumstances.

A functional analysis should be undertaken to identify individual deficits in coping skills that are likely to cause relapse after therapy or change-orientated methods. Social skills training has been shown to be effective in preventing relapse, together with a wide range of self-control or self-management programmes (Marlatt & Gordon 1985) that are designed to include the development of new skills and coping strategies.

The cognitions that are associated with these behavioural lapses can be placed in three categories: perceived inability to cope, decreased perception of control in high risk situations and positive expectancies of outcome (Donovan & Marlatt 1980). For example, if clients see a situation as stressful and feel that they do not have the necessary skills to cope, there is a decrease in perceived control. The emphasis should therefore be on the situational demands and stresses placed on an individual and the beliefs individuals hold of their own ability to deal with these stresses. The authors propose a series of cognitive and behavioural exercises designed to increase self-confidence, self-control and coping ability. These include: aggression management, anxiety management and social and relaxation skills. In order to maintain any of these behaviours the client can learn cognitive and behavioural skills designed specifically to prevent reversion to old behaviour patterns.

Short-term coping skills

Relaxation training, stress management, anxiety management and efficacy enhancing imagery are among the many techniques used in skills training and coping strategies. As the client is taught skills to help cope this leads in turn to increased confidence and perception of self-control. Relapse becomes less likely. Skills training programmes include problem-solving skills such as orientation, definition of problems, generation of alternatives and decision-making. Teaching can be in the form of basic instruction, modelling and cognitive and behavioural rehearsal:

- Assertiveness training provides the ability to express aspects of covert hostility and resentment.
- Anger control teaches the client to learn to recognise anger and its source in the environment and then to communicate the anger in a less threatening way.
- Self-control skills lead to a decrease in levels of arousal and irritability and so reduce anger and prevent aggression.
- Cognitive behavioural stress management programmes teach the client to gain control over emotional and arousal states.
- Relaxation and meditation techniques teach the client how to relax physically and mentally.

It is clear that all clients do not need social or coping skills training. However, many find that these skills provide alternative coping mechanisms.

Long-term coping strategies

Marlatt and Gordon (1985) have proposed that it is not sufficient to teach clients specific individual skills appropriate for personally defined high-risk situations. It is also necessary to develop the individual's ability to deal with a broader range of situations and to exercise general self-control strategies to reduce the likelihood of relapse in any situation.

The overall influence of negative effect on relapse (e.g. anger, frustration and depression) suggests that more general mood control strategies may also be effective. Examples are learning self-management skills; increasing involvement in pleasant activities; learning to relax; becoming more socially skilful in interpersonal relationships; controlling negative or self-defeating thoughts; increasing positive self-reinforcing thoughts; providing appropriate coping-orientated self statements and gaining constructive problem-solving skills.

Teach risk and relapse prevention skills

General improvement of confidence and coping skills, while an important part of maintenance, does not deal with specific problems of risk and relapse. There are two main methods: to help clients to modify their own cognitions and behaviours that may lead them closer to risky behaviours or relapse; and to help them to identify and modify their high risk environments.

Risk and relapse prevention can be seen as an essential part of preventing or moderating risky behaviour or as specifically maintaining treatment gains. They can similarly be seen as fast track efficient intervention to prevent further deterioration, which may involve an initial or further course of treatment. They can also involve educating and preparing the client during treatment to identify the signs of escalating problems and to recontact services as soon as possible if this occurs or is likely to occur (Moos *et al.* 1990).

The psychosocial methods summarised below are developed where research and practice have evolved substantially in the past decade in creating a series of proven techniques for helping clients master individual coping skills to prevent risky or relapsed behaviours (Marlatt & George 1984; Davidson *et al.* 1991).

The concepts of risk prevention and intervention are similar to those of relapse prevention and relapse intervention. These terms can be used to describe methods designed to stop the occurrence or recurrence of risky behaviour. Relapse intervention refers to the need for professionals to respond quickly if and when clients relapse, in order to prevent further deterioration and the redevelopment of previous psychological and social problems associated with the situation before treatment (Marlatt & Gordon 1980).

These methods derived from cognitive behavioural techniques have also been developed to help prevent relapse from various behavioural treatments. These include self-monitoring, relapse fantasies and behavioural assessment methods to assess the relative risks of particular moods and situations. Information is gained from clients through descriptions of past relapses and rehearsal of possible future relapses.

Teach clients about risk and risk management and/or relapse and relapse management

The basic aim here is to teach the client to self-monitor. Self-monitoring helps clients to gain insight into their own behaviour and learn to recognise patterns. Having done this, they can find ways of avoiding certain behaviours or situations in the future. Self-monitoring varies from the use of diaries to complex behavioural assessments.

Seemingly automatic, habitual behaviours can result in relapse to problematic situations because of a lack of self-awareness. The client simply falls back on old familiar patterns of behaviour without realising that she/he has done so; for example, 'apparently irrelevant decisions' can be made without the client realising their significance. Becoming self-aware is seen as an integral part of preventing relapse because habitual cognitions and behaviours can only be controlled through an increased understanding of each individual's own particular arousal states and patterns of behaviour. Behavioural assessment allows the client to assess the relative risks of particular moods and situations (Marlatt & Gordon 1985).

In addition to prospective self-monitoring the clients need to learn about themselves and their vulnerabilities and personal resources from their previous histories and patterns of behaviour. Information from clients' descriptions of past relapses can be invaluable in helping them acquire understanding about themselves. This information can be supplemented by learning from previous relapses and rehearsals of possible future relapses. Role play, desensitisation and self-control methods are useful here.

Help clients to modify cognitions and behaviours that may lead them closer to risky behaviours or relapse

By teaching clients to understand their own situation (including the cognitive, behavioural and emotional antecedents of behaviour), the professional can contribute to the clients' self-awareness. It is then necessary to provide the tools that the clients will need to build on this self-knowledge to modify their behaviour and environment.

In the same way that clients can learn self-awareness, they can become more adept at assessing risks in any given situation and so withdraw before they lose control of their behaviour. For example, well remembered cues may stimulate a lapse, but if an individual avoids places where these cues are likely to occur the danger of relapse is also avoided. Clients can learn to identify and respond to situational, interpersonal and intrapersonal cues as early warning signals.

It is also useful for clients to plan specific strategies for high-risk situations. It is possible to decrease the probability of risky behaviour or relapse by helping clients to plan step-by-step coping strategies for particular high risk situations involving negative emotional states, interpersonal conflicts and social pressure.

Provide rapid, easy access support in the event of a crisis or relapse

No matter how effective skills training may be, many clients will revert to risky behaviours or relapse many times throughout the life course. Therefore any maintenance service should provide rapid, easy access support in the event of a crisis or relapse.

It will probably be necessary to continue to work with clients through several periods of deterioration or relapse. The notion of meeting clients with complex needs and helping them once or twice is not helpful here. It is much more likely that the relationship will last a long time and have no immediate outcome. Instead, workers support clients through difficult or dangerous periods in their lives. They help them to regain control over their lives, to prevent relapse to old behaviours and to learn to cope after relapse. Complex problems and needs will vary during the client's life. There will be times when the client appears to have few problems and copes well and there will be times when everything seems to go wrong at once.

When clients go through therapy or change-orientated methods, the professional can help them to develop new skills and perhaps a new life-style to prevent relapse. The worker should then monitor the client's post-therapy or change-orientated methods progress in order to offer ongoing support and to be available quickly in case the client lapses or relapses back to old dangerous patterns of behaviour.

This continued support (regular phone calls, meetings and/or group support) and immediate availability at relapse should be built into the aftercare phase. At present it is not uncommon for client and worker to see the end of a therapy or change-orientated methods phase as the final 'outcome', and therefore clients may well feel any relapse is a failure and should be disguised from the worker. This misconception stems from the medical notion of a distinct time-limited programme with a clear outcome, rather than of a recurring disorder or disability where there is no 'outcome' as such, only a continued monitoring of progress and availability of support when necessary.

Aftercare support should incorporate a well-understood procedure in the event of a lapse and/or relapse. The immediate priority is to be available to the client and offer maintenance management services if necessary. This can then be followed by the opportunity to re-enter therapy or change-orientated methods. Lapse can mean anything from a single episode to a full return to old lifestyles and risky patterns of behaviour. It is therefore crucial to determine its extent before acting further. A reassessment of the client's behaviour and circumstances will be necessary.

If potential relapse is presented to clients as an expected part of the change process rather than a failure they will be more likely to return if they need help. Monitoring of progress is essential at this stage, to enable prompt intervention in the event of a lapse to prevent full relapse.

The events that cause the initial lapse may be different from those which maintain it and from those which contribute to the re-establishment of the social and behavioural routines associated with a full-blown relapse. The practical implications of this are that relapse intervention as distinct from relapse prevention should become an essential part of an aftercare programme.

Different strategies are needed at different stages of relapse. These strategies are designed to deal with temporary loss of control. It is helpful for the initial lapse to been seen as controllable. A relapse can be defined in many ways. If it is seen as a 'slip' or 'lapse' but not as a complete remission, this may make it easier to deal with. Marlatt and Gordon (1980) suggest that the interpretation placed on a single lapse may determine whether or not it develops into a full relapse. So if a client expects the lapse to precipitate a serious relapse it actually becomes more likely.

It can be seen that a professional working with change-orientated methods and a model of change is likely to see a lapse as a failure.

Identify high-risk environments and develop new safer, supportive environments

Maintenance of change is associated with psychological and social factors rather than treatment variables. The concept of change focuses attention on individual rather than more general social factors that may precipitate relapse. In contrast, it may make more sense to reduce environmental stress, either by changing the environment or simply by helping clients to adopt a less stressful lifestyle and less stressful relationships. In the past this was often achieved by providing residential accommodation such as mental hospitals; now short-term rehabilitation units are more common, and although these are often followed by some form of sheltered housing, this too is often short-term.

Too often rehabilitation is seen as developing individual skills (as above), not in developing living environments and social support, perhaps because these are not the areas of expertise of any one profession. By improving the client's social relationships and making work and social environments less stressful it may be possible to modify the situational and relationship factors which lead to risks. Supportive agencies such as social services, citizens advice bureaux and housing associations can provide essential information about welfare rights, housing and financial problems.

However, developing supportive environmental networks is normally seen as peripheral to the work of any professional and it is unclear who should take on this role (Trower *et al.* 1991). The 'case management' role of the social worker may be more appropriate after treatment completion in preventing loss of treatment gains. Sullivan *et al.* (1992), for example, suggest that professionals should take substance misuse into account in case management, by focusing on community functioning and social rehabilitation, and in this way help prevent relapse. The authors outline their plans for developing case management in this way in a later article (Sullivan & Hartmann 1994).

Although research is undeveloped in this area, it is possible that a more rewarding and less stressful lifestyle may provide a solution for certain types of vulnerable people. This can involve changes in order to reduce negative effects from stress at work or in relationships on a permanent basis. Clients can change jobs or relationships, start new activities and/or build new social support networks. Again, research on developing social environments to prevent loss of treatment gains is in its infancy. However, the alcohol field offers some indicators. Moos *et al.* (1990) have demonstrated that individual variables interact with environmental factors to cause relapse. They suggest that support from family and friends and the existence of a relatively stable social and economic situation are important factors in the maintenance of behaviour change.

Brown (1990–91) emphasises the importance of changing role demands and expectations placed on the client by the family, school or employer, particularly for clients with complex problems. In addition he advocates developing new and prosocial networks and helping clients structure their free time activities to avoid relapse. He points out that activity in the first two of these areas has been practically non-existent and is still largely undeveloped in the third.

The stigma and exclusion associated with many complex needs problems mean that this type of activity may be crucial. The importance of establishing social networks can also be seen as particularly important for this group, as sociological research indicates that there are 'deviant' subcultures and that individuals may be socialised into their way of life and learn to rely on them for safety and support. The homeless, criminals and substance misusers are examples (Young 1971; Becker 1974; Parker *et al.* 1988; Bloor *et al.* 1994). If clients are to change damaging or risky lifestyles they may need to leave these social networks and corresponding occupations and develop a complete change in lifestyle. It follows that old social networks will need to be abandoned and new ones developed. Individuals will have to change their own reactions to things and develop new skills. It is at this most crucial time that treatment ends and the help stops.

As we are aware that treatment drop-out and relapse after treatment are the norm for many complex needs clients, research is now developing into the identification of the conditions associated with relapse and focusing on areas such as employment, relationships, social settings, psychological stress and cross-addiction. Aftercare therefore consists of remedial education, vocational counselling, life skills training, family support and cognitive behavioural relapse prevention techniques. In its most extreme form, stages of treatment can be seen as preparation for aftercare rather than the other way round.

SUMMARY

Multiple problems, lack of support and an inability to cope, particularly in stressful or risky situations, are likely to precipitate difficulties. The client and professional can decide together on coping or avoidance strategies. These can involve individual skills such as learning to recognise and avoid high risk situations, increasing personal confidence and developing coping skills, together with changes in the environment, from improving stressful relationships to developing new supportive circumstances.

The professional should:

(1)   Give clients detailed, accurate information about the services and resources available. This should include teaching clients about the functions of particular types of services, which are appropriate for what problems and needs, and also which professional groups deal with what problems in what ways. Much of the difficulty comes from inaccurate expectations.

(2)   Help clients to learn to understand their own problems, their personal vulnerabilities and their own resources. This can include providing clients with a cognitive behavioural framework, in which they can understand their own behaviour patterns and practical understanding of social factors which cause them stress and distress.

(3)   Help clients to identify environments and conditions where they cannot cope, and high risk situations (including the situational, social, relationship, cognitive, behavioural and emotional causes of problems).

(4)   Help clients to modify their own cognitions and behaviours that may lead them closer to risky behaviour or relapse. Teach new cognitions and behaviours to develop new confidence, coping skills and self-control. Teach clients about relapse and relapse management.

(5)   Help clients to learn about reducing stress in their lives and to understand where and why they are particularly vulnerable. Assist them to recognise social situations and environmental conditions where they are likely to be placed under stress and help them to find and develop supportive social and environmental conditions. Teach clients to modify their own environmental antecedents, to improve relationships and to make work and social environments less stressful.

MAINTENANCE BEFORE AND AFTER INDIVIDUAL CHANGE

This chapter has highlighted the need for continuing support and help over long periods. A major drawback to psychological change-orientated methods such as cognitive behavioural and psychotherapeutic interventions is that they do not last forever. Research indicates that when clients with complex needs stop attending the services they start to develop problems again. One of the most important tasks for generic professionals is to support and maintain clients after psychological change interventions.

Equally important is the need, emphasised in Chapter 7, to prepare clients for individual cognitive or behavioural change, in order to ensure that they are both motivated and equipped to cope with the stresses inherent in making a change. While this may mean extra resources, it is likely, in view of research on interventions with complex needs clients, that the costs will be outweighed by the benefits in the long term.

It has been suggested that a period of maintenance support is necessary, both as a preparation for change and as ongoing support after change.

Preparation for change

The concepts of motivational change were appropriated for prechange preparation to ensure that the client is not only motivated to make individual changes, but that the timing is right and that he or she is well prepared and capable of both making and maintaining change. Making life changes can lead to more problems in the short term, rather than fewer. These can take the form of additional stress and anxiety or changes in relationships.

It has already been emphasised that motivation is an essential precursor to working with clients with complex needs. It is ineffective to try to make clients change their behaviour before they are ready. However, it may well be effective for professionals to intervene to postpone clients making drastic life changes until they are fully prepared. Having motivated the client, the professional's job is then to help the client prepare for change. Part of making any change is preparing the ground; assessment and aftercare plans should therefore be an integral part of any change-orientated or treatment programme.

Aftercare maintenance

The concepts and methods of relapse prevention were used to ensure that clients are self-aware of their vulnerability and can identify the risks and resources in their environment. The essence of relapse prevention is to equip clients to recognise and prepare for risky situations and cope without reverting to old behaviours (whether these be problems directly related to the diagnosis or associated risk behaviours).

Aftercare plans should be designed to maintain clients over long periods with the minimal necessary professional input and to enable the immediate re-establishment of more intensive contact if and when this is necessary. The foundation of good aftercare is a comprehensive assessment of the reasons why a client might take risks or relapse, and preparation to avoid or cope with these situations in the future. Initial preparation may involve the client developing a less stressful or dangerous lifestyle and learning the necessary relapse prevention and coping skills.

Aftercare support itself involves the development of a programme of regular aftercare contacts and procedures to re-establish contact in the event of a crisis, lapse or relapse.

The professional may therefore need actively to dissuade a client from engaging in therapy or change-orientated methods until they are sure that the client has the necessary skills and support to cope in the long term. Only when the future ground has been thoroughly prepared should changes take place. If no account is taken of conditions contributing to presenting problems in the client's everyday life then relapse is more likely.

Relapse prevention and intervention

As discussed in the previous section, relapse prevention and intervention involve teaching cognitive behavioural methods to help prevent relapse to old patterns of behaviour. Cognitive behavioural methods have been designed to prevent relapse. These methods can be used irrespective of the therapy or change-orientated methods theory itself, either to maintain abstinence or controlled drug misuse.

Social support

Post-change aftercare involves a more structured approach to developing a supportive environment. Research indicates that social support networks and individual coping skills can be critical in preventing change-orientated methods relapse and maintaining treatment gains.

Assessment before and after interventions

The increased emphasis on needs and resources before and after psychological change interventions should also be reflected in assessment procedures.

Motivational assessment is designed to assess the clients' motivation and 'readiness to change'. Aftercare assessment is designed to establish what the clients' needs will be after change interventions, to determine whether clients are capable of maintaining changes in the future and, if so, what individual resources/skills and professional support systems will be necessary.

This assessment will then provide the basic framework for aftercare support. Assessment will need to be reviewed and updated at the close of the change intervention. (It is likely that these stages will in effect form a continuum, if not actually overlap.) This also includes assessing progress to make sure that clients have resolved any underlying problems contributing to their presenting problem and have a clear understanding of their vulnerabilities in the future.

Assessment should focus on identification of potentially dangerous situations for risky behaviour and/or relapse and identification of social supports and individual resources. Following the assessment, aftercare then consists of preparing the client's social environment and developing their personal skills. This plan should outline the extent of professional support and contact necessary and clarify a procedure for dealing with crisis situations and relapses.

MAINTENANCE WITHOUT INDIVIDUAL CHANGE

Part II of this book identified one of the main difficulties in working with this group as the fact that their priorities and definitions of problems often differed from those of professionals. So, complex needs clients are often described by professionals as 'inappropriate clients', 'difficult' or 'non-compliant'. As might be expected, the clients themselves describe the services as inappropriate, and professionals as uncooperative or unhelpful.

Perhaps the most important aspect of working with this client group then is not what should be done to bring about cognitive or behavioural change, but what should not be done. In terms of specialist individual assessments for change, professionals should not assume that individual behavioural change is the best solution. They should not even assume that their specialist assessment has identified the main problem or priority for the client, before talking to the client and considering the wider picture. If a client has complex needs, the specialist expertise or service provision of any one profession or agency may not necessarily be the priority for that client.

Crisis intervention

This is particularly true if the client has accessed the service at a time of crisis. Crisis intervention services have traditionally been seen as functioning to offer immediate support, and to link clients into psychological change-orientated services, whether for therapy or rehabilitation. It has been assumed that the time of crisis is a good time to offer change-orientated interventions, as the client will feel some pressure or motivation to change at this time. However, it is also probable that the client will have less ability or resources to change when under stress. It is suggested that the time when a client is in crisis might be the least sensible time for him or her to try to change.

This is also important for those professionals working with the motivational interviewing model described in the previous chapter. While this model is useful for those clients who are capable of making and maintaining individual change (who might well be more motivated at a period of crisis), it may be less than helpful if they do not have the ability to do so or the resources to sustain it.

It is suggested that at times of crisis clients will contact a range of different professionals and that all these professionals should see crisis intervention primarily in terms of maintenance and support, with the long-term aim of ongoing support and easy access facilities on demand. Alternatively if the aim is change, it should be postponed until the period of crisis is past and the client well prepared. It is important to point out that easy access, maintenance services provided when clients are in a period of crisis, function as an incentive to link clients into all services, whether change-orientated or not.

Long-term ongoing support

The main alternative to individual change-orientated services is services which offer long-term support. Contemporary mental health and drugs agencies may offer ongoing support and maintenance service. However, many will also offer a change-orientated programme, whether treatment, therapy or rehabilitation, where clients are expected to achieve individual targets. Consequently services are terminated whether the client 'succeeds' or 'fails' to achieve personal change. These clients, whether successful or not, are then frequently allowed to reregister for another programme of treatment often after a short period such as six months (often after a crisis or relapse).

This pattern of service use is common for services with complex needs clients. For some clients the periods of service use result in gaps where they may actually be more vulnerable. This is particularly true if they have lost contact with old support structures while in treatment or rehabilitation.

Many agencies provide a sporadic ongoing maintenance service for these clients, but define their service as a series of treatment programmes and define the client as 'non-compliant', 'failing', 'succeeding' or 'relapsing'. The client, in contrast, will often move from one treatment or rehabilitation agency to another, with the aim of receiving the same kind of practical help and support from all independently of their particular professional expertise or aims. It is therefore hardly surprising that there is a lack of communication between professionals and clients.

It should be stressed that many professionals are aware of this situation, that is, they know that their professional expertise and service are appropriate for most clients but inappropriate in isolation for complex needs clients. Some professionals will turn this group away because they are not appropriate or not able to benefit and some will try to refer them elsewhere. However, some will provide as much ongoing support and help as possible. They will do this by redefining what they do in terms that are appropriate for their profession and terms that the agency contractors or funders will recognise as appropriate. So ongoing support may be redefined as 'a series of short-term treatment periods', or as 'a short-term goal with the ultimate treatment aim of individual change', or even as 'relapse prevention'. It is clear to these professionals that they will be unable to provide a useful service for complex needs clients without defining it as the same kind of service that they provide for single problem clients.

It will not then come as a surprise to realise that different types of professionals are often doing exactly the same things with complex needs clients, but defining them differently. While clients are aware of this professionals may not be, causing unnecessary obstacles to working together, as illustrated in Chapter 4.

Risk prevention

The equivalent of relapse prevention for complex needs clients who do not make individual changes is often classified as primary or secondary prevention. This involves maintaining a support structure to ensure that clients do not take unnecessary risks in the future. This can consist of the establishment of regular access to services and support and basic cognitive behavioural skills programmes (Wilson 1992).

Low threshold, easy access services

Most professional statutory services function on a referral basis only. The advantages are obvious in terms of appropriate service use and prioritising resources. However, self-referral services are practically useful for offering easy and immediate access to some level of practical support. Accident and emergency departments have traditionally offered this help; GPs and the newly developing easy access health centres also provide this type of service.

In addition, non-statutory agencies have traditionally offered a self-referral service for clients, who can then play an active role in defining their own problems and needs. These services have tended to provide practical and social support.

Social support

As for post-change interventions, ongoing maintenance should also involve a structured approach to developing a supportive environment as social support networks and individual coping skills can be critical in preventing risky behaviour on an ongoing basis.

DISCUSSION: A NEW MODEL OF CARE?

It can be seen that it is often unrealistic to try to make radical interventions with complex needs clients. Instead of changing the client or their behaviour and resolving problems completely, it may be more pragmatic to reduce environmental risks, lessen vulnerability and make life more comfortable. It has therefore been argued that change models need to be supplemented by new models of maintenance, which could build on intermediate and long-term models of care.

The professional theories and ideology that underpin work with shared complex needs client groups are largely those of the health and social care professions. The models used are therefore either those of the medical professions which focus on acute illness and its treatment and cure, or the psychological and social care professions which focus on the psychological functioning of the individual and the individual's need to change. As a consequence there is little research on theory of maintenance needs or maintenance service provision. It has been argued that a psychosocial perspective leads to different priorities and different interventions to that of treatment models which have an implicit, if not explicit, model of illness and cure (Turk *et al.* 1986). Consequently, the priorities of those who work with complex needs clients will be different from the priorities of treatment providers and single needs clients.

However, where maintenance services do exist they are often intricately bound up with treatment provision and it can be difficult to find appropriate agencies where help is available without compulsory treatment. As a consequence of medical perceptions of complex needs, such as dual diagnosis, there are not only professional misconceptions about this as a homogeneous problem, but also about the nature and efficacy of 'treatment' for this group. The main obstacle to discarding old stereotypes and developing new understandings is the lack of information about the effects of multiple problems on the client group, whether this be the mentally ill, older people or parents and children (Coleman & Cassell 1995; Rhodes *et al.* 1996; Rickford 1996).

In contrast to specialist professional work where practitioners will often focus on their specific area of expertise, it is necessary with complex needs clients to see any one problem as one of a range of difficulties experienced by these men and women. This calls for more comprehensive and complex solutions. Not only is it necessary to move away from the medical notion of cure, but also from the psychological notion of permanent individual change (independent of social circumstances). Rather than a single treatment or therapeutic episode it may be necessary to implement a range of social and psychological solutions over time in order to maintain and support vulnerable people.

For example, the term 'intervention' does not necessarily mean individual change; it can mean to prevent or modify individual or social circumstances in order to maintain quality of life. Interventions do not necessarily lead to individuals making fundamental changes to themselves or their lifestyles. The emphasis on cognitive behavioural or psychodynamic therapy and personal change can become largely redundant for many complex needs clients who need instead an emphasis on support and maintenance, particularly among the mentally ill, disabled and those with learning difficulties. Instead of attempting to 'cure' complex needs clients, practitioners should find ways to improve social and individual circumstances, to support clients, reduce risks and maintain quality of life.

If this situation is accepted for clients with complex psychological and social problems, it becomes less clear whether and when to recommend treatment as an option for any one problem. The presence of a diagnosed health or mental health problem clearly points up the need for treatment. It is the timing and psychosocial context which are important. For example, the level of clinical depression or physiological drug dependency is crucial to a medical understanding of mental health and drug misuse, which traditionally presumed that patterns of mood or drug use are consistent and regular over time. In contrast, recent advances in mental health prescribing and drug treatment identify the significance of different patterns of mood and types of drug use and their respective problems throughout the life course. These are the factors which will both determine and be determined by social and psychological problems.

Finally, it should be remembered that much professional status is attached to the more theoretically-based disciplines that bring about individual change. It is therefore often difficult for professionals to accept work that does not use their professional training or expertise. They may feel that this is not appropriate or not a priority. If these issues are to be addressed there is a clear need for training programmes across a range of professions to integrate them. If rehabilitative programmes are to be successful the importance of staff training is critical. Corrigan (1998) states that this is because the principles and skills that are part of the rehabilitation paradigm are not necessarily an integral part of conventional training. Training is also considered important in this field because of the need for knowledge about other professions and the different agencies concerned, particularly regarding such areas as accommodation, employment, financial independence/support, need for outpatient psychiatric care and quality of life (Uchtenhagen 1996; Lewis & Patterson 1998).

So, not only does practice need to change, but the beliefs and attitudes of health and social care professionals must be extended to involve a more holistic view of people and their problems. If professions are to change their attitudes and work with new models of care and within newly developing interdisciplinary services, this will need to be reflected in their training. Interprofessional training could occur at qualifying or post-qualifying levels. It could involve common core components which raise awareness of the existence and needs of shared complex needs clients and provide alternative aims and methods for working with them.

Chapter 9
New Models of Ongoing Psychosocial Care

This book has been concerned with both planning and practice for clients with complex needs. It has reviewed literature on both problems and solutions and combined original quantitative and qualitative data to provide an overview of the main issues.

Part I emphasised the importance of generic population needs assessment and planning. It suggested that this could be achieved by developing interagency databases to inform joint planning and audit, together with common interagency tariffs and screening for shared complex needs clients. Part II was concerned with obstacles to service provision for this group. It identified limitations in practice and concluded that two additional initiatives were necessary for complex needs clients: common comprehensive psychosocial assessments and maintenance-orientated interventions. Part III examined the methods and skills necessary to implement these new approaches, utilising the practical methods and expertise of a range of different professional specialists for dealing with their own clients with psychosocial problems.

PLANNING: INTERAGENCY POPULATION STUDIES TO INFORM INTERAGENCY PLANNING

Comprehensive joint planning is concerned with assessing needs and managing service provision across agency populations. This provides a foundation for interprofessional work with this group.

Two main problems were identified for planners. First, the need to assess complex needs across different agency populations as a whole and not restrict it to their specialised populations and the measures that concern them. Second, the need to plan and manage interdisciplinary service provision based on audits in conjunction with other agency planners. This form of population planning can be useful for informing the development of multiagency services and prioritising help for their complex needs clients. It provides both planners and professionals with a clearer idea of the proportions of their clients with complex needs and the particular characteristics of these clients.

In addition, this information concerning shared client groups could then make possible the negotiation of agreed interagency tariffs prioritising collaborative resources for shared clients. It can also directly inform professional interventions through the development of standardised assessment protocols or screening instruments for complex needs, based on population indicators or predictors of multiple need and service use. This will enable individual professionals to identify clients in need of comprehensive multidisciplinary assessments and/or maintenance support.

THE CONTEMPORARY POLICY CONTEXT IN THE UK

While this book is neither a policy text nor concerned only with the UK, it will be of interest to some readers to place its findings in the context of recent policy initiatives in England and Wales. The white paper *The New NHS (*DoH 2000*)* and The Health Act 1999, together with the development of the General Social Care Council and the white paper *Modernising Social Services* (DoH 1998a) stress the need to develop interagency working. These all recommend that health and social care agencies work more closely together and also work in partnership with housing, education, employment and voluntary services. In addition The Crime and Disorder Act 1998 enables all these agencies to work more closely with criminal justice agencies. Policy initiatives include health improvement programmes (DoH 1998b), single local care networks, and social and health 'care trusts'.

These initiatives place a responsibility on all agencies to assess need across their respective populations in order to develop joint assessment plans, audit procedures and joint commissioning. In addition, agencies will be required to demonstrate that they are developing 'best value' health and social care systems through the development and monitoring of 'one stop' health and social care services, multidisciplinary teams, rapid response teams, intensive rehabilitation for the elderly, intermediate care and integrated home care.

While this book has not been primarily concerned with policy, the methods outlined here can be used to inform both planning and practice within national policies concerned to develop interagency services.

PRACTICE: DEVELOPING A NEW MODEL OF MULTIDISCIPLINARY, PSYCHOSOCIAL MAINTENANCE

It is suggested that professionals should work from this interagency population planning foundation to develop multidisciplinary care, using comprehensive psychosocial assessments to decide whether maintenance and/or change goals would be more appropriate.

This book has proposed the development of a new psychosocial maintenance model of care. It has advocated that all professions should recognise the limitations of both their specialist assessments and their common change-orientated models (whether treatment, therapy, rehabilitation or reform). It would then be possible for each professional group to place their specialist assessments within a psychosocial context and to develop an additional common atheoretical approach to maintenance and support.

This would also enable the development of a common interprofessional understanding of the influence of psychological and social factors and the consequent importance of ongoing psychosocial support. Professionals may also find it easier to work together more constructively with an additional shared atheoretical or cross-disciplinary model.

It is difficult to understand and respond to complex needs clients without an appreciation of both psychological and social problems and the ways in which they interact with ill health, disability and risk. Problems such as poverty, homelessness, violence and social deficits are often outside the remit, training or resources of any one profession. Professionals are therefore ill-equipped to understand and deal with the consequences of these problems. A psychosocial approach enables an overview of the individual and the environment and the relevant social and societal constraints. Such an approach and assessment might then lead to the provision of ongoing psychosocial maintenance such as psychological skills training and the development of a supportive social environment in order to minimise risks or consequences of impairments.

Most professionals have developed practical common-sense ways of helping complex needs clients. However, beliefs about health and welfare are often seen within established professional frames of reference and these patterns of perception determine their assessments and interventions. The majority of the health and psychosocial care system is structured and intended for short specific episodes of acute illness or psychological problems that can be treated, cured or changed. Therefore, when professionals work with clients they try to fit them into this model, by making specialist assessments of clients' specific needs for change to take place. They then evaluate their intervention in terms of whether the client fails or succeeds in making this change; either way the outcome is the same for the client – the service is terminated. As a consequence, professionals are often frustrated and impatient with complex needs clients, labelling them as 'non-compliant' or 'difficult' or 'no-hopers'.

Similarly, models of chronic, intermediate and rehabilitative care in effect often serve to provide ongoing psychosocial maintenance strategies, but again within the conceptual framework of specific acute problems and their treatment. While these practices, strategies and methods have been developed over the years to be effective, it is suggested that if the constraints of these latter models are recognised, a more conceptually distinct generic model of care could then be constructed. This would facilitate the practical helping process, in terms of assessment and resource allocation, and ongoing psychosocial support.

CONCLUSION

Many complex needs clients are consistently reusing or 'revolving' through specialist change-orientated services because this is their only way of getting support and maintenance on an ongoing basis or during particularly stressful periods in their lives. The psychological and social support needs of these clients often go far beyond the remit of any one professional change-orientated model. This book has indicated that specialist ways of defining problems, assessing needs and providing services are not effective for complex needs clients and that additional methods need to be developed both for working with clients and for working with other professionals.

In addition, it has been argued that the change imperative across the professions has not only reduced the priority of clients with multiple problems but also limited the extent of maintenance management interventions as a whole. It is suggested that all health and social care professionals need to provide effective ways to provide ongoing support and reduce health and social risks and damage, in addition to their specialist aims and expertise. In doing so they may well find they are in effect developing potential areas of common ground.

It is proposed that all professionals use a common second model of care, that of psychosocial maintenance management. This should be seen as conceptually distinct from change-orientated methods and concerned with supporting clients with complex needs to prevent deterioration in their problems, and not merely as an adjunct to change programmes.

References

Acheson, E.D. (1967) *Medical Record Linkage.* Nuffield Hospitals Services, Oxford University Press, Oxford.

Acheson, E.D. & Baldwin, G. (1978) *Textbook of Medical Record Linkage.* Oxford University Press, Oxford.

American Psychiatric Association (1994) *Diagnostic and Statistical Manual of Mental Disorders,* 4th edn revised. Division of Public Affairs, American Psychiatric Association, Washington DC.

Anon (1999) Practice parameters for the assessment and treatment of children, adolescents, and adults with mental retardation and comorbid mental disorders. *Journal of the American Academy of Child and Adolescent Psychiatry,* 38 (12), 5–13.

Anthony, W.A. (1996) Integrating psychiatric rehabilitation into managed care. *Psychiatric Rehabilitation Journal,* 20 (2), 39-44.

Applebaum, R. & Austin, C. (1990) *Long Term Care and Case Management; Design and Evaluation.* Springer, New York.

Azrin, N.H., Sisson, R.W., Meyers, R. & Godley, M. (1982) Alcoholism therapy or treatment by Disulfiram and community reinforcement therapy. *Journal of Behaviour Therapy and Experimental Psychiatry,* 13, 105–12.

Baggott, R. (1994) *Health and Health Care in Britain.* 2nd edn. MacMillan, Basingstoke.

Baldock, J. (1997) Social care in old age: more than a funding problem. *Social Policy and Administration,* 31 (1), 73–89.

Balinsky, W. (1994) *Home Care; Current Problems and Future Solutions.* Jossey Bass, San Francisco.

Bandura, A. (1977) *Social Learning Theory.* Prentice Hall, Englewood Cliffs, New York.

Barbee, J.G., Clark, P.D. & Crapanzano, M.S. (1989) Alcohol and substance abuse among schizophrenic patients presenting to an emergency psychiatric service. *Journal of Nervous and Mental Disease,* 177, 400–7.

Baronet, A.M. & Gerber, G.J. (1998) Psychiatric rehabilitation: efficacy of four models. *Clinical Psychology Review,* 18 (2), 189–228.

Bartels, S.J., Drake, R.E., Wallach, M.A. & Freeman, D.H. (1991) Characteristic hostility in schizophrenic patients. *Schizophrenia Bulletin,* 17 (1), 163–71.

Bartels, S.J., Drake, R.E. & Wallach, M.A. (1995) Long-term course of substance use disorders among patients with severe mental-illness. *Psychiatric Services,* 46 (3), 248–51.

Bean P. & Wilkinson, C. (1988) Drug taking, crime and the illicit supply system. *British Journal of Addiction,* 83, 533–9.

Bearman, D., Claydon, K., Kincheloe, J. & Lodise, C. (1997) Breaking the cycle of dependency: dual diagnosis and AFDC families. *Journal of Psychoactive Drugs*, **29** (4), 359–67.

Bebbington, P.E. (1995) The content and context of compliance. *International Clinical Psychopharmacology*, **9** (S5), 41–50.

Bebout, R.R., Drake, R.E., Xie, H.Y., McHugo, G.J. & Harris, M. (1997) Housing status among formerly homeless dual diagnosed adults. *Psychiatric Services*, **48** (7), 936–41.

Beck, A.T. (1989) *Cognitive Therapy and the Emotional Disorders.* International Universities Press, Inc., New York.

Becker, M.H. (ed.) (1974) *The Health Belief Model and Personal Health Behaviour.* Thorofare, New Jersey.

Becker, M.H. & Maiman, L.A. (1975) Sociobehavioural determinants of compliance with health and medical care recommendations. *Medical Care*, **13**, 10–24.

Becker, T. & Thornicroft, G. (1998) Community care and management of schizophrenia. *Current Opinion in Psychiatry*, **11** (1), 49–54.

Bellack, A.S. & Gearon, J.S. (1998) Substance abuse treatment for people with schizophrenia. *Addictive Behaviours*, **23** (6), 749–66.

Berg, B.L. (1995) *Qualitative Research Methods for the Social Sciences*, 2nd edn. Allyn and Bacon, Boston.

Bergin, A. & Garfield, S. (eds) (1978) *Psychotherapy and Behaviour Change.* Wiley, New York.

Billings, A.G. & Moos, R.H. (1983) Psychosocial processes of recovery among alcoholics and their families: implications for clinicians and programme evaluators. *Addictive Behaviours*, **8**, 205–18.

Bloor, M., Frischer, M. & Taylor, A. (1994) Tideline and turn; possible reasons for the continuing low HIV prevalence among Glasgow's injecting drug users. *Sociological Review*, **42** (4), 738–57.

Bogenschutz, M.P. & Siegfried, S.L. (1998) Factors affecting engagement of dual diagnosis patients in outpatient treatment. *Psychiatric Services*, **49** (10), 1350–2.

Bolles, R.C. (1979) *Learning Theory.* Holt, Rinehart and Winston, New York.

Borsay, A. (1986) *Disabled People in the Community.* Bedford Square Press, London.

Brach, C., Falik, M., Law, C., Robinson, G., Trentadams, S., Ulmer, C. & Wright, A. (1995) Mental health services – critical component of integrated primary care and substance abuse treatment. *Journal of Health Care for the Poor and Undeserved*, **6**, (3), 322–41.

Breakey, W.R., Calabrese, L., Rosenblatt, A. & Crum, R.M. (1998) Detecting alcohol use disorders in the severely mentally ill. *Community Mental Health Journal*, **34** (2), 65–174.

Breen, R. & Thornhill, J.T. (1998) Noncompliance with medication for psychiatric disorders – reasons and remedies. *Central Nervous System: Drugs*, **9** (6), 457–71.

Brown B.S. (1979) *Addicts and aftercare: community integration of the former drug user.* Sage Publications, Beverly Hills, California.

Brown, B.S. (1990–91) Relapse prevention in substance misuse. Introduction. *International Journal of the Addictions*, **25** (9A and 10A), 1081–3.

Brown, B.S. & Ashery, R.S. (1979) Aftercare in drug abuse programming. In *Handbook on Drug Abuse* (eds R.I. DuPont, A. Goldstein and J. O'Donnell). National Institute of Drug Abuse, US Government Printing Office, Washington DC.

Burgess, R.W. (1988) *Conducting Qualitative Research*. JAI Press, London.

Carroll, K.M., Rounsaville, B.J. & Bryant, K.J. (1993) Alcoholism in therapy or treatment-seeking cocaine abusers: clinical and prognostic significance. *Journal of Studies on Alcohol*, **54** (2), 199–208.

Cartwright, D. (1979) Contemporary social psychology in historical context. *Social Psychology Quarterly*, **42**, 82–93.

Catalano, R.F. & Hawkins, J.D. (1985) Project skills: preliminary results from a theoretically based aftercare experiment. In *Progress in the Development of Cost-Effective Therapy or Treatment for Drug Abuse* (ed. R.S. Ashery). National Institute on Drug Abuse, Rockville, Maryland.

Catalano, R.F., Hawkins, J.D., Wells, C.A. & Miller, J. (1990–91) Evaluation of effectiveness of adolescent drug use treatment, assessment of risks for relapse and promising approaches for relapse prevention. *International Journal of Addictions*, **25** (9A and 10A), 1085–140.

Catania, C. & Harnad, S. (eds) (1988) *The Selection of Behaviour*. Cambridge University Press, Cambridge.

Clark, D.B. & Bukstein, O.G. (1999) Psychopathology in adolescent alcohol abuse and dependence. *Alcohol Health & Research World*, **22** (2), 117–21.

Cohen, P. (1989) Balancing Act. *Social Work Today*, **22**, 18–19.

Coleman, R. & Cassell, D. (1995) Parents who misuse drugs and alcohol. In *Assessment and Parenting: Psychiatric and Psychological Contributions* (eds P. Reder and C. Lucey). Routledge, London.

Collins, S. & Keene, J. (2000) *Alcohol, Social Work and Community Care*. Venture Press, London.

Conrad, P. (1992) Medicalization and social control. *Annual Review of Sociology*, **18**, 209–32.

Conrad, P. & Schneider, J.W. (1992) *Deviance and Medicalization: From Badness to Sickness*. Temple University Press, Philadelphia.

Corney, R. (1985) The health of patients referred to social workers in an intake team. *Social Science and Medicine*, **21** (8), 873–8.

Corrigan, P.W. (1998) Building teams and programs for effective rehabilitation. *Psychiatric Quarterly*, **69** (3), 193–209.

Craig, R.J. & Olson, R.E. (1990) MCMI comparisons of cocaine abusers and heroin addicts. *Journal of Clinical Psychology*, **46**, 230–7.

Crinson, L. (1995) The impact of the patients charter on accident and emergency departments. *British Journal of Nursing*, **4** (22), 1321–5.

Cronkite, R.C. & Moos, R.H. (1980) Determinants of post therapy or treatment functioning of alcoholic patients: a conceptual framework. *Journal of Consulting and Clinical Psychology*, **48**, 305–16.

Davidson, R., Rollnick, S. & MacEwan, I. (eds) (1991) *Counselling Problem Drinkers*. Routledge, London.

Davies, M. (1985) *The Essential Social Worker: a guide to positive practice*. Community Care Practice Handbooks, Ashgate, Hants.

Deakin, E.Y., Levy, J.C. & Wells, V.W. (1987) Adolescent depression, alcohol and drug abuse. *American Journal of Public Health*, **77**, 178–82.

Dermott, F. & Pyett, P. (1994) Co-existent psychiatric illness and drug abuse: a community study. *Psychiatry Psychology and Law*, 45–52.

Deykin, E.Y., Buka, S.L. & Zeena, T.H. (1992) Depressive illness among chemically dependent adolescents. *American Journal of Psychiatry*, **149** (10) 1341–7.

Dhooper, S., Green, S.M., Huff, M.B. & Austin Murphy, J. (1993) Efficiency of a group approach to reducing depression in nursing home elderly residents. *Journal of Gerontological Social Work*, **20**, 87–100.

Dhooper, S.S. (1991) Caregivers of Alzheimer's disease patients. A review of the literature. *Journal of Gerontological Social Work*, **18**, 19–37.

Dillon, A.S. & Dollieslager, L.P. (2000) Overcoming barriers to individualised psychosocial rehabilitation in an acute treatment unit of a state hospital. *Psychiatric Services*, **51** (3), 313–17.

Dingwall, R. & Lewis, P. (1989) *The Sociology of The Professions; Lawyers, Doctors and Others*. MacMillan, London.

DoH (1996) *The Task Force To Review Services For Drug Misusers; Report Of An Independent Review Of Drug Treatment Services In England*. Department of Health, London.

DoH (1998a) *Modernising Social Services*. The Stationery Office, London.

DoH (1998b) *Health Improvement Programmes: Planning for Better Health and Better Health Care*. HSC98/167, The Stationery Office, London.

DoH (2000) *The New NHS*. The Stationery Office, London.

Donovan, D.M. & Marlatt, G.A. (1980) Assessment of expectancies and behaviours associated with alcohol consumption: a cognitive behavioural approach. *Journal of Studies on Alcohol*, **41**, 1156–85.

Drake, R.E., Mercer-McFadden, C., Mueser, K.T., McHugo, G.J. & Bond, G.R. (1998) Review of integrated mental health and substance abuse treatment for patients with dual disorders. *Schizophrenia Bulletin*, **24** (4), 589–608.

Ducq, H., Guesdon, I. & Roelandt, J.L. (1997) Psychiatric morbidity of homeless persons: a critical review of Anglo-Saxon literature. *Encephale-Revue de Psychiatrie Clinique Biologique et Therapeutique*, **23** (6), 420–30.

Edelman, M.J. (1974) *American Politics: Policies, Power and Change*. Lexington Press, Lexington, Mass.

Edens, J.F., Peters, R.H. & Hills, H.A. (1997) Treating prison inmates with co-occurring disorders: An integrative review of existing programs. *Behavioral Sciences & The Law*, **15** (4), 439–57.

Egan, G. (1990) *The Skilled Helper: A Systematic Approach to Effective Helping*. Brooks Cole, California.

ElandGoossensen, M.A., VandeGoor, L.A.M., Garretsen, H.F.L. & Schudel, W.J. (1997) Screening for psychopathology in the clinical practice. *Journal of Substance Abuse Treatment*, **14** (6), 585–91.

Ellis, A.(1962) *Reason and Emotion in Psychotherapy*. Lyle Stuart, New York.

Ellis, A. (1987) The evolution of rational-emotive therapy (RET) and cognitive-behaviour therapy (CBT). In *The Evolution of Psychotherapy* (ed. J. Zeig). Brunner/Mazel, New York.

Evans, R.l., Connis, R.T., Hendricks, R.D. & Haselkorn, J.K (1995) Multidisciplinary rehabilitation versus medical-care – a meta-analysis. *Social Science & Medicine,* **40** (12), 1699–706.

Finney, J.W., Moos, R.H. & Mewborn, C.R. (1980) Post therapy or treatment experiences and therapy or treatment outcome of alcoholic patients six months and two years after hospitalisation. *Journal of Consulting and Clinical Psychology,* **48,** 17–29.

Fiorentine, R., Pilati, M.L. & Hillhouse, M.P. (1999) Drug treatment outcomes: investigating the long-term effects of sexual and physical abuse histories. *Journal of Psychoactive Drugs,* **31** (4), 363–72.

Fishbein, M. & Ajzen, I. (1975) *Belief, attitude, intention and behaviour: An introduction to theory and research.* Addison-Wesley, Reading, Mass.

Fisher, M.S. & Bentley, K.J. (1996) Two group therapy models for clients with a dual diagnosis of substance abuse and personality disorder. *Psychiatric Services,* **47** (11), 1244–50.

Fowler, I.L., Carr, V.J., Carter, N.T. & Lewin, T.J. (1998) Patterns of current and lifetime substance use in schizophrenia. *Schizophrenia Bulletin,* **24** (3), 443–55.

Friedmann, P.D., Alexander, J.A., Jin, L. & D'Aunno, T.A. (1999) On-site primary care and mental health services in outpatient drug abuse treatment units. *Journal of Behavioral Health Services and Research,* **26** (1), 80–94.

Fuller, C.G. & Sabatino, D.A. (1998) Diagnosis and treatment considerations with comorbid developmentally disabled populations. *Journal of Clinical Psychology,* **54** (1), 1–10.

Gafoor, M. & Rassool, G.H. (1998) The co-existence of psychiatric disorders and substance misuse: working with dual diagnosis patients. *Journal of Advanced Nursing,* **27** (3), 497–502.

Gentry, W.D. (ed.) (1984) *Handbook of Behavioral Medicine.* Guilford Press, New York.

Glaser, B. G. & Strauss, A. (1970) *The Discovery of Grounded Theory.* Aldine Press, New York.

Goldfried, S.L. & Bergin, A.E. (eds) (1986) *Handbook of Psychotherapy and Behaviour Change.* John Wiley, New York.

Gordon, J.R. (1998) Harm reduction psychotherapy comes out of the closet. *Psychotherapy In Practice,* **4** (1), 69–77.

Greene, R.R. (1982) Families and the nursing home social worker. *Social Work in Health Care,* **7** (3), 57–67.

Grella, C.E. (1997) Services for perinatal women with substance abuse and mental health disorders: the unmet need. *Journal of Psychoactive Drugs,* **29** (1), 67–78.

Hall, W. & Farrell, M. (1997) Comorbidity of mental disorder with substance abuse. *British Journal of Psychiatry,* **171,** 4–5.

Hammersley, R., Forsyth. A. & Lavelle, T. (1990) The criminality of new drug users in Glasgow. *British Journal of Addiction,* **85,** 1583–94.

Hanks, R.A. & Lichtenberg, P.A. (1996) Physical, psychological, and social outcomes in geriatric rehabilitation patients. *Archives of Physical Medicine and Rehabilitation,* **77** (8), 783–92.

Harrison, A. & Dixon, J. (2000) *The NHS. Facing the Future.* Kings Fund, London.

Hawkins, J.D. & Catalano, R. (1985) Aftercare in drug abuse therapy or treatment. *International Journal of Addictions,* **20,** 917–45.

Hien, D., Zimberg, S., Weisman, S., First, M. & Ackerman, S. (1997) Dual diagnosis subtypes in urban substance abuse and mental health clinics. *Psychiatric Services*, **48** (8), 1058–63.

Hill, M. (1986) *Analysing Social Policy*. Blackwell, Oxford.

Hoff, R.A. & Rosenheck, R.A. (1998) Long-term patterns of service use and cost among patients with both psychiatric and substance abuse disorders. *Medical Care*, **36** (6), 835–43.

Holland, M. (1996) Substance use and mental health problems: meeting the challenge. *British Journal of Nursing*, **7** (15), 896–900.

Holland, M. (1999) How substance use affects people with mental illness. *Nursing Times*, **95** (24), 46–8.

Hoptman, M.J., Yates, K.F., Patalinjug, M.B., Wack, R.C. & Convit, A. (1999) Clinical prediction of assaultive behavior among male psychiatric patients at a maximum-security forensic facility. *Psychiatric Services*, **50** (11), 1461–6.

Horvath, A.T. (1994) Comorbidity of addictive behavior and mental disorder – outpatient practice guidelines (for those who prefer not to treat addictive behavior). *Cognitive and Behavioral Practice*, **1** (1), 93–109.

Hunt, G.H. & Azrin, N.H. (1973) A community-reinforcement approach to alcoholism. *Behaviour Research and Therapy*, **11**, 91–104.

Iguchi, M.Y., Handelsman, L., Bickel, W.K. & Griffiths, R.R. (1993) Benzodiazepine and sedative use/abuse by methadone maintenance clients. *Drug and Alcohol Dependence*, **32** (3), 257–66.

Jarvis, T.J. & Copeland, J. (1997) Child sexual abuse as a predictor of psychiatric co-morbidity and its implications for drug and alcohol treatment. *Drug and Alcohol Dependence*, **49** (1), 61–9.

Jenkins, W.I. (1978) *Policy Analysis: A Political and Organisational Perspective*. Martin Robertson, London.

Jerrell, J.M. & Ridgely, M.S. (1997) Dual diagnosis care for severe and persistent disorders: A comparison of three methods. *Behavioral Healthcare Tomorrow*, **6** (3), 26–33.

Jerrell, J.M. & Wilson, J.L. (1997) Ethnic differences in the treatment of dual mental and substance disorders – a preliminary analysis. *Journal of Substance Abuse Treatment*, **14** (2), 133–40.

Johnstone, B., Schopp, L.H. & Frank, R.G. (1997) Managed care and rehabilitation: Issues related to cognitive rehabilitation. *Neurorehabilitation*, **8** (1), 57–65.

Kadden, R. & Kranzler, H. (1992) Alcohol and drug abuse treatment at the University of Connecticut Health Centre. *British Journal of Addiction*, **87** (4), 521–6.

Kandel, D.B. (1982) Epidemiological and psychosocial perspectives on adolescent drug use. *Journal of the American Academy of Child Psychology*, **4**, 328–47.

Kane, S. (1991) HIV, heroin and heterosexual relations. *Social Science and Medicine*, **32**, 991–1037.

Kane, R.A. & Kane, R.A (1987) *Long Term Care; Principles, Programmes and Policies*. Springer, New York.

Kanfer, F. & Goldstein, A. (eds) (1986) *Helping People Change: A Textbook of Methods*. Pergamon Press, Oxford.

Kearney, P. & Norman-Bruce, G. (1993) The Children Act. *Druglink*, **8** (1), 10–12.

Keene, J. (1997) *Drug Misuse: Prevention, Harm Minimisation and Treatment*. Chapman and Hall, London.

Keene, J. (2000) Do therapeutic models limit comprehensive assessment, interventions and evaluation? A qualitative study of substance misuse agencies. *International Journal of Drug Policy*, **11**, 337–49.

Keene, J., Willner, P. & Love, A.C. (1999) The relevance of problems and models to treatment outcome: A comparative study of two agencies. *Substance Use and Misuse*, **34** (10), 1347–69.

Khantzian, E.J. (1985) The self medication hypothesis of addictive disorders; focus on heroin and cocaine dependence. *American Journal of Psychiatry*, **142**, 1259–64.

Kidorf, M. & Stitzer, M.L. (1993) Descriptive analysis of cocaine use of methadone patients. *Drug and Alcohol Dependence*, **32** (3), 267–75.

Kitsuse, J. & Cicourel, A.B. (1963), Combining analysis of records with survey data. A note on the use of official statistics. *Social Problems*, **11**, 113–19.

Kofoed, L. (1993) Outpatient vs. inpatient therapy or treatment for the chronically mentally ill with substance use disorders. *Journal of Addictive Diseases*, **12** (3), 123–37.

Kozarickovacic, D., Folnegovicsmalc, V., Folnegovic, Z. & Marusic, A. (1995) Influence of alcoholism on the prognosis of schizophrenic patients. *Journal of Studies on Alcohol*, **56** (6), 622–7.

Krueger, M.W., Nachison, C., Robertson, J., Stacks, M. & Staines, G. (1997) MHS/CSAT collaborative demonstration program for homeless individuals. *Journal of Social Distress and the Homeless*, **6** (4), 261–74.

Lamb, H.R. (1994) A century and a half of psychiatric rehabilitation in the United States. *Hospital and Community Psychiatry*, **45** (10), 1015–20.

Lambert, E.Y. & Caces, M.F. (1995) Correlates of drug-abuse among homeless and transient people in the Washington, DC, Metropolitan-area in 1991. *Public Health Reports*, **110** (4), 455–61.

Lambie, I., Bullen, D., Rodetz, A. & Seymour, F. (1997) Psychiatric rehabilitation: Development of group programs in hospital and community settings. *Psychiatric Rehabilitation Journal*, **21** (1), 51–8.

Landry, M.J., Smith, D.E., McDuff, D.R. & Baughman, O.L. (1991) Anxiety and substance use disorders: the therapy or treatment of high-risk patients. *Journal of the American Board of Family Practice*, **4** (6), 447–56.

Launay, C., Petitjean, F., Perdereau, F. & Antoine, D. (1998) Addictive behavior in mental disorders: a survey in the Paris area. *Annales Medico-Psychologiques*, **156** (7), 482–5.

Lawson, M.P. (1986) Functional assessment. In *Geropsychological Assessment and Treatment* (eds L. Teri and P.M. Lewinson). Springer, New York.

Lee, A.J., Huber, J. & Stason, W.B. (1996) Post-stroke rehabilitation in older Americans – the Medicare experience. *Medical Care*, **34** (8), 811–25.

Leff, J. (1993) All the homeless people – where do they come from? *British Medical Journal*, **306** (6879), 669–70.

Lehman, W.E.K., Barrett, M.E. & Simpson, D.D. (1990) Alcohol use by heroin addicts 12 years after drug abuse therapy or treatment. *Journal of Studies on Alcohol*, **51**, 233–44.

Leukefeld, C.G. & Tims, F. M. (1989) Relapse and recovery in drug abuse: research and practice. *International Journal of the Addictions*, **24** (3), 189–201.

Leventhal, H. & Cameron, L. (1987) Behavioural theories and the problem of compliance. *Patient Education and Counselling*, **10**, 117–38.

Leventhal, H. & Nerenz, D. (1985) The assessment of illness cognition. In *Measurement Strategies in Health Psychology* (ed. P. Karoly). Wiley and Sons, New York.

Levine, S. & Lilienfeld, A. (1987) *Epidemiology and Health Policy*. Tavistock Publications, London.

Levy, M., Saemann, R. & Oepen, G. (1996) Neurological comorbidity in treatment-resistant dual diagnosis patients. *Journal of Psychoactive Drugs*, **28** (2), 103–10.

Lewis, S. & Patterson, J.B. (1998) Training needs of rehabilitation counselors and rehabilitation teachers in state vocational rehabilitation agencies serving individuals with visual disabilities. *Journal of Rehabilitation*, **64** (2), 46–50.

Lindqvist, P. & Skipworth, J. (2000) Evidence-based rehabilitation in forensic psychiatry. *British Journal of Psychiatry*, April, **176**, 320–3.

Lindstrom, L. (1992) *Managing Alcoholism. Matching Clients to Treatments*. Oxford University Press, Oxford.

Luke, D.A., Mowbray, C.T., Klump, K., Herman, S.E. & Boots-Miller, B. (1996) Exploring the diversity of dual diagnosis; utility of cluster analysis for program planning. *Journal of Mental Health Administration*, **23** (3), 298–316.

Macdonald, K.M. (1995) *The Sociology of the Professions*. Sage, London.

Macpherson, R. (1996) Psychosis and substance misuse comorbidity: ethical dilemmas. *Psychiatric Bulletin*, **20** (8), 463–5.

Magruder-Habib, K., Hubbard, R.L. & Ginzburg, H.M. (1992) Effects of drug misuse therapy or treatment on symptoms of depression and suicide. *International Journal of the Addictions*, **27** (9), 1035–65.

Maisto, S.A. & Carey, K.B. (1987) Therapy or treatment of alcohol abuse. In *Developments in the Assessment and Therapy or Treatment of Addictive Behaviours* (eds T.D. Nirenberg & S.A. Maisto). Abllex, Norwood, New Jersey.

Maisto, S.A., Carey, K.B., Carey, M.P., Purnine, D.M. & Barnes, K.L. (1999) Methods of changing patterns of substance use among individuals with co-occurring schizophrenia and substance use disorder. *Journal of Substance Abuse Treatment*. **17** (3), 221–7.

Mallams, J.H., Godley, M., Hall, G.M. & Meyers, R. (1982) A social systems approach to resocialising alcoholics in the community. *Journal of Studies on Alcohol*, **43**, 1115–23.

Marlatt, G.A. (1985) Cognitive assessment and intervention procedures. In *Maintenance Strategies in the Treatment of Addictive Behaviours* (eds G.A. Marlatt & J.R. Gordon). Guilford Press, New York.

Marlatt, G.A. & George, W.H. (1984) Relapse prevention: introduction and overview of the model. *British Journal of Addiction*, **79**, (3), 261–73.

Marlatt, G.A. & Gordon, J.R. (1980) Determinants of relapse: implications for the maintenance of behaviour change. In *Behavioural Medicine: Changing Health Lifestyles* (eds P. Davidson & S. Davidson). Plenum, New York.

Marlatt, G.A. & Gordon, J.R. (1985) *Relapse Prevention; Maintenance Strategies in the Treatment of Addictive Behaviors.* Guilford Press, New York.

Marshall, J.R. (1997) Alcohol and substance abuse in panic disorder. *Journal of Clinical Psychiatry,* **58** (S2), 46–50.

Marshall, M., Nehring, J., Taylto, C. & Gath, D. (1994) Characteristics of homeless mentally-ill people who lose contact with caring agencies. *Irish Journal of Psychological Medicine,* **11** (4), 160–3.

Matson, J.L. & Bamberg, J.W. (1998) Reliability of the assessment of dual diagnosis (ADD). *Research in Developmental Disabilities,* **19** (1), 89–95.

Mayer, E. & Timms, N. (1970) *The Client Speaks: Working Class Impressions Of Case Work.* Routledge and Kegan Paul, London.

McKeown, M., Stowell-Smith, M., Derricott, J. & Mercer, D. (1998) Dual diagnosis as social control. *Addiction Research,* **6** (1), 63–70.

McKinlay, J.B. (1972) Some approaches and problems in the study of the use of services, an overview. *Journal of Health and Social Behaviour,* **13**, 115–53.

McLellan, A.T., Woody, G.E. & Metzer, D. (1996) Evaluating the effectiveness of addiction treatments: reasonable expectations, appropriate comparisons. *Millbank Quarterly,* **74** (1), 55–86.

Menezes, P.R., Johnson, S., Thornicroft, G., Marshall, J. & De Crespigny, P.K. (1996) Drug and alcohol problems among individuals with severe mental illnesses in South London. *British Journal of Psychiatry,* **168** (5), 612–19.

Miller, W.R. (1983) Motivational interviewing with problem drinkers. *Behavioural Psychotherapy,* **11** (2), 147–72.

Miller, W.R., Sovereign, R.G. & Krege, B. (1988) Motivational interviewing with problem drinkers II: the drinker's check-up as a preventive intervention. *Behavioural Psychotherapy,* **16**, 251–68.

Mittler, P. (1973) *The Psychological Assessment of Mental and Physical Handicaps.* Methuen, London.

Moggi, F., Ouimette, P.C., Finney, J.W. & Moos, R.H. (1999) Effectiveness of treatment for substance abuse and dependence for dual diagnosis patients: A model of treatment factors associated with one-year outcomes. *Journal of Studies on Alcohol,* **60** (6), 856–66.

Moos, R.H. (ed.) (1984) *Coping with Physical Illness, Vol 2: New perspectives.* Plenum, New York.

Moos, R.H., Finney, J.W. & Chan, D.A. (1981) The recovery process from alcoholism: 1 Comparing patients and matched controls. *Journal of Studies on Alcohol,* **42**, 383–402.

Moos, R.H., Finney, J.W. & Cronkite, R.C. (1990) *Alcoholism Therapy or Treatment. Context, Process and Outcome.* Oxford University Press, Oxford.

Mowbray, C.T., Ribisl, K.M., Solomon, M., Luke, DA. & Kewson, T.P. (1997) Characteristics of dual diagnosis patients admitted to an urban, public psychiatric hospital: an examination of individual, social, and community domains. *American Journal of Drug and Alcohol Abuse,* **23** (2), 309–26.

Mowbray, C.T., Jordan, L.C., Ribisl, K.M., Kewalramani, A., Luke, D., Herman, S. & Bybee, D. (1999) Analysis of postdischarge change in a dual diagnosis population. *Health and Social Work,* **24** (2), 91–101.

Mueser, K.T., Drake, R.E. & Wallach, M.A. (1998) Dual diagnosis: a review of etiological theories. *Addictive Behaviours,* **23** (6), 717–34.

Nachmias, D. & Nachmias, F.N. (2000) *Research methods in the Social Sciences,* 6th edn. Worth, New York.

Najavits, L.M., Weiss, R.D. & Shaw, S.R. (1999) A clinical profile of women with posttraumatic stress disorder and substance dependence. *Psychology of Addictive Behaviors,* **13** (2), 98–104.

Nordstrom, G. & Burglund, M. (1986) Successful adjustment in alcoholism; relationships between causes of improvement, personality and social factors. *The Journal of Nervous and Mental Disease,* **174**, 664–8.

Nurco, D.M., Wegner, N., Stephenson, P., Makofsky, A. & Shaffer, J.W. (1983) *Ex-Addicts Self-Help Groups.* Praeger, New York.

Ouimette, P.C., Brown, P.J. & Najavits, L.M. (1998) Course and treatment of patients with both substance use and posttraumatic stress disorders. *Addictive Behaviors,* **23** (6), 785–95.

Parker, H., Baker, K. & Newcombe R. (1988) *Living With Heroin.* Open University Press, Buckingham.

Paton, S.M., Kessler, R. & Kandel, D. (1977) Depressive mood and adolescent illegal drug use; a longitudinal analysis. *Journal of Genetic Psychology,* **31**, 267–89.

Peters, R.H., Strozier, A.L., Murrin, M.R. & Kearns, W.D. (1997) Treatment of substance-abusing jail inmates – examination of gender differences. *Journal of Substance Abuse Treatment,* **14** (4), 339–49.

Pitts, M. & Phillips, K. (1991) *The Psychology of Health, An Introduction.* Routledge, London.

Polcin, D.L. (1997) The etiology and diagnosis of alcohol dependence: differences in the professional literature. *Psychotherapy,* **34** (3), 297–306.

Powell, J.E. & Taylor, D. (1992) Anger, depression, and anxiety following heroin withdrawal. *International Journal of the Addictions,* **27** (1), 25–35.

Pozzi, G., Bacigalupi, M. & Tempesta, E. (1997) Comorbidity of drug dependence and other mental disorders: A two-phase study of prevalence at outpatient treatment centres in Italy. *Drug and Alcohol Dependence,* **46** (1–2), 69–77.

Prendergast, P.J. (1995) Integration of psychiatric rehabilitation in the long-term management of schizophrenia. *Canadian Journal of Psychiatry,* **40** (3), 18–21.

Prochaska, J.O. (1979) *Systems of Psychotherapy: A Transtheoretical Perspective.* Dorsey Press, Homewood, Ill.

Prochaska, J.O. & DiClemente, C.C. (1982) Transtheoretical therapy, towards a more integrative model of change. *Psychotherapy Theory, Research and Practice,* **19** (3), 276–88.

Prochaska, J.O. & Diclemente, C.C. (1983) Stages and processes of self change of smoking: toward an integrative model of change. *Journal of Consulting and Clinical Psychology,* **51**, 390–5.

Prochaska, J.O. & DiClemente, C.C. (1986) Towards a comprehensive model of change. In *Treating Addictive Behaviours: Processes of Change* (eds W.R. Miller and N. Heather). Plenum, New York.

Prochaska, J.O. & DiClemente, C.C. (1994) *The Transtheoretical Approach: Crossing Traditional Boundaries of Therapy.* Daw-Jones, Irwin, New York.

Pyles, D.A.M., Muniz, K., Cade, A. & Silva, R. (1997) A behavioral diagnostic paradigm for integrating behavior-analytic and psychopharmacological interventions for people with a dual diagnosis. *Research in Developmental Disabilities*, **18** (3), 185–214.

Quinton, D., Gulliver, L. & Rutter, M. (1995) A 15–20 year follow-up of adult psychiatric patients. *Psychiatric Disorder and Social Functioning*, **167** (8), 315–23.

Ravndal, E. & Vaglum, P. (1994) Treatment of female addicts: the importance of relationships to parents, partners, and peers for the outcome. *International Journal of the Addictions*, **29** (1), 115–25.

Reder, P., Duncan, S. & Gray, M. (1993) *Beyond Blame: Child Abuse Tragedies Revisited*. Routledge, London.

Reed, B.G. (1985) Drug misuse and dependency in women: the meaning and implication of being considered a special population or minority group. *International Journal of Addictions*, **20**, 13–62.

Rees, S. (1979) *Social Work Face to Face: Client's and Social Worker's Perception of the Content and Outcomes of Their Meetings*. Columbia University Press, New York.

Regier, D.A., Narrow, W.E. & Rae, D.S. (1990) The epidemiology of anxiety disorders – the epidemiologic catchment area (ECA) experience. *Journal of Psychiatric Research*, **24** (Suppl.2), 3–14.

Rhodes, T. (1995) Social relations of risk among heroin users. In *Aids: Safety, Sexuality and Risk* (eds P. Aggleton, P. Davies & G. Hart). Taylor and Francis, London.

Rhodes, T., Stimson, G.V. & Quirk, A. (1996) Sex, drugs interventions and research from the individual to the social. *Substance Use and Misuse*, **31** (3), 375–407.

Rickford, F. (1996) Bad habit. *Community Care*, February, 20–21.

Rickford, F. (2000) The future is looking intermediate. *Community Care*. September–October, 20–21.

Ries, R.K., Russo, J., Wingerson, D., Snowde, M., Comtois, K.A., Srebnik, D. & Roy-Byrne, P. (1998) Schizophrenia and severe affective illness alternating over time in some patients: a hypothesis. *Psychiatry – Interpersonal and Biological Processes*, **61** (3) 262–8.

Ries, R.K., Russo, J., Wingerson, D., Snowde, M., Comtois, K.A., Srebnik, D. & Roy-Byrne, P. (2000) Shorter hospital stays and more rapid improvement among patients with schizophrenia and substance disorders. *Psychiatric Services*, **51** (2), 210–15.

Rogers, C.R. (1967) *Client Centred Therapy in Current Practices, Implications and Theory*. Houghton Mifflin, Boston.

Rosenstock, I.M. (1966) Why people use health services. *Millbank Memorial Fund Quarterly*, **44**, 94.

Ross, R.L. (1988) *Government and Private Sector – who should do what?* Crane Russak, New York.

Ross, H.E., Gavin, D.R. & Skinner, H.A. (1990) Diagnostic validity of the MAST and the alcohol dependency scale in the assessment of DSM III alcohol disorders. *Journal of Studies in Alcohol*, **6**, 506–13.

Rothschild, D. (1998) Treating the resistant substance abuser: Harm reduction (re)emerges as sound clinical practice. *Psychotherapy in Practice*, **4** (1), 25–35.

Rounsaville, B.J. (1986) *Clinical Implications of Relapse Research*. National Institute of Drug Abuse Research Monographs Series, 72, Rockville, Maryland.

Royal College of Physicians (1992) *Smoking and the Young*. Royal College of Physicians, London.

Sainsbury, E., Nixon, S. & Phillips, D. (1982) *Social Work in Focus: Client's and Social Worker's Perceptions in Long term Social Work*. Routledge and Kegan Paul, London.

Salaman, M.J. (1986) *A Basic Guide to Working with Elders*. Springer, New York.

Salloum, I.M., Moss, H.B,. Daley, D.C., Cornelius, J.R., Kirisci, L. & Al Maalouf, M. (1998) Drug use problem awareness and treatment readiness in dual-diagnosis patients. *American Journal on Addictions*, 7 (1), 35–42.

San, L., Tato, J., Torens, M. & Castillo, C. (1993a) Flunetrazepam consumption among heroin addicts admitted for TH – patient detoxification. *Drug and Alcohol Dependence*, **32** (3), 281–6.

San, L., Torrens, M., Castillo, C. & Porta, M. (1993b) Consumption of buprenorphine and other drugs among heroin addicts under ambulatory therapy or treatment: results from cross-sectional studies in 1988 and 1990. *Addiction*, **88** (10), 1341–9.

Saunders, J.B. & Aasland, O.G. (1987) *WHO Collaborative project on the identification and therapy or treatment of persons with harmful alcohol consumption*. Report on phase 1 development of a screening instrument. WHO, Geneva.

Saunders, W.M. & Kershaw, P.W. (1979) Spontaneous remission from alcoholism: a community study. *British Journal of Addiction*, **74**, 251–65.

Saxon, A.J. & Caslyn, D.A. (1995) Effects of psychiatric care for dual diagnosis patients treated in a drug dependence clinic. *American Journal of Drug and Alcohol Abuse*, **21** (3), 303–13.

Schon, D. (1990) *Educating the Reflective Practitioner*. Jossey Bass, New York.

Schubiner, H., Tzelepis, A., Isaacson, J.H., Warbasse, L.H., Zacharek, M. & Musial, J. (1995) The dual diagnosis of attention-deficit hyperactivity disorder and substance-abuse – case-reports and literature-review. *Journal of Clinical Psychiatry*, **56** (4), 146–50.

Scoping Study Committee (1999) *Review of the Mental Health Act Draft Outline Proposals*. The Stationery Office, London.

Sestoft, D. (1996) Trends in Danish research on crime and mental health (1970–94): a review. *Nordic Journal of Psychiatry*, **50** (2), 161–8.

Sheppard, S. (1990) Social work and community psychiatric nursing. In *The Sociology of the Caring Professions* (eds P. Abbot and C. Wallace). Falmer Press, London.

Silver, R.L. & Wortman, C.B. (1980) Coping with undesirable life events. In *Human Helplessness* (eds J. Garber & M. Seligman). Academic Press, New York.

Silverstein, S.M., Schenkel, L.S., Valone, C. & Nuernberger, S.W. (1998) Cognitive deficits and psychiatric rehabilitation outcomes in schizophrenia. *Psychiatric Quarterly*, **69** (3), 169–91.

Simpson, D.D. & Sells, S.B. (1982) *Effectiveness of therapy or treatment for drug abuse*. Institute of Behavioural Research, report 81-1, Texas Christian University, Fort Worth.

Sisson, R.W. & Azrin, N.H. (1986) Family-member involvement, to initiate and promote therapy or treatment of problem drinkers. *Journal of Behaviour Therapy and Experimental Psychiatry*, **17**, 15–21.

Sloan, K.L. & Rowe, G. (1995) Substance-abuse and psychiatric-illness: psychosocial correlates. *American Journal on Addictions*, **4** (1), 60–69.

Smith, J. & Hucker, S. (1993) Dual diagnosis patients: substance abuse by the severely mentally ill. *British Journal of Hospital Medicine*, **50** (11), 650–4.

Snyder, C.R. (ed.) (1999) *Coping. The Psychology of What Works*. Oxford University Press, Oxford.

Solomon, R. (1983) Serving families of the institutionalised aged. The four crises. In Sommerville 1985 (below).

Sommerville, G.S. (1985) *Community Development in Health: Addressing the Confusions*. Kings Fund Centre, London.

Soyka, M. (1996) Dual diagnosis in patients with schizophrenia. Issues in pharmocological treatment. *American Journal on Addictions*, **5** (6), 414–25.

Stallones, R.A. (1980) To advance epidemiology. *Annual Review of Public Health*, **1**, 69–82.

Starkey, D. & Leadholm, B.A. (1997) PRISM: The Psychiatric Rehabilitation Integrated Service Model – A public psychiatric hospital model for the 1990s. *Administration and Policy in Mental Health*, **24** (6), 497–508.

Steel, J. (1995) Inappropriate – the patient or the service? *Accident and Emergency Nursing*, **3** (3), 146–9.

Steptoe, A. & Matthews, A. (ed.) (1984) *Health Care and Human Behaviour*. Academic Press, London.

Stone, G.C., Cohen, F. & Adler, N.E. (eds) (1979) *Health Psychology: A Handbook*. Jossey-Bass, San Francisco.

Sturmey, P. (1998) Classification and diagnosis of psychiatric disorders in persons with developmental disabilities. *Journal of Developmental and Physical Disabilities*, **10** (4), 317–30.

Sullivan, W.P. & Hartmann, D. J. (1994) Implementing case management in alcohol and drug treatment. *Families in Society*, **75** (2), 67–73.

Sullivan, W.P., Wolk, J .L. & Hartmann, D. J. (1992) Case management in alcohol and drug treatment: improving client outcomes. *Families in Society*, **73**, 195–204.

Sutton, S.R. (1992) Commentaries. *British Journal of Addiction*, **87**, 24.

Swanson, J.W., Holzer, C.E., Ganju, V.K. & Jono, R.T. (1990) Violence and psychiatric disorder in the community. *Hospital and Community Psychiatry*, **41** (7), 761–70.

Szasz, T.S. (1976) *The Myth of Madness: Foundations of a Theory of Personal Conduct*. Perennial Library, New York.

Talbott, G.D. (1989) Alcoholism should be treated as a disease. In *Chemical Dependency: Opposing Viewpoints* (ed. B. Leone). Greenhaven, San Diego.

Thomson, L.D.G. (1999) Substance abuse and criminality. *Current Opinion in Psychiatry*, **12** (6), 653–7.

Toombs, D.L. (2000) *Introduction to Addictive Behaviors*, 2nd edn. Guilford Press, New York.

Trinder, H. & Keene, J. (1997) Comparing substance misuse agencies: different substances, clients and models, but the same methods? *Journal of Substance Misuse*, **2**, 24–30.

Trocchio, J. (1993) Community partnerships for nursing homes. *Nursing Homes*, Nov/Dec, 18–19, 24.

Trower, P., Casey, A. & Dryden, W. (1991) *Cognitive-Behavioural Counselling in Action*. Sage, London.

Truax, C. & Carhuff, R. (1967) *Towards Effective Counselling and Psychotherapy*. Aldine, Chicago.

Tsang, W.H.H. & Pearson, V. (1999) A conceptual framework for work-related social skills in psychiatric rehabilitation. *Journal of Rehabilitation*, **62** (3), 61–7.

Tsuang, D., Cowley, D., Ries, R., Dunner, D.L. & RoyByrne, P.P. (1995) The effects of substance use disorder on the clinical presentation of anxiety and depression in an outpatient psychiatric clinic. *Journal of Clinical Psychiatry*, **56** (12), 549–55.

Tucker, P. (1999) Attention-deficit/hyperactivity disorder in the drug and alcohol clinic. *Drug And Alcohol Review*, **18** (3), 337–44.

Turk, D.C., Rudy, T.E. & Salovey, P. (1986) Implicit models of illness. *Journal of Behavioural Medicine*, **9** (5), 453–74.

Uchtenhagen, A. (1996) Psychiatric rehabilitation in Switzerland. *European Psychiatry*, **11** (2), 90–6.

Ungerson C. (1994) *Becoming Consumers of Community Care*. Joseph Rowntree Foundation, York.

Valliant, G.E. (1983) *The Natural History of Alcoholism; Causes, Patterns and Paths to Recovery*. Harvard University Press, Cambridge, Mass.

Wallace, C.J. (1993) Psychiatric rehabilitation. *Psychopharmacology Bulletin*, **29** (4), 537–48.

Walsh, M. (1995) The health belief model and the use of accident and emergency by the general public. *Journal of Advanced Nursing*, **22** (4), 694–9.

Weale, A. (1983) *Political Theory and Social Policy*. Macmillan, London.

Weinmann, J. (1987) *An Outline of Psychology as Applied to Medicine*. Butterworth-Heinmann Ltd, Oxford.

Wilkinson, J.D. & Campbell, E.A. (1997) *Psychology in Counselling and Therapeutic Practice*. John Wiley and Sons, Chichester.

Wilson, P. (1992) *Principles and Practice of Relapse Prevention*. Guilford Press, New York.

Wolff, N. (1998) Interactions between mental health and law enforcement systems: Problems and prospects for cooperation. *Journal of Health Politics Policy and Law*, **23** (1), 133–74.

Woods, M.E. & Hollis, F. (2000) *Casework: a Psychosocial Therapy*, 5th edn. McGraw Hill, Boston.

Woogh, C.M. (1990) Patients with multiple admissions in psychiatric record linkage system. *Canadian Journal of Psychiatry*, **35**, 401–6.

Yalisove, D. (1998) The origins and evolution of the disease concept of treatment. *Journal of Studies on Alcohol*, **59**, 469–76.

Young, J. (1971) *The Drug Takers*. McGibbon and Kee, London.

Ziedonis, D. & Brady, K. (1997) Dual diagnosis in primary care – detecting and treating both the addiction and mental illness. *Medical Clinics of North America*, **81** (4), 1017.

Index